Plate I

Currituck County, North Carolina Eighteenth Century Tax & Militia Records

William Doub Bennett

CLEARFIELD

Reprinted for
Clearfield Company, Inc. by
Genealogical Publishing Co., Inc.
Baltimore, Maryland
1994, 2000

International Standard Book Number: 0-8063-4987-5

Made in the United States of America

CONTENTS

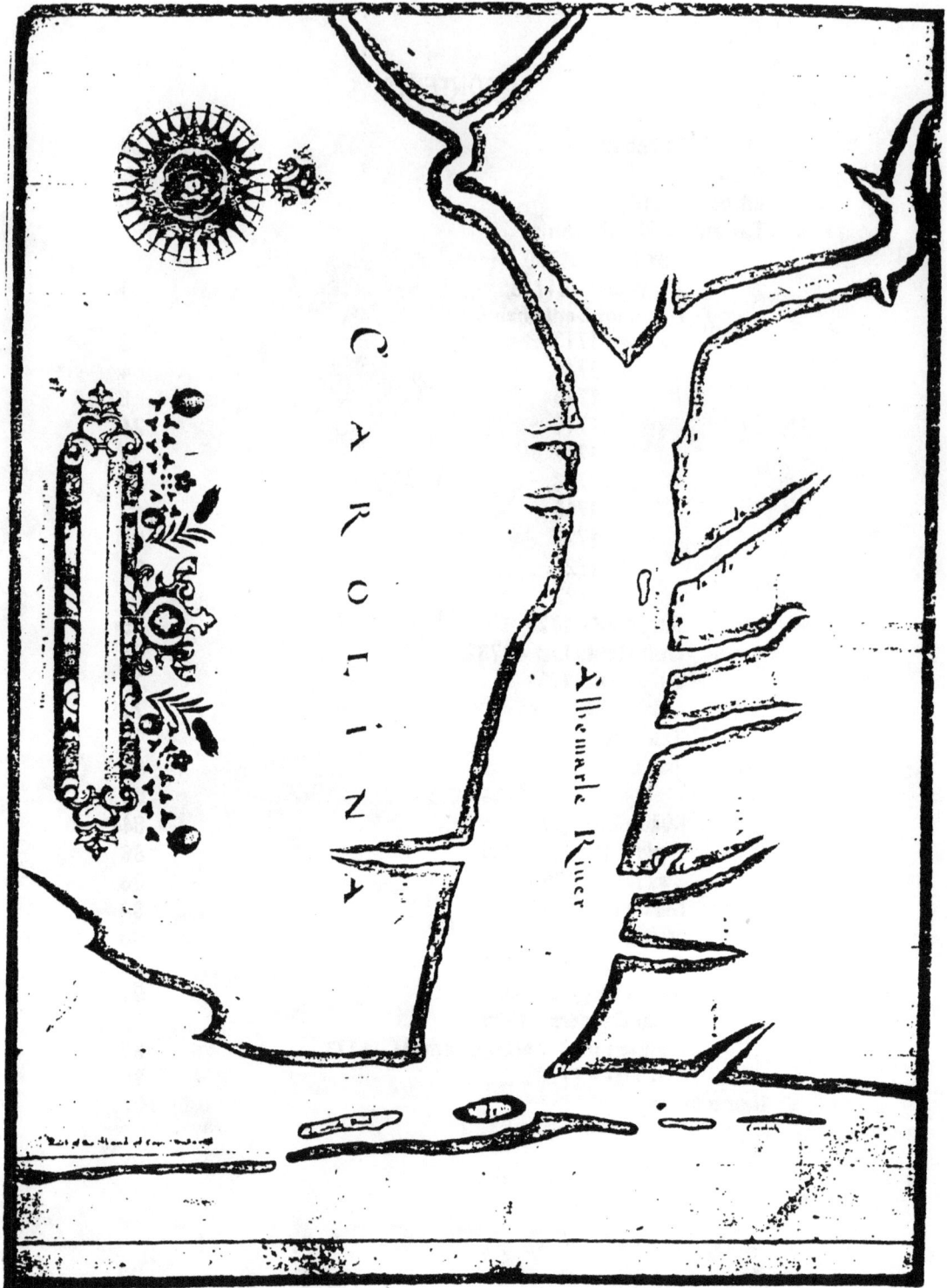

CAROLINA

Albemarle River

Plate II

LIST OF ILLUSTRATIONS

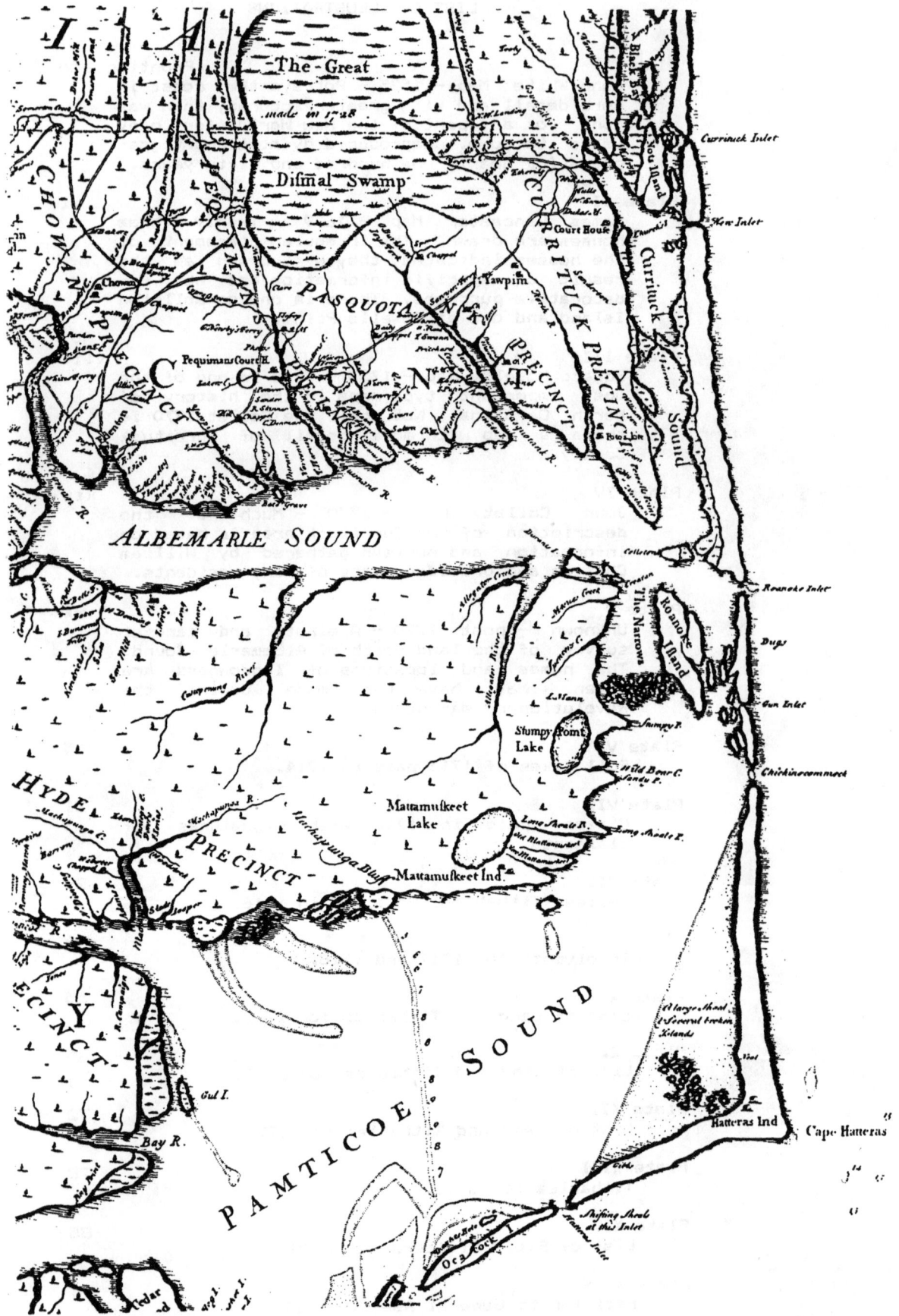

The-Great

Dismal Swamp

made in 1728

CHOWAN PRECINCT

PEQUIMANS PRECINCT

Pequimans Court H.

PASQUOTANK PRECINCT

Yawpim

COUNT

CURRITUCK PRECINCT

Court Houſe

Currituck Sound

Currituck Inlet

New Inlet

ALBEMARLE SOUND

Colleton

The Narrows

Roanoke Iſland

Roanoke Inlet

Dugs

Gun Inlet

Stumpy Point Lake

Stumpy P.

Wild Bear C.

Chickinecommock

HYDE PRECINCT

Mattamuſkeet Lake

Machapunga Bluff

Mattamuſkeet Ind.

Long Shoals R.

Long Shoals P.

Y PRECINCT

Gul I.

Bay R.

PAMTICOE SOUND

A large Shoal & ſeveral broken Iſlands

Hatteras Ind

Cape Hatteras

Shifting Shoals at this Inlet

Ocacock I.

Cedar

Plate III

FOREWORD

In 1989 William D. Bennett was voted Historian of the Year by the North Carolina Society of Historians. The following year he received the North Carolina Genealogical Society Award of Excellence for his service to the society and to other genealogists. When he was certified in 1986 as a genealogist by the Board for Certification of Genealogists, one of the judges wrote, "His knowledge of the history, genealogy, social customs, and people of early North Carolina is awe inspiring, and his ability to weave this information into his reports results in informative and entertaining family history."

Reputed to know more about the records in the North Carolina State Archives than the professional archivists, Mr. Bennett has, since his retirement, published the earliest records of North Carolina from the counties that have suffered the greatest loss of records, some twenty volumes or there abouts, and more than forty articles for learned journals. Additionally, he lectures widely about the country, sharing his expertise and also conducts symposiums for the North Carolina State Archives. He is a past director of the Friends of the North Carolina State Archives, the North Carolina Society of Historians, and the Wake County Historical Society, an honorary life member of the Wake County Genealogical Society, and Registrar of the North Carolina Society of SAR.

Because he knows the value of the complete record, Mr. Bennett's compilations supply all the available information therein.

This compilation of the tax and militia records of Currituck, an original precinct established in 1670, is particularly important because the deeds and court minutes of the colonial period are no longer extant for that area where the spillover from Virginia was significant. The lists, culled from the corn lists, the quit rents lists, jurymen lists, tithable lists, tax lists, petitions, and militia lists from the Military Collection at the North Carolina State Archives, from the British Public Record Office, from the Colonial Court Records, and the Treasurer's and Comptroller's Papers present the names of men in the area from 1700 until the Revolution with a single index.

Often relationships are stated for taxable-aged sons in a household; some lists are divided to show married men and single men; mulattoes are identified; free negroes and some slaves are named, some of them can be identified subsequently in the households of descendants. Sometimes the acreage is given and the notation as to whether the land is a survey, a deed, or a patent ["patten"]. Sometimes descriptive locations of the land are given. Some lists mention land held by Virginians; some show delinquents or say "not to be found." That comment suggests migration and movement.

Sometimes a man is taxed for land owned by a land company, thus supplying evidence of his occupation and another record source to be consulted. An idea of economic situation supplies hints as to other record groupings that may provide information.

Since most of the lists are not alphabetized, the reader gains a knowledge of neighbors, important information in establishing migration. Analyses of lists indicate when sons come of age, when a wife becomes a widow and is suddenly taxed for land previously charged to a man. A run of lists covering the colonial period is a boon in any area but particularly in one where the majority of the early records are missing.

The militia lists provide the names and ranks of commissioned officers and soldiers, providing proof of service for hereditary societies.

The most important function of the lists, however, is to place specific persons in an exact area at a particular time. Gentleman William D. Bennett has again, with painstaking persistance and patience provided with the publication of these lists further proof of his dedicated service to historians and genealogists.

Jo White Linn
Past president,
North Carolina
Genealogical Society

INTRODUCTION

Currituck County was one of the original precincts established in Albemarle County by 1670. The original county (precinct) included present Currituck County and Dare County and parts of Hyde and Tyrrell Counties. Nearly all of the early records of Currituck County at the county level have been lost. The deed books begin in the 1760s and include a few land records from the early eighteenth century. The minute books begin in 1799 and there are a scattering of loose papers from about 1780. Currituck County played an important part in the economy of the colony during its formative years. Currituck Inlet, now closed, provided easy access to the inland sounds without the dangers of Diamond Shoals encountered when using inlets to the south. For this reason, some New England merchants established offices along the western shores of Currituck Sound in the area known today as Currituck Shores. In the seventeenth century records, one finds numerous bonds that were payable in produce delivered to Currituck. While the Carolina Charter of 1665 had established the northern boundary of the province as the "North end of Carahtuke River or Gullet" (the north side of old Currituck Inlet), the Virginia Colony continually tried to exercise authority of much of northern Currituck County. Virginia claimed that the Charter of 1665 was not valid and in the early 1680s undertook to collect quit rents and taxes in Currituck. Around 1696, the sheriff of Princes Anne County, Virginia, seized goods, in an attachment, that were located on Crow Island in Currituck Sound. This island was clearly within the bounds of the Carolina Province. In another instance, an arrest warrant was issued for Christopher Merchant, clerk of court and collector of customs for Currituck, on charges that he had attempted to act as collector of customs in Princess Anne County. A document published by J. R. B. Hathaway in 1903 from records then at the courthouse in Edenton, North Carolina (North Carolina State Archives, Albemarle County Records, Shelf Mark CR 02.002), is a petition from inhabitants living along the North West River, in northern Currituck. This document reads in part, "Being soe ner as is Supposed to the Line of Virginia that many of us are great Sufferers to the Loss of Several Tracts of Land by Surveys and patents granted out of Virginia." That they "in the time of the Right Honoble John Archdale Esqr then Governor" (Archdale was acting Governor about 1685) brought a petition that the Governor and Council "thought it reasonable that we Inhabitants Should not be forced to take patents or pay Quitt Rents for our land untill the Line be runn between her Maties Dominion of Virginia and this Governmt." This document was signed by Richd. Sanderson Junr., Richd. Cominfort, Ben Tulle, Thos. Taylor, and Wm. Bateman and is tentatively dated 1705 or early 1706.

Although most of the early county records are missing, a thorough study of *North Carolina Colonial Records* and the Higher Court records and Executive Council minutes in *The Colonial Records of North Carolina Series II* provides data on many of the people living in Currituck County during its first hundred years. This volume is an attempt to bring together the lists of inhabitants of Currituck County from 1700 to 1780 found in the various colony and British records. An initial study of the records leaves one amazed at the amount of material which has survived from the colonial period. However, a more in-depth study of the laws of the colony leaves one wondering what happened to the many records generated at the time which have not survived. Some of these lists are available scattered in other publications. Approximately half of this volume consists of tax records for the first quarter century with which most researchers are unfamiliar. One of the earliest records listing land owners in Currituck Precinct is a volume entitled "Book of Warrants and Surveys: 1681-1706." This volume is found in the Secretary of State Papers, North Carolina State Archives, shelf mark S. S. 978.1. While this volume was generated in the mid1690s, it includes data as early as 1669. The volume consists primarily of lists of headrights, surveys, and grants. Transcriptions of this volume are available from Weynette Parks Haun, 243 Argonne Drive, Durham, NC 27704. The following are listed as land owners in Currituck Precinct: Thomas Cox 640 acres adjoins Jno. Bennitt [headrights: Tho. Cox, Ruth his wife, Edw. & Eliz. Cox, Jno. Buck & 8 negroes]; Richard Bright 550 acres adjoins John Stroud [headrights: Richard Bartenshall, Pricilla his wife, Richard & Susan their children assigned to Bright by Bartenshall and Jos. Sambrin, Jno. Souther, Jno. Smith, John Tully, Tho. Jackson, Ralph Madren, & Ffra. Robison assigned by Jos. Chase]; Richard Harris 268 acres adjoins Richard Comingford [headrights: Richard Harris, Susan Harris, Richardson Harris, Eliz. Harris, Mary Harris, Barbary Hodge]; Dennis Cassaul 290 acres adjoins Saml. Barnes and Ann Bayley [headrights: Tho. Bayley, Jno. Thorogood, Dennis Cassaul, his wife, Wm. Green]; Andrew Cashaul 150 acres adjoins Richard Harris [headrights: Jane Vandermulen, Tho. Lamb, Andrew Cashall, and W. Green]; John Stroud 300 acres adjoins Danl. Glascock [headrights: six negroes]; Edward Warren 350 acres on Thomas Tulls Creek [headrights: Edw. Warren, Eliz. his wife, Mary Warren, Mary Barton, Jacob Mash, Richard Richards, and Eliz. his wife]; John Sanderson 300 acres [headrights: Jno. Sanderson, Ellinor his wife, Walter McClenahan, Christopher Cnapper, Eliz. Warren, and one Indian woman]; George Bullock 550 acres adjoins W. Williams, Edw. Warren, and An Balden [headrights: eleven negroes]; Benjamin Reynaud 300 acres adjoins Edw. Warren [headrights: Benj. Reynaud, Mary his wife, Olimpa, Morgan, & Mary his children]; and Samuel Jones 203 acres on Holly Neck Point on North West River adjoins Capt. Christopher Marchant [headrights: Samuel Jones, Jno. Millington, Giles Chandler, and Luke Neale].

Thanks to the publications of J. R. B. Hathaway, two lists which appear to have disappeared during this century can be found in issues of *North Carolina Genealogical and Historical Register*. The first of these is an undated Quit Rents Roll of Albemarle County (J. R. B. Hathaway, *North Carolina Genealogical & Historical Register*, Vol. 2). Because of known data concerning some of those on the list, it would appear this list is from the late 1690s. Those listed as living in Currituck or known to have lived in Currituck include: George Bullock, Tull's Creek, Coratuck, 550 acres; Benj. Regnuad, Coratuck, 300 acres; John Sanderson, Coinjock Bay, Coratuck, 300 acres; John Shroud, Majork Creek, Coratuck, 300 acres, Edward Warren, Tull's Creek, Coratuck, 350 acres; Sam'l. Jones, Holly Neck Point, Coratuck, 203 acres; Andrew Cashnal, Coratuck, 50 acres; Dennis Cashnal, do., 290 acres; Richard Harris, Coratuck, 268 acres; Richard Bright, Majork Creek, Coratuck, 550 acres; Wm. Stafford, do., 640 acres; Henry Slade, 299 acres; Thos. Taylor, 352 acres; Thos. Vandermullen, 800 acres; Christopher Merchant, 908 acres; Edward Jones, 610 acres; Richard Sanderson, 895 acres; and Richard Sanderson, Jr., 1101 acres. It is possible this list is an abstract Hathaway made from the previously cited volume. If so, pages are now missing from the surviving volume.

The second list is an undated list of tithables for Currituck County (J. R. B.

CURRITUCK COUNTY TAX AND MILITIA LISTS

Hathaway, *North Carolina Genealogical and Historical Register*, Vol. 3, page 257). This list appears on page 1 of this volume and appears to have been made in the period between 1700 and 1705.

The next group of records are currently filed under "Higher Court Records" at the North Carolina State Archives and are found in Box CCR 190. These records in reality are "Treasurer's and Comptroller's Papers." They are settlements between the county treasurer and the treasurer of the colony or are reports from the treasurer of the colony to the governor and executive council. The first list is referred to as a "Corn List." Because of the shortage of any form of money in the colony, nearly all taxes were paid in produce. The first record of a corn tax being imposed comes from the minutes of the Executive Council for February 1711/12 and reads:

> Ordered that five hundred bushels of corn be immediately raised and sent round to Bath County for the use and subsistence of the forces now come from South Carolina.

That the inhabitants had already been taxed in corn seems apparent from the minutes of the Executive Council for March 1711/12 which read:

> Capt. Edwd. Adlard shall depart with his Sloop "Core Sound Merchant" to Pasquotank River and there take from on board "The Return" so much corn as will load his sloop and that he embrace the first fair wind and weather to go to Bath County and there apply himself to the Hon. Jno. Barnwell Esqr. Genl. of all the forces of Carolina.

In April 1712, the minutes read:

> That there have not been impressed above twelve hundred bushels of corn ordered and directed to be impressed by Act of Assembly.

Undated corn lists prior to 1715 appear to be complete lists for the year and this corn tax continued for several years. The only surviving act which called for a corn tax is found in the Laws of 1715. Chapter LXII was entitled: "An Act for raising Corn to satisfy the Debt due from this Government to the Homourable Charles Craven, Esq., Governor of South Carolina; and for the Subsistance of such Forces as shall be raised for the necessary Defense of the Frontiers of this Government." This act provided for a poll tax of one bushel of corn per poll. The corn collected in Currituck was to be sent to South Carolina as reimbursement for arms and ammunition which had been sent in 1712. While this list has been dated 1715 - 1716 by the North Carolina State Archives, at least one man on this list was dead by January 1715; thus it would appear that the list is for the period 1713 or 1714.

The next group of lists consist of the settlements between the treasurer of Currituck, both William Bell and James Brown, and the treasurer of the colony, Edward Mosely. These records cover the period from 1714 through 1721 and are found at the North Carolina State Archives filed under Colonial Court

Records, shelf mark CCR 190, Taxes and Accounts 1679-1754, folder "Tax Lists - Currituck - No Date, 1714-1721, 1751, 1752". The first list is the 1715 Corn Tax. From surviving records it would appear that the poll tax charged in 1713 was five shillings per poll. There is no complete list for 1713. The next list is a list of the 1713 poll taxes which were not paid until 1714.

In November 1714, the General Assembly ordered that each person's total assets be valued for the imposition of a tax. There appears to have been a poll tax also. Included are the lists for 1714 of ad valorem taxes paid, ad valorem taxes due but not paid, payments made by the county treasurer, and poll taxes due.

The Laws of 1715 provided for "An Act for raising the sum of two thousand Pounds annually till the publick Debts are answered." This act was necessary because of the irregularities and mismanagement committed in the manner of assessing the earlier estate and poll tax. Under this act tithables were charged fifteen shillings and landowners were charged two shillings six pence per hundred acres. This act also provided that land should be listed with the clerk of each precinct before the first day of February and taxes were to be paid by the 21st day of March.

The earliest act concerning liability for poll tax is found in the Laws of 1715. Chapter LI reads:

> All Males not being slaves in this Government shall be Tythable at the Age of Sixteen Years And All Slaves Male or Female, either imported or born in this Country shall be Tythable at the Age of Twelve Years.

A strict interpretation of this act would indicate that free blacks, mullattos, and Indians were not subject to a poll tax until they reached the age of sixteen. It was this same year that the Assembly passed an act requiring that "From henceforward the Militia of this Govermt. shall consist of all the Freemen within the same between the ages of Sixteen years and Sixty." It is this provision that has left some researchers with the feeling that free males over sixty were exempt from paying a poll tax. Nothing has been found in the laws to substantiate this presumption.

From 1715 until sometime in the 1720s there was both a land tax and a poll tax. The county treasurer's settlements for this period provide us with the lists of land taxes charged, poll taxes charged, taxes collected, payments made to indivuals for service to the county, and those delinquent in payment of taxes. It was the duty of each taxable to list his land with the Clerk before the first of February and taxes were due to be paid on the 21 of March. In 1715 and 1716. The treasurer kept a separate journal for claims he paid which primarily concerned the Tuscarora Indian War and the Indian conflicts which immediately followed it. In this journal he listed all claims he paid; the claimant was required to sign the journal. From this journal we have the signatures of a number of the early residents in Currituck County.

The Laws of 1720 reduced the tax on land from two shillings six pence per hundred acres to one shilling eight pence and the poll tax from fifteen shillings to ten shillings. This act provided for a method of listing taxes that would remain in effect for a number of years. The act provided that each constable should go to "ye Dwelling house of each housekeeper in his District on or before 11 December & demand of such housekeeper a true List of Tythables which List every housekeeper is required to give in writeing ye Number Name & Condition of every Tythable person he or they ought to pay Tax for, & in ye said List shall mention whether the same Tythable or Tythables be free, Servt., or Slave Negro Indian or Mulato, Men or Women." The Clerk was required to take this list and prepare an alphbetical account containing "An Account of each person Mastr. or Mrs. of a family who are charged with Land & Pole Tax & and plainly set down to each person ye several parcels of Land holden or Claimed by Patent, Survey or Deed." When these lists were completed, a copy was to be given the commissioner appointed by the Assembly for filing with the colony records. Included are the tax lists for 1720, 1721, and 1722.

The next list (from the British Public Record Office) is a list of those men in Currituck who were qualified to serve as jurymen at General Court. This list was originally from the Laws of 1723. The earliest copy of this law is found in correspondence from Governor Burrington, about 1729, which is deposited in the Colonial Office Papers, Class 5, Volume 293, folio 245b. These papers are Colonial Office papers concerning *America and West Indies, North Carolina*, and consists of original correspondence. The particular document concerns North Carolina Acts passed by the General Assembly with marginalia by Governor Burrington. This document, like all those included from the Public Record Office are reproduced with permission of the Copyright Officer, Public Record Office. The 1723 Act provided a list of names of all those in the colony who were qualified to serve as jurymen. Unfortunately, the land holding requirements have not been found, but ownership of at least one hundred acres was probably required.

It is over ten years later, 1735, before we find another list of the inhabitants of Currituck County. The next document is from the British Public Record Office and is found in the Treasury Papers, Accounts Departmental, Colonies: North Carolina, Class 38, Volume 277, Folio 76-78. This record is dated 12 June 1735 and is probably a result of an order of the Executive Council of 18 February 1734 (O.S.). Many of the colonists were several years in arrears in paying their quit rents. When the Lords Proprietors sold the colony to the Crown, there was question as to whom was qualified to collect the quit rents. There was extended delay in appointing a Receiver General who felt he was qualified to collect the quit rents. The Executive Council approved an order which provided that the colonists could pay one half of the arrears in June 1735 and the remaining half at a later date. This list is not a complete list of the monies that were due to be paid, it is a list only of those monies actually collected in Currituck.

The Laws of 1727 provided that additional names be added to the list of jurymen included in the Laws of 1723. Unfortunately, the surviving copy of that act included names only from Chowan, Perquimans, and Pasquotank Precincts. The Laws of 1739 in the Vestry Act provide the names of more individuals whose names were added to the list of jurymen. The surviving copy of this act is found in the British Public Record Office in the Colonial Office Papers, America & West Indies, North Carolina: Sessional Papers - Assembly, Council, Council in Assembly, 1735-1741, Class 5, Volume 344, folios 174, 174b, and 175. This record is from the North Carolina Journal of the Lower House of Assembly, 5-27 February 1739/40

In each Militia Act, starting with the Laws of 1715, the captain of each company was required to prepare a list of the men in his company each year at General Muster. These lists were to be forwarded to the Secretary of the colony. The earliest such list for Currituck County is a list of c1748 of the soldiers in the company of William Bray. This document is in the Military Collection at the North Carolina State Archives.

The next tax lists are those for 1751 and 1752. These lists are filed under Colonial Court Records in Box CCR 190. The Laws of 1749 again redefined those who were taxable. It reads:

> All and every White Person, Male, of the Age of Sixteen Years, and upwards, all Negroes, Mulattoes male or Female, and all Persons of Mixt Blood, to the Fourth Generation, of the Age of Twelve Years, and upwards, and all white Persons intermarrying with any Negro, mulatto. or Mustee, or other Person of mixt Blood, while so intermarried, and no other Person or Persons whatsoever, shall be deemed Taxables.

This act also redefined the method of listing taxes, reading:

> Every Master or Mistress of a Family, or Overseer of a Plantation, of which there is no Master or Mistress, although not summoned, is hereby required to appear before one of his Majesty's Justices of the Peace, and to give his or her List of Taxables, setting forth in such List, the Name and Sex of each Taxable Person, whether white or black, bond or free, and distinguishing such Male Slaves as are Sixcteen Years of Age, and upwards.

Those with no place of residence were required to get some householder to list them.

A list of officers in the Regiment of Currituck County in 1754 is found in the Military Collection at the North Carolina State Archives. There is also the list of the men in the company of Jacob Farrow. While this list is dated 1754, it is apparently of slightly later date. In 1754, Jacob Farrow was only a junior officer in the company. There is also the field return for the Currituck County Regiment for 1751 which provides a list of the names of the officers of each company at that date. The next list is that of the tithables of Currituck County in 1755 from a list prepared by William Shergold in 1756. The original of this list is found in the Treasurer's and Comptroller's Papers, County Settlements, Tax Lists, Box 1. The next list is that of the militia company of John Woodhouse dated c1758 the Military Collection. This list, undated, is probably of a year or two earlier since a list dated 1758 indicates that Joseph Sanderson is dead. There is also a field return of the Currituck Militia for 1763 which lists only the company comanders. The muster roll of the Currituck County Regiment from the mid 1760s provides a good list of the taxable males in the county. This list is also from the Military Collection. The field return of 1771 provides only the names of the officers of the Currituck County Militia. In the loose papers from the General Assembly for the 1773 Session can be found a petition from inhabitants in the north eastern part of Currituck County near Tull's Creek. By providing signatures of these inhabitants it may more clearly identify these men.

Attention should be called to another volume which includes many military records. This volume is *Journal "A", 1775-1776*, from the Treasurers and Comptrollers Papers. This is the record of expenses paid by Richard Caswell as Treasurer of the Southern District of North Carolina. At this time the colony was divided into two districts: the Northern District which included the Granville Proprietary and the Southern District which included the Crown lands. Included in this volume are records of expenses paid for two of the three campaigns by North Carolina troops against the British prior to the Declaration of Independence. The two included here were the campaign which led to the Battle of Great Bridge which ultimately drove Governor Dunsmore from Norfolk and the campaign that led to the Battle of Moores Creek Bridge which destroyed the Loyalist strength until Cornwallis invaded the state in 1780. There are records of several Currituck County troops involved in the Battle of Great Bridge. Among those listed were Peter Dauge, Dempsey Gregory, Thos. Relf, James Sumner, Gideon Lamb, Thomas Nuby[Newby], Mathias Brickel, John Watkins, James Garrett, Joseph Murphey, Joseph Dickinson, Thos. Beadingfield, Arthur Cotton Timothy Etheridge, Samuel Jarvis, Jos. Jones, Jas. Williams, Charles Perkins, Wm. Perkins, Robt. Heath, Saml. Linton, Thos. Coper, Saml. Halstead, Benja. Crabb, Saml. Philips, John Cockton, Elisabeth Jones, John Stanley, Jeremiah Mercer, Evan, Stanley, John Stuart, Joshua Baxter, Thos. Mercer, John Slaughter, John Hutchins, Nathan Poyner, Solomon Smith, Mr. Slacks, James White, Wm. Holloway, Hodges Brinsham, Lewis Williams, Thomas Jarvis, John Hall, Nathan Hall, Thos. Allin, Thos. Walker, Wm. Wooten, David Lindsey, Thos. Barrot, Saml. Walker, John Adams, David Hill, Josiah Cooper, William Wooton, John McCay, John Overton, William Melson, Jonathon Duke, James Gamwell, Peter Padrick Jur., Permenas Smith, Peter Gordon, Wm. Focker, Taylor Jones, Jeremiah Sexton, Isaac Simmons, Robert Poyner, and George Powers.

The last tax list in this volume is the 1779 tax list. Unfortunately, the ink of the original has faded to a light tan and the paper has also turned to a light tan and it is impossible to obtain a reproducible copy of the original. The tax for 1779 was based on the valuation of the individual's estate. Married men and single men with an estate of less than one hundred pounds were charged a poll tax. The tax in 1779 was one pound for such single men and five shillings for such married men. For this reason you will find these two groups listed separately at the end of the list.

The editor would like to express appreciation to some of the people involved in the preparation of this manuscript. First, to Mr. J. R. Lankford, Jr., Assistant State Archivist, North Carolina State Archives, for his assitance in trying to procure legible copies of each of these documents. Thanks also to the British Public Record Office for permission to reproduce records deposited with them and Clements Library, University of Michigan, Ann Arbor, Michigan, for permission to reproduce the post 1770 map of Currituck County. I would also like to thank Clearfield Company of Baltimore, the publisher, for their interest and willingness to publish this volume. And finally, but definitely not least, I would like to thank Mrs. Jo White Linn of Salisbury, North Carolina, for her interest, encouragement, and work in bringing this volume to fruition. Her constant, though subtle, insistence pressured me to complete this work.

William D. Bennett
1804 Lafayette Avenue
Rocky Mount, North Carolina 27803

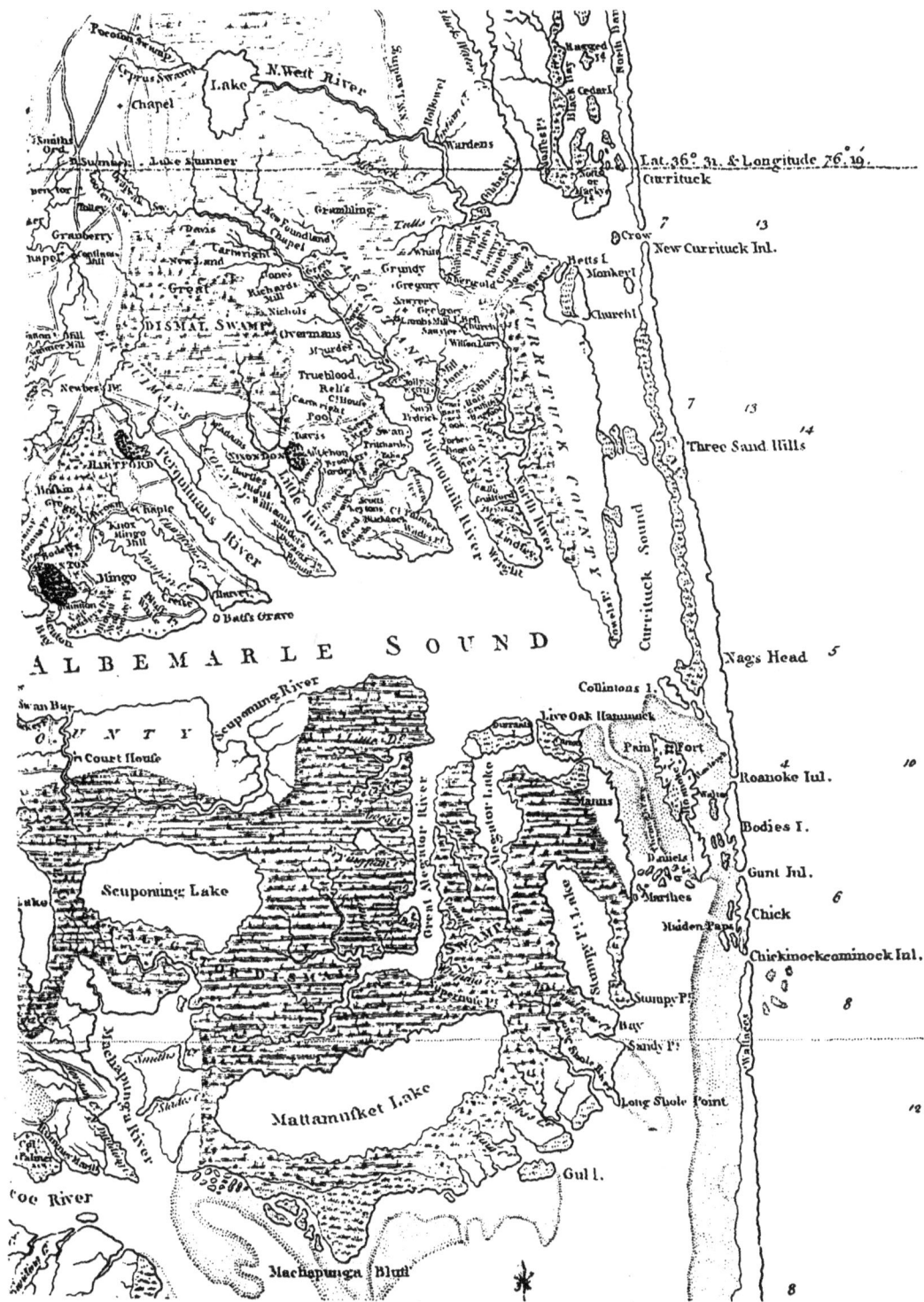

ALBEMARLE SOUND

DISMAL SWAMP

Mattamuſket Lake

Scuponing Lake

Nags Head

Roanoke Iul.

Bodies I.

Gunt Iul.

Chickinockeominock Iul.

Lat. 36° 31. & Longitude 76.19.

Plate IV

xix

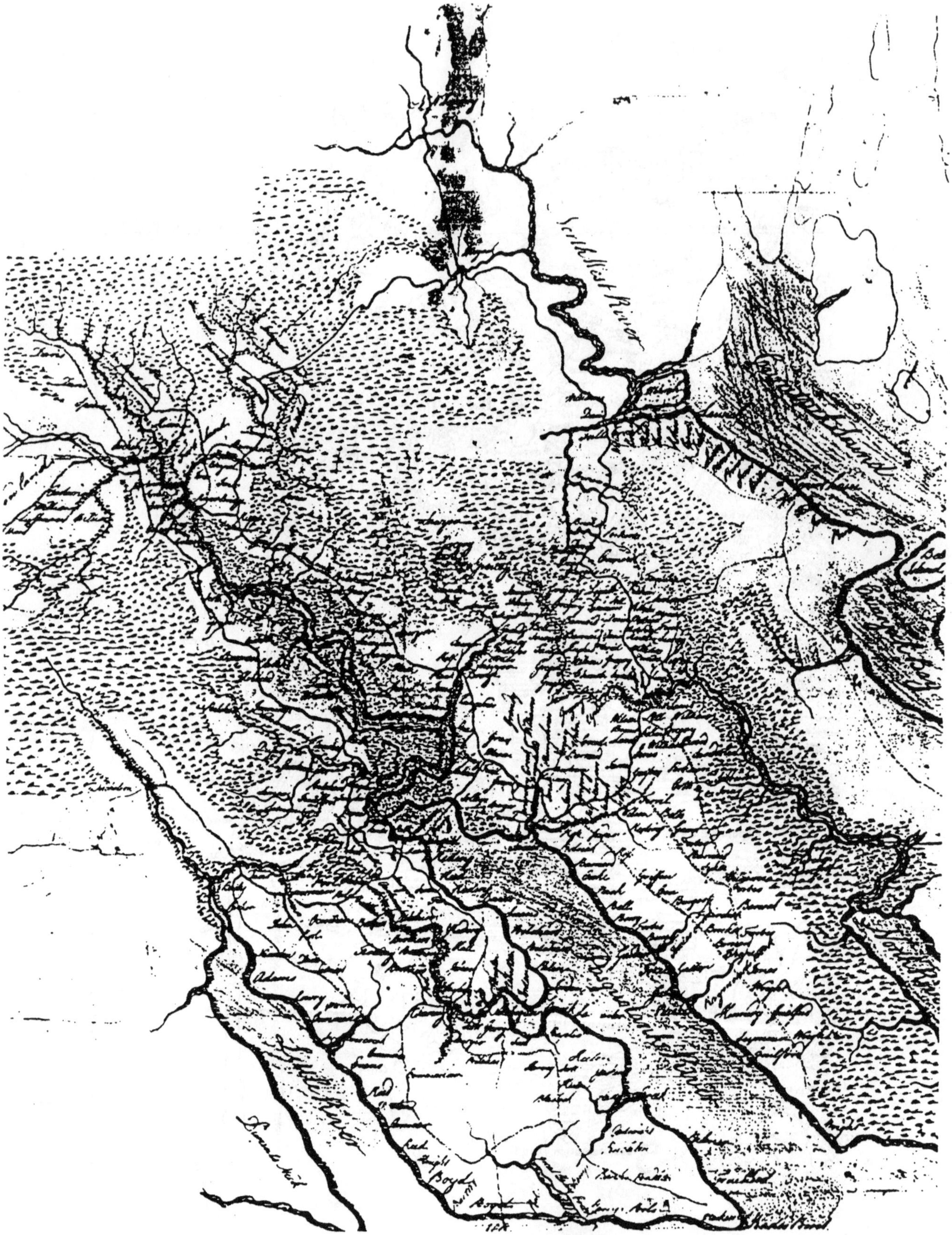

Plate V

CURRITUCK COUNTY 18TH CENTURY TAX & MILITIA RECORDS

List of Tithables in Coratuck [Undated]

Edward Mullen	1	Richard Sanderson, Jr.	3	Est[ate of] John Sanderson	1
William Steel	1	Henry Slade	4	Samuel Barnes	2
Matthias Towler	2	Richard Sanderson, Sr.	5	Thomas Vince	1
Mr. Caroon	1	Rob't Gard	1	Humphrey Vince	3
John Lewin	1	Charles Draper	1	Richard Cominfort	1
David Blake	3	Thomas Lowd	2	Rich. Harris	1
Robert Kitching	1	George Richards	1	John Baker	1
Jacob Petterson	7	Wm. Corry	1	Andrew Consoll	1
Henry Jonson	1	Edward Taylor	1	Peter Parker	1
Timothy Pead	1	Foster Gervis	7	Robert Jones	1
Mark Tully	1	Lend Smith	2	Thos. Jains [Jarvis?]	1
Thomas Young	1	Thomas Taylor	1	Thos. Vandermulen	5
John Scarborough	1	George Cooper	1	Wm. Basnett	3
Edward Jelfe	2	John Bell	4	Thos. Grandy	5
John Billet [Bennet?]	1	John Pell	1	Thomas Tulle	3
Richard Gespar	1	Wm. Fuller	1	Edmond Barron [Bowren?]	1
				Wm. Bray	1

Hathaway, J. R. B., Ed., North Carolina Historical and Genealogical Register, Volume III, p. 257.[This is not a listing of the entire precinct, rather a constable's list of one district. The original has not been found.]

Colonial Court Records; Tax Accounts; 1679-1754; Corn Lists; Loose Papers (There are two copies of this lists; One prepared in the county and the other a compilation of all the precincts.)

Couratuck Corn List [Undated]

Mr. Reading List		Mr Averidge List		Tho Poyner	1
John Bales	1	Edwd Galf	1	Wm Williams	3
John Jones Senr	2	Wm Hampton	1	John Dixon	1
Jack ye Negroe	1	Chris Burston	1	Wm Swann	4
John Woodhouse	1	Tho Spencer	1	Tho Vandermulen	4
Mr Sanderson Senr	11	Tho Evens	1	Evin Miller	1
Capt Sanderson	4	John Masson	2	John Swindall	1
Ralph Love	1	Adol Hanson	2	Aron Prescod	2
Wm Leury	2	Danl Linsey	1	Wm Parker	2
Richd Ballance	1	Saml Paine	2	Richd Cannady	1
Joseph Sanderson	4	James Corone	1	Tho Vince	2
Abra Moore	1	Petter Dauge	1	Wm Russell	1
Henry Gibson	1	John Jones	1	Tho Simons	1
Henry Hude	2	Richd Smith	2	John Walker	1
Isaac Jones	1	Petter Parker	2	John Pell	1
Azar Parker	2	John Barber	1	Thos Tayler	2
Michl Wenter	1	Richd Etheridge	2	Wm Bell	3
Robert Burrus	1		25	James Douglas	1
Henry Woodhouse	2	Mr. Vince List		Levi Smith	1
James Corowine	1/2	Thos. Hensaw	1	Jerri Smith	1
Will Willson	1	Petter Piner	1	Tho Tayler Senr	4
Tho Johnson	1	Joseph Poyner	1	Pettere Poyner	1
	41				

CURRITUCK COUNTY TAX AND MILITIA LISTS

James Roe	1	James Marttin	1	Andw Consaule	1
Ffoster Jarvis	4	Wm Ross	1	James Poyner	1
Joseph Church	7	Edwd Poyner	1	Ffr. Jarvis	1
John Mills	1	Wm Poyner	1	Humph Vince	5
John Ives	1	Saml Poyner	1	Charles Barber	1
John Lewis	1	Michl Oneal	1	Joseph Cooper	1
					76

[The list of Thomas Miller was included with Pasquotank County]
Pasquotank Precinct List

Mr. Millers List		Marm: Etheridge	3	Edwd: Cox	1
Jams: Brown	2	Jno: Nolan	3	Thos: Cox	1
Wm: Luffman	3	Marm: Capele	1	Thos: Muncrief	1
Thos: Davis	3	Geo: Thompson	2	Sam: Jones	1
Chas: Brant	1	Wm: Stafford	1	Jno: Ledget	1
Dan: Glascock	1	Edwd: Stafford	1	Dan: Suel	1
Timo: Royale	1	Cha: Stickway	1	Southwd: Denby	1
Josph: Bennet	1	Rd: Bright	1	Sam: Bateman	1
Thos: Williams	4	Jno: Harris	1	Thos: Miller	4
Ral: Doe	1	Chas: CCrib	1	Rbt: Heath	1
And: Etheridge	3	Benjn: Bennet	1	Jno: Wicker	3
Hen: Bret Senr.	2	Martin Bowlin	1		62
Hen: Bret	1	Rd: Brickhouse	3		

Colonial Court Records, Taxes & Accounts, 1679-1754, CCR 190, Tax Lists - Currituck - No Date, 1714-1721, 1751, 1752, Loose Papers

An account of Tax for ye year of 1713 payed in The year of 1714 per me Wm Bell Treasurer for Corotuck presint.

	£	S	D		£	S
Hanary Davis	1	5		John Mayson	2	10
Thomas Johnson ml	1	5		Wm Hartly	1	5
Mr Wm Swann	5			Wm Lufman Junr		15
Thomas Williamsun		12	6	John Evans	1	
Edward Cox		4	6	John Haris	1	5
Wm Wells	1	5		Nicklis Marshal	1	5
Southwood Denby	1			Edward Jones	1	5
Wm Bell	3	14		James Jones	2	10
Wm Chanse	1	5		John Hobs	1	5
Thomas Moncreef	1	5		John Pomar	1	5
Andrew Consaul		5		Wm Stool		5
John Pell	1	5		John Backly	1	5
Jos Banit		5		Wm Booling	1	5
Jos Wicker	1	5		Danil Linsy	2	10
Wm Poyner	1	5		Hanary Gibsun	1	5
Peter Parker		12		Fransis Faro	1	5
Wm Scot		5		George Salsbary		15
Mosis Royonal	1	5		Wm Johnsun	1	5
Arch Hartly	1	5		George Scarbro	1	5
Richd Smith	2	10				

An account of pol Tax for ij year of 1713 paid in
The year of 1714 pr ms wm Boll Treasurer for
Corotuck presinct —

Hearcey Harris	1	5	John Evans	1
Thomas Johnson ml	1	5	John harris	1 5
mr wm swann		5	nicklis marshall	1 5
Thomas williamson		12	Edward Jones	1 5
Edward Cox		4	James Jones	2 11
wm rolls	1	5	John hobs	1 5
southwood Denby	1		John Poman	1 5
wm Boll	3	14	wm stool	1 5
wm Charss	1	5	John Backly	1 5
Thomas muncrof	1	5	wm Cowling	1 5
Andrew Conseal		5	Daniel Linby	2 10
John poll	1	5	Hearcey Gibson	1 5
Jos Barrit		5	frances foro	1 5
Jos wicker	1	5	george sallbany	1 5
wm poyner	1	5	wm Johnson	1 5
Peter parker		10	george scanbro	1 5
wm scot		5	Moneys paid	
Moses Roynal	1	5	Reed by Wm	
Arch heatly	1	5	Bell in Corotuck	
Rich smith	2	10		
John mayhun	2	10		
wm Heatly	1	5		
wm Lufman iunr		15		

Plate VI

3

CURRITUCK COUNTY TAX AND MILITIA LISTS

In Obediance to An Act of Assembly made and Ratified ye 6th Day of November anno dom. 1714 Impowering and Commanding to ye commissioners To Take a Trew Accot of ye Estates of ye iinhabitants of Corotuck That a Just Rate Tax Might be Laid which accot. orderly followeth - Vizt- [Valuations in pounds]

Name	Value	Name	Value	Name	Value
John Mannin	10	Alexdr Maccoy	5	John Whidbe	40
Henr. Davis	10	John Beckly	1	John Jones Jr.	10
Fra. Farrow	5	Adalphus Hanson	5	Isaac Jones	12
Dav'd Jones Sen	30	Richd Smith	50	Henr. Woodhouse	40
Dav'd Jones Jr	10	John Mason	10	Edwd Poyner	30
Rich'd Johnson	20	Mathias Towler	5	Capt Lionell Reading	300
John Neal	150	John Evans	15	Capt Richard Sanderson	400
Wm Wells	20	Geo Scarbrough	5	[Jo]hn Smith free negro	26
Thos Spencer Sen	40	Danll Linsey	10	Wm Lerry	100
Henr. Gibbs	10	Levi Smith	50	Timo Ives	50
Geo Barnes	10	James Duglas	10	Abraham Boom	5
Moses R_____	10	Peter Poyner Jr	12	Henr. Gibson	5
Wm Johnson	10	Wm. Bell	200	John Sanderson	300
Dav'd Linsey	5	Richd Etheridge	60	Rich Sanderson Esqr	750
Ralph Mathan	20	John Bailes	25	John Woodhouse	700
Wm Hanson	20	[Josi]ah White 1 year	18	James Rowe	10
Thos Spencer Jr	20	[Jam]es Carron Senr	20	Azricam Parker	70
Edwd Jelfe	1	[Jam]es Carron Jr	6	Foster Jervis	210
Christ. Bustin	1	Sam'£ Paine	30	Jos. Church	360
Ambros Maccoy	30	Capt James Dauge	65	John Mills	10
Michal Winter	5	Wm Linton	15	Benja Tully	87
Conl Wm Reed	500	Danl Makefasion	7	Southwood Denby	30
John Selley	120	Martin Boulin	5	Peter Parker	60
Michl Oneal	75	Elizabeth William	5	Rich Dauge	20
John Pell	40	Robt Bell	5	Peter Dauge	10
Tho. Taylor Jr	65	Thos Davis	120	Leach Jacob	35
Wm Russell	70	Thos Miller	270	Elizabeth Northan	110
Thos Simons	10	John Brent	12	John Lewis	5
Margtt Morris	10	Luke White	40	Wm Hunter	25
John Walker	7	Humph Vince	220	Rich Jones	2
Wm Carsewell	5	Thos Vince	80	James Martine	15
Darby Bartlitt	25	Catrine Evans	12	Thos Creed	28
Henr. Slade Sr	60	Richd Cannady	2	Wm Davis	5
Alex Brent	30	Aron Precod	39	Edwd Bonny	5
Wm Scott	10	Wm Parker	30	Jos Berkley	15
James Brown	75	Richd Morton	10	Benja Beaselly	2
Wm Johnson malatto	5	John Swindall	10	Ralph Love	15
Richd Ferrill	6	Saml Wentworth and		Wm Hancock & Edmd	
Saml Jones	45	Compa Merchants		Ashley of Virginia	34
Thos Muncrief	12	of Boston	80	John Jones	130
Charles Brent	20	Tho Vandermulen	180	Geo Draper	15
Willoughby Merchant	35	Wm Swann	220	Samuel Poyner	5
Danl Glasco Jr	6:10:0	Evan Miller	6	James Poyner	2
Andr Etheridge	50	Jos Poyner	24	Wm Wilson	14
Marmeduke Capell	25	Peter Poyner Sen	35	Richd Ballance	21
Geo Thomson	30	John Dickson one year		Timo Matthews	15
Charles Sinqua	20	in the gov'rent	40	Jeremiah Smith	2:10:0
Adam Peavey	10	James Keath one year in the gov	30		

CURRITUCK COUNTY TAX AND MILITIA LISTS

Wm Lufman	80	John Harris	5	Fra Jones	31
Jos Bennit	30	Wallis Bray	70	Henr Claten	53
Robt Heath	45	Charles Barbor	15	Wm Stevens	45
Thos Cox	15	John Barbor	15	Geo Duran	10
Thos Cox Jr	8	Jos Cooper	18	Wm Wamoth &	
Wm Stafford	90	John Perkins, Jr	16	Rob't Wamoth	15
Richd Bright Sen	60	Danll Savell	15	Jonathon Jacocks	30
Henr Bright Sen	35	Marmeduke Ehteridge	78	John Wade	45
Richd Bright Jr	10	John Etheridge	2	Capt. John Palin	5
Benja Bennit	50	Thos Fanshaw	35	Wido Scarbrough	6
Edwd Jones	55	Thos Poyner	10	Conl Thos Boyd	80
James Jones	25	Wm Poyner	9	Capt Cornl Jones	40
John Worrill	10	Fras Jervis	35	Eman Low	45
Wm Etheridge	15	Thos Swann	80	Patrick Callehan	1
Nicho Mershll	25	Andr Consaul	25	Wm Powell	5
Henr. Etheridge	35	John Legatt	20	Thos Tayler	200
Saml Ballance	15	Thos Dudley	9	Wm Nicholson	108
Wm Williams	88	Thos Williamson	12	Tho Johnson	15
Jos Wicker	140	Tho Williams	200		

Given under our hands this 12 day of Jan 1714/15

Tho Taylor   Wm Nicholson   John Jones   Tho Williams   Wm Williams   Tho Williamson

Vera copia test   [Joseph] Wicker   Clerk to the Commissioners1

November ye 15th day 1714 Then This Acount was Drawn out of my book of what monny Is payed out of the publick Treasury per me Wm Bell

Cap Richard Sanderson	50=05=0	John Smith	2=07=6
Tho Tayler	6=05=0	Lews Smith	14=0
Wm Wallis	8=05=0	Wm Russel	1=00=0
John Woodhouse	18=12=6	Tho Underwood	10=0
Sam Poyner	6=05=0	Jams Poynar	2=00=0
Tim Mathis	15=15=0	Richard Johnsun ___	2=00=0
Asaricum Parker	30=00=0	Michil Onall	5=09=0
Joseph Church	8=15=0	Richard Canady	2=15=0
Wm Bell	33=02=6	Hanary Woodhouse	2=10=0
Wm Bray	34=05=0	George Tomsun	17=10=0
Peter Poyner	2=00=0	Tho Milar	5=10=0
Evan Mil[Torn]	8=02=0	John Mixson	5=10=0
Moses Pos[Torn]	5=05=0	James Martin	1=04=0
Danis Ro[Torn]	7=00=0	Robard Bucknar	5=00=0
Torn]	5=15=0	Wm Hughs	5=10=0
Tho Poyn[Torn]	10=00=0	Joseph Sandersun	3=09=10
Sam Payn[Torn]	9=10=0	Sam Ballans	5=0
Tho Taylor Senr	3=06=0	Hugh Jons	2=00=0
Jams Duglis	7=10=0	Isack Jacobs	10=0
Wm Poynar	5=00=0	John Barbar	2=00=0
John Lagit	1=00=0	Charles Barbar	2=00=0
John Pirkins Junr	2=00=0	Hanary Slad	1=10=0
Cap John Walstar	9=05=0	John Wallis	3=10=0
Wm Lurry	8=18=0	John Tobe	1=10=0
Tho Muncref	1=00=0	Charles Hill	1=05=0
Peter Dauge	8=05=0	[Torn]	
Boniaman Tulle	11=10=0	Tho Johnson	5=10=0

CURRITUCK COUNTY TAX AND MILITIA LISTS

John Atharidge	15=0	Jams Caran	6=00=0
Gras Darnal	2=00=0	John Caron	10=0
John Wicker	15=0	John Mackuin	2=15=0
Humfrey Vince	2=00=0	John Onall	2=10=0
Richard Ballans	21=05=0	Hanary Gibs	2=10=0
Jame Dauge	5=06=4	Tho Evins	3=15=0
Hanary Gibson	5=05=0	Wm Ros	10=0
Sam Miller	2=00=0	James Moon	2=10=0
Peter Parker	1=15=0	John Pirkins Senr	1=14=0
Tho Vandermulen	1=15=0	Wm Parker	5=0
Fostar Jarvis	13=05=0	Tho Spenser	10=0
Tho Johnson malato	5=0	Robard Burrus	10=0
Wm Rolloson	5=00=0	John Butsun	1=00=0
Mr Wm Swann	8=11=0	Cornelas Rogar	3=10=0
Richard Sanderson Senr	12=19=8	Wm Nickalson	1=15=0
Joseph Ward	4=01=0	John Jons	3=05=0
_____ [Torn]	2=10=0	Hanary Davis	5=05=0
Richard Jon[Torn]	2=00=0	Wm Rolin	5=10=0
John Powil	4=00=0		

An Acount of Delinquin Bills

Peter Poynar Junr	2=10=0	Hanary [Torn]	5=00=0
Mr. Wm Swann	2=10=0	Tho Mas[Torn]	5=00=0
Edward Cox	2=10=0	Andrew [Torn]	5=00=0
Charles Brunt	2=10=0	Jams Pa[Torn]	5=00=0
Tho Muncref	2=10=0	Marma[Torn]	2=10=0
Tho Simons	2=10=0	Tim Eives	2=10=0
Edward Jons	2=10=0	Wm Rolls	5=00=0
Jams Jons	2=10=0	Hanary Gibs	5=00=0
Wm Scot	2=10=0	John Mackuin	5=00=0
Wm Nickalsun	2=10=0	David Jons	5=00=0
Ben Brickhous	5=00=0	Nick Marshal	5=00=0
Andrew Consall	5=00=0	Wm Johnsun malto	5=00=0
John Mixsun	2=10=0	John Polk	2=10=0
Wm Johnsun	5=00=0	Southwold Denbigh	5=00=0
John Hobs	5=00=0		

November ye 16th Day 1714
An acount of what munny Is Reseved in to the Treasury for Laves per me Wm Bell

Tim Mathis	1= 5=	Richard Tharp	1= 5=
Evin Milar	1= 5=	Aron Pescod	2=10=
Richard Ballans	1= 5=	John Woodhous	1= 5=
Wm Russil	1= 5=	Hanary Woodhous	1= 5=
Jams Dauge	1= 5=	Ralf Love	1= 5=
Sarah Borin	1= 5=	Luke White	1= 5=
Love Smith	2=10=	Humfre Vincs	6= 5=
Richard Cannady	1= 5=	Wm Williams	3=15=
Richard Brite Senr	3=15=	Tho Taylar	7=10=
Richard Brite	1= 5=	John Swindal	1= 5=
George Tomsun	1= 5=	[Illegible]	1= 5=
John Nixson	1= 5=	Peter Poyner junr	1= 5=

Joseph Coopar	1= 5=		Jams Duglis	1= 5=
Beniaman Tulle	2=10=		Jams Caron Senr	2=10=
Sam Ballans	1= 5=		Sam Payn	1= 5=
John Jons	1= 5=		Jams Caron	1= 5=
John Jons [Torn]	1= 5=		Tho John[son]	1= 5=
Wm Bray	5= 0=		John [Torn]	1= 5=
Charles Barbar	1= 5=		Hanary [Torn]	1= 5=
John Barbar	1= 5=		Tho [Torn]	1= 5=
Wm Willsun	1= 5=		John [Torn]	1= 5=
Wm Nickalsun	1= 5=		Richard [Torn]un	1= 5=
Richard Dauge	1= 5=		Tim Eives [Torn]	5= =
John Smith	1= 5=		Michil Onall Senr	2=10=
Tho Vincs	2=10=		Peter Poynar Senr	1= 5=
Joseph Poynar	1= 5=		Tho Vandermulin	5= =
Charles Brunt	1= 5=		Fostar Jarvis	5= =
Sam Poynar	1= 5=		Asaricum Parker	2=10=
Hanary Slade	2=10=		Tho Evins	1= 5=
Wm Lurre	2=10=		Wm Ros	1= 5=
Wm Frost	1= 5=		Edward Poynar	1= 5=
John Mills	1= 5=		Tho Poynar	1= 5=
Wm Parker	2=10=		Danil Glasco	1= 5=
Joseph Church	8=15=		Hanary Brite	3=15=
Peter Parker	2= =		Edward Cox	1= =
John Walker	1= 5=		Tho Cox	1= 5=
Sam Jons	1= 5=		Tim Royal	1= 5=
Wm Stafard	1= 5=		Wm Muncreef	1= 5=
Tho Fanshaw	2=10=		Tho Cox Junr	1= 5=
Tho Spensur	1= 5=		Jams Poyner	1= 5=
Richard Atharidge	1= 5=		Wm Scot	1= =
Cap Richard Sandarsun	7=10=		Joseph Wickar	2=10=
John Pirkins	1= 5=		Tho Williamsun	12=6
Joseph Sandarsun	6= 5=		John Lagit	1= 5=
John Sholar	1= 5=		Daniel Sisils	1= 5=
Marmarduke Atharidge	3=15=		Andrew Consall	1= =
Tho Brunt	1= 5=		Ben Brickhous	1= 5=
Tho Davis	3=15=		Southwood Denbe	5=
Robard Booth	1= 5=		Hanary Pirkins Junr	1= 5=
Richard Sandarsun Senr	10= =		Robard Burrus	1= 5=
Tho Williams	5= =		Wm Boll	1= 6=
Ambrus Maccoy	3=15=		Widdo Hutsun	1= 5=
Tho Simans	1= 5=		Isak Jacobs	1= 5=
Wm Hamton	1= 5=		Cornl. W[Torn]	4=14=
John Bay[Torn]	1= 5=		Joseph W[Torn]	2=10=
John Whid[bee]	15=		Fransis Jarvis	1= 5=
John Br[Torn]	1= 5=		Adam Pave	1= 5=
Widdo Noth[Torn]	2=10=		Charles Singuay	1= 5=
David Jons	2=10=		Wm Linton Senr	1= 5=
Wm Lufman Senr	2=10=		Wm Atharidge	2=10=
Marmarduke Capil	1= 5=		John Warin	1= 5=
Jams Martin	1= 5=		Hanary Lanly	1= 5=
Fredarick Moris			Sam Millar	1= 5=
Wm Stool	1= =		Tho Swann	1= 5=

Robard Boll	1= 5=	Wm Lufman Junr	10=
Wm Johnsun	2=10=	Jams Patesall	1= 5=
Richard Morton	1= 5=	Hanary Atharidge	1= 5=
Andrew Atharidge	2=10=	Ben Banit	1= 5=
Tho Millar	3=15=	John Evins	5=
Joseph Banit	1= =	Wm Davis	1= 5=

A List of Tithables for ye Prect of Corotuck for ye Yearr 1715 Taken By ye Clk of Said Prect In Obediance to An Act of Assembly Vizt

Richd Etheridge	2	Henr Slad[e] Senr	3	James Ro[we]	1
James Carron Senr	1	Wm Wilson	1	Azricam Parker	2
Peter Dauge	1	Lionel Reading Esqr	4	John Rannalls	1
James Dauge	1	Wm Lerry	2	Ffoster Jervis	5
John Whidbee	1	Henr Woodhouse	3	Joseph Church	7
John Bailes	1	Henr Gibson [torn]		John Mills	1
Josiah White	1	Robt Gurris [torn]		Robt Bell	1
Conl Wm Reed	8	Richd Sanderson Esqr	10	Thos Tayler Senr	4
John Jones Senr	3	Joseph Sanderson	5	Levi Smith	1
John Jones Jnr	1	John Smi[th] free negr	1	Jeremiah Smith	1
Isaac Jones	1	John Wood[hou]se	1	James Duglis	1
Wm Bell	3	Marmeduke Etheridge	3	Thos Swann	2
John Pell	1	Thos Johnson mallato	1	Richd Dauge	1
Michl Oneal	1	Robt Heath	1	Benja Tulle	1
Wm Carsewell	1	John Brent	1	Joseph Berkly	1
Wm Nicholson	1	Charles Brent	1	Ralph Love	1
Luke White	1	Thos Brent	1	Edwd Cox	1
Thos Vince	2	Thos Davis	2	Thos Cox Junr	1
Humphry Vince	6	James Brown	4	Richd Smith	2
Wm Parker	2	Obediah Rich	1	Geo Thomson	2
Aron Prescod	2	Wm Powill	1	Geo Scarbrough	1
Evan Miller	1	Saml Jones	1	John Evans	1
John Swindell	1	Danl Glasco Senr	1	Thos Simons	1
Thos Vandermulen	4	Danl Glasco Jur	1	Adolphus Hanson	1
Wm Swann	4	Thos Muncri[ef]	1	Wm Poyner	1
[Jo]seph Poyner	1	Timo Royall	1	Saml Poyner	1
[Ja]mes Poyner	1	Thos Miller	5	[E]dwd Poyner	1
[W]ido Poyner	1	Thos Williams	4	[Th]os Evins	1
A]ndr Consaul	1	Andr Etheridge	2	[John] Mason	1
P]eter Poyner	1	Luke Ethe[ridge]	1	[____] Linsey	1
[J]ohn Dickson	1	Chris Loansdaile	1	Chris Bustin	1
Wallis Bray	2	John Kite	2	[A]mbros Maccoy	2
Wm Williams	2	Joseph Bennit	1	[A]rchbl Hartley	1
[Jo]seph Cooper	1	Benja Bennit	1	Wm Johnson	1
[Jo]hn Perkins Senr	1	Wm Lufman	2	Thos Spencer	1
Charles Barber	1	Henr Brite Senr	1	Wm Hanton [Horton?]	2
John Barber	2	Richd Brite Senr	1	Thos Williamson	1
Peter Parker	2	Richd Brite Jur	1	John Ives	1
John Perkins Jur	1	Richd Brite son to Henr Brite	1	James Marten	1
Danl Savell	1	Henr Brite Jur	1	Thos Tayler	2
Southwood Denby	1	Wm Stafford	1	Wm Russell	2
John Legatt	2	Edwd Stafford	1	Wm Scott	1
Ffra Jervis	1	Charles Sinqua	1	Benja Brickhouse	1

CURRITUCK COUNTY TAX AND MILITIA LISTS

Name		Name		Name	
Thos Fanshaw Senr	2	Adam Peavey	1	James Carron Jur	1
Thos Fanshaw Jur	1	Marten Boling	1	John Carron	1
John Fanshaw	1	Edwd Jones	2	Joseph Wicker 2 slaves	2
John Northern	1	James Jones	1		

vera Copia Test Jos Wicker Clk Cot

Levies Receved In Corrytuck for the year 1715 pr James Browne Treas.

March		lev	£	S
9	Samuell Jones	1		15
12	Andrew Etherige	3	02	05
12	John Northen	3	02	05
13	Robert Heath	1		15
14	Henry Slade	3	02	05
14	Joseph Poyner	1		15
16	William Scote	1		15
16	Richard Dauge	1		15
17	Henry Bright Ser	1		15
17	Thomas Cox Jur.	1		15
17	Martien Bowlin	1		15
17	Henry Bright Jur.	1		15
17	Thomas Miller	5	03	15
17	Nickcolas Mershall	1		15
19	Charles Brunt	1		15
19	William Bell	3	02	05
19	William Caswell	1		15
19	Thomas Tayler Ser.	4	03	
19	Sarah Smith	1		15
19	Thomas Tayler Jur.	2	01	10
19	James Duglas	1		15
20	Michll. Winter	1		15
20	Richard Sanderson Esqr	10.	07	10
20	James Martin	1		15
20	Lionell Reding	4	03	
20	William Willson	1		15
21	James Carron Ser.	1		15
21	James Carron Jur	1		15
21	Adolphus Hanson	1		15
21	John Jones Ser.	2	01	10
21	John Carron	1		15
21	Isaac Jones	1		15
22	Abraham Bome	1		15
22	Petter Dauge	1		15
22	John Smith free Negro	1		15
22	William Lerry	2	01	10
22	Robert Borres	1		15
22	Henry Woodhouse	3	02	05
22	Henry Gibson	1		15
22	Coll. William Reed	8	06	
23	Michall Oneall Ser.	2	01	10
23	John Pell	1		15
24	Thomas Simons	1		15

March		lev	£	S
24	Thomas Spencer Chekencomick	2	01	10
24	Capt. William Nickalls	1		15
24	Humphry Vince	6	04	10
24	John Mills	1		15
24	Thomas Vince	2	01	10
27	Mermeduck Etherige	3	02	05
27	Daniell Glasco Ser.	1		15
27	Danieli Glasco Jur.	1		15
28	James Browne	4	03	
29	Benjemen Tull	2	01	10
31	Daniell Savell	1		15
31	Thomas Fansha Ser	2	01	10
31	John Fansha	1		15
31	Thomas Fansha Jur.	1		15
31	Henry Etherige	1		15
April				
2	John Kitts	2	01	15
2	John Haris	1		15
2	Edward Stafford	1		15
2	William Stafford	1		15
2	Walis Bray	2	01	10
2	John Dixson	1		15
3	Benjemen Bennet	1		15
3	John Pirkens Ser.	1		15
3	Moses Linton	1		15
3	John Waron	1		15
3	Richard Ballones	1		15
3	John Liggit	2	01	10
3	Frances Jervis	1		15
4	Azricom Parker	3	02	05
9	Benjemen Brickhouse	1		15
9	Adam Pavey	1		15
9	Thomas Brunt	1		15
9	Widow Poyner	1		15
9	Petter Poyner	1		15
9	Edward Cox	1		15
9	Charles Sinqua	1		15
10	John Woodhouse	1		15
10	William Poyner	1		15
10	Edward Poyner	1		15
10	Thomas Evens	1		15
10	Luke White	2	01	10

CURRITUCK COUNTY TAX AND MILITIA LISTS

April		lev	£	S
10	Henry Gibs	1		15
10	David Jones Ser.	1		15
10	David Jones Jur	1		15
10	John Oneal	1		15
10	John Lewist	1		15
10	William Wells	1		15
10	Richard Jonston	1		15
10	Mr. Joseph Church	7	05	05
10	Mr. Foster Jervis	5	03	15
10	Aron Prescot	2	01	10
10	Even Miller	1		15
10	Jerimiah Smith	1		15
10	John Ives	1		15
10	Southerd Danby	1		15
10	Samuell Poyner	1		15
10	John Jones Jur.	1		15
10	Joseph Sanderson	5	03	15
11	Petter Parker	2	01	10
11	William Parker	1		15
11	Ralph Love	1		15
11	Joseph Beckly	1		15
11	William Rusell	2	01	10
11	John Man	3	02	05
11	John Robertson	1		15
11	Thomas Williams	4	03	
11	Richard Etherige	2	01	10
11	Mr. Thomas Vandermulen	4	03	
14	Charles Williamson	1		15
14	Edward Bonny	1		15
14	Thomas Williamson	1		15
14	James Poyner	1		15
14	Richard Bright Son to Henry Bright	1		15
14	Thomas Muncref	1		15
14	William Hamton	2	01	10
14	John Barber	2	01	10
14	Charles Barber	1		15
16	Obedyah Rich	1		15
25	Andrew Consales	1		15
25	John Pirkens Jur.	1		15
27	Thomas Spencer rown ocke banks	1		15
27	John Evins	1		15
27	Daniell Linsey	1		15
27	John Mason	1		15
27	John Bailes	1		15

April		lev	£	S
27	Josiah White	1		15
27	Christopher Bustian	1		15
28	Mr. Thomas Swann	2	01	10
28	Joseph Cuper	1		15
30	Christopher Lonsdale	1		15
May				
3	Joseph Bennet	1		15
3	Benjemen Beasley	1		15
9	Thomas Davis	2	01	10
12	Robert Tucker	1		15
17	William Luffman	4	03	
21	John Whedbe	1		15
28	Thomas Jonston	1		15
29	Mr. William Williams	2	01	10
29	John Brunt	1		15
30	John Swindall	1		15
June				
1	Temothy Royall	1		15
2	William Jonston rown oke banks	1		15
18	Mr. William Swann	4	03	
21	Henry Laley	1		15
21	George Solsbery	1		15
22	William Powell	1		15
25	Richard Bright Ser.	3	02	05
25	Richard Bright Jur.	1		15
July				
9	James Jones	1		15
9	Edward Jones	2	01	10
10	Mermeduk Caple	2	01	10
12	George Scarborow	1		15
12	Ralfe Doe	1		15
12	Joseph Wicker	2	01	10
13	James Roe	1		15
21	Thomas Poyner	1		15
August				
24	John Chant	1		15
27	Ann Thomson	2	01	10
30	James Man	1		15
Septr.				
17	William Muncref	1		15
19	William Davis	1		15
Octobr.				
20	Richard Morlon	1		15
23	Samuell Burges	1		15

Land Taxes Receved in Corrytuck for the year 1715 per James Browne Treasr.

March		tra	aker	£	S	D
9	Samuel Jones	2	320		8	
12	Andrew Etherige	2	325		8	1 1/2

March		tra	aker	£	S	D
12	John Northen	2	450		11	3
13	Robert Heath	1	550		13	9

CURRITUCK COUNTY TAX AND MILITIA LISTS

March		tra	akers	£	S	D	April		tra	akers	£	S	D
14	Joseph Poyner	1	100		2	6	2	John Haris	1	150		3	9
17	Thomas Cox	1	100		2	6	2	Wallis Bray	1	260		6	6
17	Martin Bowlin	1	100		2	6	2	Benjemen Bennet	5	550		13	9
17	Henry Bright	2	340		8	6	3	John Pirkins Ser.	1	150		3	9
17	Thomas Miller	4	900	1	2	6	3	Moses Linton	1	110		2	9
17	Daniell McFerson	1	150		3	9	3	John Warren	1	200		5	
17	Daniell West	1	130		3	3	3	Richard Ballence	1	310		7	9
17	Daniell McCay	1	150		3	9	3	John Liggit	1	140		3	6
17	Samuel Ballence	1	279		7		4	Frances Jervis	1	100		2	6
17	Andrew McFerson	1	350		8	9	4	Azricom Parker	2	650		16	3
17	Nicklas Mershall	1	100		2	6	4	John Renalls	1	60		1	6
19	Charles Brunt	1	200		5		9	Widow Poyner	1	100		2	6
19	Mr William Bell	2	900	1	2	6	9	Edward Cox	1	640		16	
19	Mr Thomas Tayler	3	1060	1	6	6	9	Charles Sinqua	1	150		3	9
19	Sarah Smith	1	190		4	9	10	John Whodhous	1	150		3	9
19	Thomas Tayler Jur	1	450.		11	3	10	Edward Poyner	2	100		2	6
19	James Duglas	1	050		1	3	10	Richard Jones					
20	Richard Sanderson							of nots Island	1	100		2	6
	Esqr	3	1260.	1	11	6	10	Thomas Evens	1	300		7	6
20	John Henriks	2	850	1	1	3	10	Thomas Evens	1	300		7	6
20	William Wilson	1	300		7	6	10	Luke White	2	279		7	
21	James Carron	1	200		5		10	Henry Gibs	2	600		15	
21	John Jones Ser	3	720		18		10	David Jones Ser	1	400		10	
21	John Jones Ser.						10	John Oneall	1	350		8	9
	For Drapers land	1	550		13	9	10	William Wells	1	440		11	
21	Isaac Jones	1	240		6		10	Richard Jonston	1	600		15	
21	John Jones Jur.	1	200		5		10	Mr. Joseph Church	1	425		10	7
22	Petter Dauge	2	490		12	3	10	Mr. Foster Jervis	2	530		13	3
22	Petter Dauge						10	Thomas Simons	1	100		2	6
	for Jas. Dauge	1	530		13	3	10	Michal Oneall Ser	3	550		13	9
22	John Smith						10	Aron Prescot	2	160		4	
	free Negro	1	300		7	6	10	Even Miller	2	250		6	3
22	Henry Gibson	1	300		7	6	10	Jerimiyah Smith	1	100		2	6
22	Coll. William Reed	8	3370	4	4	3	10	John Ives	3	800	1		
23	John Pell	1	250		6	3	10	Southerd Danby	2	150		3	9
24	Thomas Spencer						10	John Jones Jur	1	250		6	3
	Chekencomik	1	100		2	6	10	Joseph Sanderson	4	1130	1	8	3
24	Capt. William						10	William Lerey	2	850	1	1	3
	Nickallls	2	650		16	3	11	Petter Parker	2	280		7	
24	Humphry Vince	1	450		11	3	11	William Parker	1	075		1	10 1/2
24	Thomas Vince	1	400		10		11	Ralfe Love	1	300		7	6
27	Thomas Stonhouse	1	300		7	6	11	William Rose	1	130		3	3
27	Mermeduck Etherige	2	360		9		11	Thomas Williams	3	1300	1	12	6
27	Daniell Glasco	1	260		6	6	11	Richard Etherige	2	660		16	6
28	James Browne	1	250		6	3	11	Richard Smith	3	700		17	6
29	Benjemen Tull	1	400		10		11	Mr. Thomas					
31	Daniell Savell	1	50		1	3		Vandermulen	1	400		10	
31	Thomas Fansha	2	570		14	3	14	Thomas Muncref	1	160		4	
31	Henry Etherige	1	110		2	9	14	John Barber	2	120		3	
Apr.							14	Charles Barber	2	120		3	
2	William Stafford	2	780		19	6	16	Obedyah Rich	1	260		6	6

	tra	aker	£ S D		tra	aker	£ S D
April				**June**			
26 William Hamton	1	600	15	18 Mr. William Swann	10	3020	3 15 6
27 Thomas Spencer	1	100	2 6	25 Richard Bright Ser.	2	730	18 3
27 John Mason	1	460	11 6	**July**			
28 Darby Bartlet	1	300	7 6	9 James Jones	1	240	6
28 Mr. Thomas Swann	1	200	5	9 Edward Jones	1	240	6
May				9 Charles Brunt for			
3 Joseph Bennet	2	280	7	John Cref	1	160	4
9 Thomas Davis	2	130	3 3	10 Mermeduck Caple	1	200	5
12 Robert Tuker	1	50	1 3	12 Joseph Wicker	1	400	10
17 William Luffman	2	400	10	**Augst**			
21 John Whedbe	2	400	10	23 Joseph Wicker for ye new			
21 William Rusell	1	150	3 9	England Company	1	580	14 6
29 Mr. William Williams	3	900	1 2 6	27 George Solsbery	1	300	7 6
Jun				30 Joseph Boatman	1	200	5
1 Elizibeth Williams	1	100	2 6	**Septr**			
2 John Dizson	1	360	9	17 William Muncref	1	160	4
2 Samuell Simons	2	200	5	17 Moses Ramse	1	50	1 3
2 David Liggit	1	140	3 6	17 Thomas Brunt	1	100	2 6
11 John Ives	1	600	15				

September ye 29th 1715

Then This Account was drawn out of my Book of what munny I have payed out of ye Treasury Since I made up my accounts with The Commissioners at Conl. Ed Mosslys in December the tenth 1714 = a true account per me Wm Bell Treasurer for Corotuck -

Edward Poyner Ma	14 6	Richd Sanderson	44 16	Robard Heeth	3 6
Marmarduke Capel	3 5 0	Richd Sanderson	3 9	John Pell	2 16
Wm Hamton	1 10 10	Richd Sanderson	3 14	Hanery Slade	5 17
Rd Sanderson Sen	24 3	Richd Sanderson	3 14	James Brown	15
Aron Pescot	2 12 6	James Dauge	2 16	Wm Lerry	2 16
Jos Sanderson	10	John Jones	5 12	Andrew Consaul	6 3
Jos Sanderson	2 16	Wallis Bray	3 9	Asaricom Parker	2
Even Millar	2 16	John Smith negrro	2 4	Foster Jarvis	5 12
John Barbar	4 19	Jos Church	5 12	Tho Taylor	5 3
Paul Wakefeeld	2 7	Jos Church	4	Wm Willson	1
Richd Smith	10 9	Levi Smith	5 12	John Bayls	17
James Dauge	7 8	George Tomson	5 12	Wm Wallis	4 6
Wm Williams	16 9	Richard Smith	11 4	Malloki Winter	1 2
Wm Williams	2 9	Richd Smith	4	Wm Nickalson	11 7
John Pell	1 10	Wm Poyner	2 16	Thomas Millar	7
Michill Onall	1 15	Richd Ballans	14	Benjamin Tull	4 6
Michill Onall	5 12	Wm Nickalson	5 12	Benjamin Tull	15
Peter Poyner	2 16	Dannil Linsy	1 14	Wm Swann	2 16
John Pirkins	2 9	Dannel Linsy	10	Wm Rissill	8
Tho Williams	5 12	Jos Wicker	5 12	Wm Russill	5 12
Humfry Vincs	18 4	John Wabstar	2 16	Samewell Poynar	2 4
Tho Vincs	4 10	Jos Wicker	1 5	Samewell Poynar	14
Jeremyah Smith	2 16	Jos Wicker	3 9	John Jones	1 8
Tho Spensur	5 12	Robard Heeth	2 16	Wm Parker	2
Tho Spensur	10	Marmarduke Etheridge	216	Jos Coopar	2
Richd Sanderson	29 14 10	Marmarduke Etheridge	1 12 6	Col. Wm Reed	5 18

Name	£	s	d	Name	£	s	d	Name	£	s	d
Captn.Lyonel Reeding	20	6	5	Hanery Davis		10		Peter Parker		12	
John Evens		4		John Carron		3		Wm Swann	1	14	
Wm Williams	3	2	7	Richd Ballans	1	15		Wm Swann		16	8
Jos Wicker	1	4		John Ives	2	19	2	Wm Swann	3	2	
Thomas Simans [Deleted]				Peter Dauge	5	11	4	John Lagit	1		
Abraham Boom		4		Thomas Williams	2	14		Wm Bell	3	14	
Thomas Simans	3	3		James Mohun	3	14		Edward Cox	4	6	
Andrew Consaul	3	2		Thomas Vandermulin	2	16		James Dauge	2	10	
Capn Richd Sanderson	6	16		Thomas Swann	5	12		Thomas Jonson	1	5	
Thomas Vincs	2	16		Ambras Maccoy		10		Richd Smith		5	
Charles Barbar	4	16		Wm Jonson		10		Arch Hartly	2	3	
Thomas Vincs	10	6		Wm Hunter	2	1	8	Arch Hartly		10	
Conl Wm Reed	2	9		Thomas Williamson		15		Wm Poynar	1	5	
Thomas Davis	3	6		Adam Pave		10		Thomas Muncreef	1		
				Hanery Davis		10		Wm Rees		8	
				Wm Hartly	1	14					

September ye 29th 1715

Then This account was Drawn out of my Book of what munny I Have Receved of State Tax and pol Tax Sencs I made up my accounts with The Commishanars at Conl Edward Mosslys in December The Tenth 1714 This is a True account per me Wm Bell Treasurer for Corotuck presint

Name	£	s	d	Name	£	s	d	Name	£	s	d
Richd Etheridge	1	10		Richd Etheridge		17		Cristofur Bustin			6
Richd Johnson malato		10		Richd Johnson		2		Ralph Matham		10	
John Bayls		12	6	John Bayls		2		John Evens		7	6
Wm Russil	1	15		Wm Russil		4		John Mils		5	
Jos Banit		15		Jos Banit		3		Jos Sandarsun	7	10	
Elisabeth Notharn	2	15		Elisabeth Notharn		4		Beniaman Tulls	2	3	6
Marmar Etheridge	2			Marmarduke Etheridge		6		James Brown	1	17	6
Thomas Fansar		12	6	Thomas Fansar		19		Love Smith	1	5	
Richard Brite Senr	1	10		Richd Brite Senr		6		Jeremiah Smith	1	3	
Richd Brite Junr		5		Richd Brite		2		James Caron Senr		10	
Peter Poynar Senr		17	6	Peter Poynar		2		Sam Payn		15	
Jos Poynar		12		Jos Poyn.		2		Thomas Evens	1	10	
Robard Heeth	1	2	6	Robard Heeth		2		Wm Staford	2	5	
James Martin		7	6	James Martin		2		Edward Cox		7	6
John Jones Senr	3	5		John Jones		19		Charls Brent		10	
John Jones		5		John Jones		2		Wm Scot		5	
Isack Jones		6		Isack Jones		15		Wm Lufman Senr	2		
Hanary Slade	1	10		Hanary Slade		4		John Haris		2	6
Wm Lurry	2	10		Wm Lurry		4		Luke White	1		
Hanary Woodhous	17			Hanary Woodhous	____			Dannil Linsy		5	
Richd Ballans		7	6	Robard Buras		2		Thomas Taylor Senr	1	12	6
Wm Willson		7		Wm Willson		2		Wm Poynar		5	
Benjaman Banit	1	5		Benjamin Banit		2		Andrew Etheridge	1	5	
Charles Sinqua		10		Charles Sinqua		2		Thomas Millar	6	15	
Martin Bolin		2	6	Martin Bolin		15		Dannil Glasco Junr		3	3
Jos White		9		Edward Jones		5		Thomas Muncreef		6	
Edward Jones	1	7	6	James Jones		5		Wm Caswell		2	6
James Jones		12	6	Dolfus Hansun		2	6	John Swindal		5	
Samewell Ballans		4	6	John Masun		5		Maloky Winter		2	6
George Draper		7	6	Mathe Towler		2	6	Foster Jarvis	5	5	

CURRITUCK COUNTY TAX AND MILITIA LISTS

Name	£ s d	Name	£ s d	Name	£ s d
Jos Church	9	Sam Poynar	2 6	Thomas Vincs	4
Darbe Bartlit	12 6	Dannil Makfasson	3 6	Thomas Spensur	2
Hanary Etheridge	17 6	Thomas Vandermulin	4 10	Even Millar	3
Richd Morton	5	John Dixon	1	Captn Richd Sanarsun	2
Dolfus Hansun	4	James Duglis	5	Thomas Bront	2
John Masun	2	Wm Williams	2 4	Wallis Bray	
Mathe Towler	2	John Brent	6	Jos Coopar	2
Cristofur Bustin	15	Michil Onall	1 17 6	John Smith	2
Ralph Matham	15	John Pell	1	John Whidbe	13 3
John Evens	5	Dannil Sifils	7 6	George Tomsun	17
John Mils	2	Peter Parker	1 10	John Navil	2
Jos Sandarsun	5	Peter Poynar	6	Richd Smith	10
Beniaman Tulle	19	Thomas Williams	4 15	Hanary Brite Junr	2
James Brown	17	Humfry Vincs	5 10	John Woodhous	2 10
Love Smith	2	Thomas Vincs	2	Wm Nickalsun	2 14
Jeremiah Smith	2	Thomas Spensur	10	Asaricum Parker	1 15
James Caron	4	Captn Rd Sandarsun	10	David Linsy	2 6
Sam Payn	4	Elisabeth Williams	2 6	James Poynar	1
Thomas Evens	2	Wallis Bray	1 15 6	David Jones Senr	15
Wm Staford	2	Jos Coopar	9	David Jones	5
Edward Cox	2	John Smith negro	13	Jos Wicker	3 10
Charls Brent	2	John Whidbe	1	Cap John Wabstor	2
Wm Scot	2	George Tomsun	15	Thomas Davis	3
Wm Lufman	4	John Navil	5	Hanary Gibsun	2 6
John Haris	5	Richd Smith	1 5	Thomas Spensur Senr	1
Luke White	2	John Pirkens	2	Captn Lional Reeding	7 10
Dannil Linsy	5	Southwood Donby	4 5	Thomas Dudly	4 6
Thomas Taylor	4	Richd Dauge	2	Andrew Consaul	12 6
Wm Poynar	2	Peter Dauge	2	Mr Thomas Taylor Sr	5
Andrew Etheridge	4	Tim Royal	2	James Roo	5
Thomas Millar	1 1	Sam Jones	2	Richd Cannady	1
Dannil Glasco	15	Hanary Brite	11	Mr Thomas Swann	2
Thomas Muncreef	2	Ralph Love	2	Thomas Simans	5
Wm Caswell	2	Edward Poynar	2	Margret Moris	5
John Swindal	2	Wm Davis	2	Wilaby Marchant	17 6
Malloky Winter	15	Sam Poynar	2	Wm Parker	15
Foster Jarvis	8	Ralf Doo	15	Fransis Jarvis	17 6
Jos Church	14	Thomas Vandermulin	8	Thomas Johnsun	7 6
John Shapard	15	John Dixon	15	Conl Wm Reed	13 15
Hanary Etheridge	2	James Duhlis	2	Mr Wm Swann	5 10
Richd Morton	7	Wm Williams	6	Wm Bell	5
John Pirkins	8	John Brent	2	Alos Brunt	15
South Wood Donby	15	Michil Onall	4	Thomas Poynar	5
Richd Dauge	10	John Pell	2	Timothy Eives	15
Peter Dauge	5	Dannil Sifils	2	John Lewis	2 6
Yoansis Jones	15 6	Peter Parker	4	James Carron Jun	3
Sam Jones	1 2 6	Peter Poynar	2	John Onall	3 15
Hamary Geite	17 6	Thomas Williams	8	Marduke Capil	12 6
Jos Backly	7 6	Humfry Vincs	10	Wm Hamtun	10
Ralph Love	7 6			Richd Sandersun Sqir	20
Edward Poynar	15			Aron Pescot	19 6
Wm Davis	2 6				

14

CURRITUCK COUNTY TAX AND MILITIA LISTS

Name		Name				Name		
John Woodhous	17	John Onall		2		Robard Bell	2	6
Wm Nickalsun	2	Marduke Capil		2		Richd Jones	1	
Asaricum Parker	2	Wm Hamtun		2		Wm Roos	3	
David Linsy	5	Richd Sandarsun	3	1		James Keeth	10	
James Poynar	2	Arun Pescot		4		John Barbar	2	
David Jones	4	Even Millar		2		Charls Barbar	2	
David Jones	____	James Keeth	15			James Dauge	17	
Jos Wicker	6	John Barbar	7	6		James Man	15	
Ben Brickhous	2	Charles Barbar	7	6		Ambrus Maccoy	1	
Thomas Davis	6	James Dauge	1 12	6		Wm Muncreef	2	
Hanary Gibsun	5	Thomas Cox Senr	17	6		Fransis Faro	5	
Thomas Spensur	17	Ambrus Maccoy	15			Abraham Boom	15	
Cap Lional Reeding	____	Elexsander Maccoy	2	6		Wm Etheridge	10	
Wm Lufman	4	Fransis Faro	2	6		Wm Linton	____	
Andrew Consaul	3	Abraham Boom	2	6		Wm Linton	____	
Thomas Taylor	8	Wm Etheridge	7	6		Nick Marshal	5	
James Roo	15	Wm Linton	7	6		Thomas Godard	5	
Richd Canady	2	Nick Marshal	12	6		Tim Mathis	2	
Mr Thomas Swann	4	Wm Powil	2	6		Ben Beesle	15	
Thomas Simans	2	Tim Mathis	7	6		Hanary Gibns	5	
Edward Staford	15	Ben Beesle	1	3		Wm Wells	5	
Luke Etheridge	2	Hanary Gibs	5			Hanary Lawly	2	
Wm Parker	4	Wm Wells	10			Wm Johnsun	5	
Fransis Jarvis	2	Wm Johnsun	5			George Scarbro	5	
Thomas Johnsun	2	George Scarbro	2	6		Moses Rinor	5	
Conl Wm Reed	12	Moses Rinor	5			Thomas Johnson lato	5	
Mr Wm Swann	1	John Hendrix	15			Richd Brite Junr	2	
Wm Bell	12	Thomas Williamson	6			Thomas Williamson	18	6
Danil Glasco Senr	2	Catarn Evens	6			Edward Bonny	15	
Thomas Poynar	2	Edward Bonny	2	6		Adam Pane	2	
Arch Hartly	5	Adam Pane	5			Hanary Davis	5	
John Lewis	15	Hanary Davis	5			Robard Bell	2	
John Eives	2	Wm Hunter	12	6		Robard Tucker	15	
Wm Roos	2	Saman Burgis	15					

The End of this account per me Dated this Sixteenth day of November 1715 per me W Bell

A List of the Contrys Corne Receved In Corrytuck for the year 1715 pr Humphry Vince

Name		Name		Name	
Ralph Love	1	John Pell	1	Thos: Vandermulen	4
John Ives	1	Thomas Tayler Jur.	2	William Swann	4
Wm: Davis	1	Wm: Caswell	1	John Dixson	1
Benjemen Beasly	1	Thomas Simons	1	Wallis Bray	1
Edward Poyner	1	Michall Oneall Ser.	1	Wm: Williams	2
Wm: Poyner	1	William Nickallson	1	Joseph Poyner	1
Samuell Poyner	1	Michall Oneall Jur.	1	Petter Parker	1
Foster Jervis	5	Samuell Burgos	1	Petter Poyner	1
Joseph Church	6	Luke White	1	Elizabeth Poyner	1
John Mills	1	Thomas Vince	2	John Barber	1
Michall Winter	1	Aron Prescot	1	John Pirkens	1
Thomas Tayler Ser.	4	Moses Prescot	1	Joseph Coper	1
Sarah Smith	1	William Parker	1	Humphry Vince	6
James Duglas	1	James Poyner	1	Thomas Fanshaw	1
William Bell	3	Andrew Consall	1	Thomas Poyner	1

CURRITUCK COUNTY TAX AND MILITIA LISTS

A List of the Contrys Corne Receved in Corrytuck for ye year 1715 per Thomas Miller

Andrew Etherige	3	Benjemen Brickhouse	1	Richard Bright	3
William Stafford	1	Joseph Bennet	1	Henry Etherige	1
Sanuell Jones	1	Nicklus Mershall	1	Francis Jervis	1
John Kitt	2	Robert Heath	1	John Ligitt	2
Richard Bright	1	Temothey Royall	1	Thomas Muncref	1
Henry Bright Ser.	1	Thomas Jonston	1	Benjemen Tull	2
Henry Bright Jur.	1	John Harris	1	John Brunt	1
Edward Jones	1	George Solsbery	1	Charles Brunt	1
James Jones	1	Edward Cox	1	Thomas Brunt	1
Daniell Glasco Ser.	1	James Browne	4	Charles Sinqua	1
Daniel Glasco Jur.	1	William Luffman	3	Adam Pavey	1
Robert Tucker	1	Thos: Miller	5	John Chance	1
John Etherige	3	Joseph Wicker	2	James Man	1
John Northen	3	Obediah Rich	1	Mertin Bowlen	1
Thomas Davis	2	Benjemen Bennet	1	John Pirkins Senr.	1
Thomas Williams	2	Wm: Muncref	1	Thos: Swann	2
William Scot	1	Edward Stafford	1	George Thomson	2

Corn Receved in Corrytuck pr. Lyoel. Reading

John Woodhouse	1	John Renalls	1	Isaac Jones	1
Richard Sanderson Esqr.	10	Azricom Parker	3	Henry Slade	2
		James Marten	1	Richard Ballone	1
Robert Borrows	1	Henry Woodhouse	2	Lyoel: Reading	4
James Roe	1	Abraham Boome	1	William Lurry	2
John Smith negro	1	John Jones Ser.	3	William Willson	1

Corn Receved in Corrytuck pr Richard Etherige

Richard Etherige	1	Thomas Spencer	1	William Powell	1
Christopher Bastian	1	William Hamton	1	Joseph Sanderson	5
Josiah White	1	Mermeduck Caple	2	Luke White	1
John Bales	1	Edward Jones	1		

A list of the delqts. that has not paid their Corne in Corrytuck

James Carron Ser.	1	Richard Bright Jur.	1	William Wells	1
Petter Dauge	1	Richard Dauge	1	John Lewist	1
John Whidbe	1	Joseph Beckly	1	Henry Gibs	1
Coll: Wm: Reed	8	Thos: Cox Jur.	1	David Jones Ser.	1
Henry Slade	1	Richard Smith	2	David Jones Jur.	1
Henry Woodhouse	1	John Evens	1	Richard Jonston	1
Henry Gibson	1	Adallphus Hanson	1	John Man	3
Joseph Church	1	Thos: Evens	1	John Robertson	1
Jeremiah Smith	1	John Mason	1	Fransis Farow	1
Wm: Parker	4	Daniell Linsay	1	Henry Davis	1
Even Miller	1	Ambros Mckay	2	Edward Bonny	1
Charles Barber	1	Archebald Hartly	1	Charles Williamson	1
John Barber	1	William Jonston	1	George Scarborow	1
Petter Parker	1	Thos: Williamson	1	Daniell Davis	1
Daniell Savill	1	William Rusell	2	Thos: Spencer	
Southerd Danby	1	James Carron Jur.	1	Chekencomic	2
Thos: Williams	2	John Carron	1	Edward Bright	1
Christopher Lousdall	1	John Oneall	1	William Linton	1

CURRITUCK COUNTY TAX AND MILITIA LISTS

Moses Linton	1	Henry Lawly	1	Bryhan Callyhan	1
Samuell Miller	1	John Warren	1	Ralf Doo	1
William Etherige	1	Richard Morton	1		

A list of Corrytuck Clams not paid by Wm: Bell

Andrew Barber			Samuell Sparks	2
141 days	7 1		John Lewist	15 2
John Muncref	12 6		James Dauge	12
Richard Thorpe	3 6		Henry Davis	2 18 6
Daniell Mckay	1 9		Adam Pavey	1 10
William Ballone	7		William Wells	2
Richard Hogges	1 9		William Rose	3 17
John Huttson	3 6			
Thomas Brunt	3 6		Corrytuck Clams not paid per Jas. Brown	
Henry Etherige	1 9		Andrew Barber	
John Hobs	4 4		141 days	7 1
William Stafford	5 3		John Callihan	10
John Callihan	10		Jacob Barber	4
Erasmus Haslive	5 11		Cornelyas Royall	9
Aron Prescot	3 6		John Lewist	15 2
James Carron	8 9		James Dauge	12
Cornelyus Royall	9		Henry Davis	2 18 6

A list of Consealled Tithables in Corrytuck in the year 1715

	tith	£ S D			
Francis Farow	1	15	Samuell Miller	1	15
Henry Davis	1	15	William Etherige	1	15
Edward Brighrt	1	15	Bryan Callyhan of Crotan	1	15
William Linton	1	15	Daniell Davis	1	15
Ambros Mckay and Archibald Hartly has not paid					3

Colonial Court Records, Tax and Accounts, 1679-1754, Claims, Loose Paper
Rects. for Currytuck Clames

Currytuck March ye 19th 1715/6
Then Receved of Jas. Browne Eight pounds Currant monys it being a Clame due to Wm Caswell for on hundred and Sixty days Service I Say Receved by me   Tho« Taylor

Currytuck March ye 20th 1715/6
Then Receved of Jas. Browne on pound currant money it being a clame due for Cattell kild I Say Receved by me   Michall Winter

Currytuck March ye 20th 1715/6
Then Receved of Jas. Browne on pound teen Shillings Currant money it Being a clame due for 30 days boat hire I say Recd. pr me   Ly: Leading

Currytuck March ye 20th 1715/6
Then Receved of Jas. Browne five pounds nine Shillings Currant money it being a clame due for 109 days Servis I Say Receved pr me   Wm Willson

Currytuck March ye 21th 1715/6
Then Receved of Jas. Browne three pounds Currant money it being a Clame due for Sundry
Servises due for ye Cuntry I Say Receved pr me   Ja Carron

Currytuck March ye 21th 1715/6
Then Receved of Jas. Browne two pounds Eighteen Shillings it being a clam due for 38 days
Servis and a hiefer I Say Receved pr me   Jno Carron

Currytuck March ye 22th 1715/6
Then Receved of Jas. Browne two shillings & six pence it being a Clame due for landing the
burgers wth cannon I Say receved pr me   Abraham Boom

Currytuck March ye 22th 1715/6
Then Receved of Jas. Browne three pounds eight Shillings it being a Clame due for sixty eight
days Servis I say Receved pr me   John Smith negro

Currytuck March ye 22th 1715/6
Then Receved of Jas. Browne two pounds three shillings & ten ipence it being a Clame due for
526 pounds of beef I Say Receved pr me   Wm Reed

Currytuck March ye 22th 1715/6
Then Receved of Jas. Browne two pounds Currant money it being a Clame due to my Husband
who has departed this land about three years Since I Say received pr me   Judith Sparks

Currytuck March ye 23d 1715/6
Then Receved of Jas. Browne twelve shillings Currant money it being a Clame due for Eight days
Servis I Say Receved pr me   Michial Oneall

Currytuck March ye 24th 1715/6
Then Receved of Jas. Browne two pounds Corrant monny it being a Clame due for Raissing of
Soulders and Horse to assembly I Say Receved pr me   Wm Nichols

Currytuck March ye 24th 1715/16
Then Receved of Jas. Browne fouer pounds it being a claim due For a gun. I Say Rec. pr me.
                                   Luke White

Currytuck March ye 24th 1715/6
Then Receved of Jas. Browne fouer pounds Eighteen Shillings it being a Clame due for Sundry
Commodities and Servises don I Say Receved pr me   John Northon

Currytuck March ye 27th 1716
Then Receved of Jas. Browne fouer Shillings it being a Clame due for four days servis pr me
                                   Jobe Etherige

Currytuck March ye 28th 1716
Then Receved of my selfe teen Shillings it being due for four days Servis & three Shillings and six
pence upon ye acompt of John Hudson it being due for wheat pr me   Jas: Browne

Currytuck March ye 29th 1716
Then Receved of James Browne three pounds teen Shillings it being a Clame due for a gun I Say
Receved pr me   Benja Tulle

18

Currytuck March ye 31th 1716
Then Receved of James Browne one pound teen Shillings it being a Clame due for thirty eight
days Servis I Say Receved pr me   Daniell Savell

Currytuck March ye 31th 1716
Then Receved of James Browne fouer Shillings it being a Clame due for fouer days Servis I Say
Receved pr me   John Fushore

Currytuck April ye 2d 1716
Then Receved of James Browne two Shillings & three pence it being a Clame due for wheat
Receved pr me   Wm Stafford

Currytuck April ye 3d 1716
Then Receved of James Browne Seven Shillings Currant money it being a Clame due for two
bushels of wheat I Say Receved pr me   William Ballone

Currytuck April ye 3d 1716
Then Receved of James Browne two Shillings Currant money it being a Clame due for dyett for
Soulders Receved pr me   John Pirkins

Currytuck April ye 4th 1716
Then Receved of James Browne Sixteen Shillings Currant mony it being a Clame due for Sixteen
day Servis Receved pr me   Azricam Parker

Currytuck April ye 5th 1716
Then Receved of James Browne twelve Shillings and Six pence Currant mony it being a Clame
due to John Muncref I Say Receved pr me   Charls Brunt

Currytuck April ye 5th 1716
Then Receved of James Browne four Shillings Currant mony it being due for four day Servis
Receved pr me   Benjiman Brickhouse

Currytuck April ye 7th 1716
Then Receved of James Browne fouer Shillings Currant monny it being due for fouer days Servis
Receved pr me   Wm Grea

Currytuck April ye 9th 1716 Then Receved of James Browne one pound teen Shillings it being a
Clame due for Servises done pr me   Adam Peavy

Currytuck April ye 9th 1716
Then Receved of James Browne three Shillings & Six pence it being a Clame due for wheat to
Tho Brunt Receved pr me   Ealsa Brunt

Currytuck April ye 9th 1716
Then Receved of James Browne two pounds three Shillings it being a Clame due for fourty three
days Servis Receved pr me   Thomas Pyner

Currytuck April ye 10th 1716
Then Receved of James Browne teen Shillings it being a Clam due for teen day servis Receved pr
me   William Poyner

Currytuck April ye 10th 1716
Then Received of James Browne two pounds Currant monny it being a Clame due for Care of
Wallis Received pr me   Edward Pyner

Currytuck April ye 10th 1716
Then Received of James Browne Eight Shillings and nine pence Currant monny pr me   Ja Caron

Currytuck April ye 10th 1716 Then Received of James Browne two pounds Curt: monny it being a
Clame due for Servis done Received pr me   Wm Woll

Currytuck April ye 10th 1716
Then Received of James Browne Sixteen Shillings it being a Clame due for Servis Received pr me
                                                  Jos Church

Currytuck April ye 10th 1716
Then Received of James Browne three Shillings Six pence it being due for wheat pr me
                                                  Aron Prescoat

Currytuck April ye 10th 1716
Then Received of James Browne two pound teen Shillings it being a Clame due for a gun Received
pr me   John Jones Juner

Currytuck April ye 11th 1716 Then Received of James Browne three pounds Seventeen Shillings it
being due for Servises don pr me

                                                Wm Rose

Currytuck April ye 14th 1716
Then Received of James Browne three pound two Shillings it being a Clame due for Sixty two days
Servis Received pr me   James Pynor

Currytuck April ye 14th 1716
Then Received of James Browne two pounds it being a Clame due for fourty days Servis Received
pr. me   John Barber

Currytuck April ye 19th 1716
Then Received of James Browne five pounds Corrant monnys it being a portion allowed to Wm
Wallis Received pr me   John Wallis

Currytuck April ye 25th 1716
Then Received of James Browne Eight Shillings it being a Clame due for Eight days Servis
Received pr me   Andrew Consale

Currytuck April ye 27th 1716 Then Received of James Browne four pounds Eight Shillings Currant
imonny it being a Clame due for Six qutr: of ould Stear and dyett to Soulders & teen days Servis
Received pr me   Tho Spencer

Currytuck April ye 27th 1716
Then Received of James Browne twelve Shillings and Six pence Currant monny it being a Clame
due to Christopher Bustian for landing the Burgers Received pr me   Tho Spencer

Corrytuck may y 17th: 1716
Then Recevod of James Browne two pound
Sixteen Shilling, it being due for a delinqua
bill paid to Mr Wm Swann, p me

Ed McLufman

Corrytuck may y [...]
Then Recevod of James Browne three pound
Ninteen Shillings & Sixpence by order of John
Whedbee it being due for thirty six days Servis
and a Cow and a quarter of beef Recevod p me

his
Wm W Russell
mark

Corrytuck may y 29th: 1716
Then Recevod of James Browne one pound
Eighteen Shillings it being a Clame due for
Sunday Services. Recevod p me

Wm Williams

Corrytuck may y 31th: 1716
Then Recevod of James Browne two p
Sixteen Shillings it being due for a delinq...
bill Recevod p me

Rd Bland

Corrytuck Jun y 14th: 1716.
Then Recevod of James Browne three Shillings
and Six pence it being due for one bushell
of wheat Recevod p me
his
Richard R Thorpe
mark

Plate VII

21

Currytuck April ye 28th 1716
Then Receved of James Browne five pounds Eleven Shillings by order of Ann Cowin
Administratrix to Erasmus Harlist Receved per me   Tho Swann

Currytuck May ye 9th 1716
Then receved of James Browne on Shilling nine pence by order of Daniel McKay it being due for
one halfe busshell of wheat pr me   Richard Hodges

Currytuck May ye 9th 1716
Then receved of James Browne one Shilling nine pence by order of Henry Etherig it being due
for one halfe busshell of wheat pr me   Richard Hodges

Currytuck May ye 9th 1716
Then Receved of James Browne one Shilling nine pence it being due for one Halfe Busshell of
wheat per me   Richard Hodges

Currytuck May ye 12th 1716
Then Receved of James Browne four Shillings it being due for four days Servis pr me
                    Robert Tucker

Currytuck May ye 17th 1716
Then receved of James Browne two pounds Sixteen Shillings it being due for a delinquent bill paid
to Mr. Swann pr me   Wm Lufman

Currytuck May ye 21th 1716
Then Receved of James Browne three pounds thirteen Shillings & Six pence by order of John
Whedbee it being due for thirty Six days Servis and a Cow and a quarter of beef Received pr me
                    Wm Russell

Currytuck May ye 29th 1716
Then received of James Browne one pound Eighteen Shillings it being a Clame due for Sundry
Servises Receved pr me   Wm Williams

Currytuck May ye 31th 1716
Then received of James Browne two pounds Sixteen Shillings it being due for a delinquent Bill
Receved pr me   Rd Balance

Currytuck June ye 14th 1716
Then Receved of James Browne three Shillings and Six pence it being due for one busshell of
wheat Receved per me   Richard Thorpe

Currytuck June ye 18th 1716
Then Receved of James Browne Seven pound Six Shillings Currant monny it being a Clame due
for Sundry Servises pr me   Wm Swann

Currytuck June ye 25th 1716
Then Receved of James Brown two pound Sixteen Shillings Currant munnys it being due for a
delinquent Bill Recevd. pr me   Richard Bright

Currytuck July ye 11th 1716
Then Received of James Browne Sixteen Shillings it being a Clame due for beef Receved pr me
                                                                                            Thomas Evans
Currytuck August ye 10th 1716
Then Received of James Browne four Shillings it being due for four days Servis Received pr me
                                                                                            Charles Kitt

Currytuck August ye 25th 1716
Then Received of James Browne four Shillings it being due for four days Servis Red. pr me
                                                                                            Marten Bowlen

Currytuck August ye 29th 1716
Then receved of James Browne four Shillings it being due for four days Servis Red. pr me
                                                                                            Thomas Golherd

Currytuck August ye 30th 1716
Then Received of James Browne two pound Sixteen Shillings it being due for a delinqt. bill pr me
                                                                                            Thos Miller

Currytuck August ye 30th 1716
Then receved of James Browne four Shillings it being due for four days Servis pr me
                                                                                            Joseph Boatman

Currytuck Sept ye 26th 1716
Then Received of James Browne four Shillings and four pence it being due for wheat
                                                                                            John Hobs

Currytuck October ye 23d 1716
Then Received of James Browne two pound Sixteen Shillings it being due to Humphrey Vince for a
deliqt. Bill Received pr me   Wm Swann

(A Summary of the Preceding Receipts)
Corrytuck Clams paid in the year 1715 & 1716 per James Browne

March		£	S	D
19	Wm Caswell 160 days paid to Thos Tayler	8		
20	Michall Winter for Calf Kild	1		
20	Lionel Riding for 30 days for Boat	1	10	

		£	S	D
20	William Willson 109 days Servis	5	9	
21	James Carron for Sundry Servises dun	3		
21	John Carron for 38 days & a hiefer	2	18	
22	Abraham Bome connon with burgers		2	6
22	John Smith free negrow 13 days wth burgers	3	8	
22	Coll Wm Reed for 526 pound of beef	2	3	10
22	Judith Sparks in behalf of hir husband	2		
23	Michall Oneall for 8 days Servis		12	
24	Capt. Wm Nickalls for Servis don	2		
24	Luke White for a gun	4		
27	John Nothen fo Sundry Servises don	4	18	
27	Jobe Etherige for four days Servis		4	
28	James Browne for 4 days Ensigns wth men		10	
28	James Browne for a clam due [John] Hudson	3	6	
29	Benjemen Tull for a gun	3	10	
31	John Fansha for 4 days Servis		4	

April

		£	S	D
2	William Stafford for wheat		7	3
3	William Ballone for wheat		5	
3	John Pirkins dyett for Soulders		5	
4	Azricom Parker for 16 days Servis		16	
5	Charles Brunt for wheat due to Jon Muncref		12	6
5	Benjemen Brickhouse for 4 days Servis		4	
7	William Grea for 4 days Servis		4	
9	Adam Pavey for Servis don	1	10	
9	Eals Brunt for wheat due to hir husband		3	6
9	Thomas Poyner for 43 days Servis	2	3	
10	William Poyner for 10 days Servis		10	
10	Edward Poyner for ye care of Wallis	5		
10	James Carron		8	9
	William Wells	2		

Corrytuck Clames Paid in ye year 1716

April

		£	S	D
10	Joseph Church for 16 days Servis		16	
10	Aron Prescot for wheat		3	6
10	John Jones for a gun	2	10	
11	William Rose	3	17	
14	James Poyner for 62 days Servis	3	2	
14	John Barber for 40 days Servis	2		
19	William Wallis pentioner	5		
25	Andrew Consaule for 8 days Servis		8	
27	Thos Spencer for 6 quarter oul Stear & Servis	4	8	
27	Christopher Bustian for landing burgers		12	6
28	Thos Swann for Ann Lowing adtx to Harlis	5	11	

May

		£	S	D
9	Daniell McCoy for wheat		1	9
9	Henry Etherige for wheat		1	9
9	Richard Hogges for wheat		1	9
12	Robert Tucker for 4 days Servis		4	
17	William Lufman a delin. bill paid to Wm Swann	2	16	
21	John Whedbe for 36 days Servis & beef	3	13	6

29	William Williams for Sundry Servises	1	18	
31	Richard Ballones for a delin. bill	2	16	
Jun				
14	Richard Thorpe for wheat		3	6
18	William Swann for Sundry Services	7	6	
25	Richard Bright for a deliqt. bill	2	16	
July				
12	Thos Evens for beef		16	
Aug				
16	Charles Kitt for four days Servis		4	
30	Thos Miller for a delit. bill	2	16	
30	Joseph Boatman for 4 days Servis		4	
Sept				
26	John Hobs for wheat		4	4
Octor				
23	Humphry Vince for a deliqt. bill	2	16	

An a Compt of the Contrys Corne Sould in Corrytuck pr James Browne Treasr. in ye year 1716

		busls	£	S	D
July					
13	To Petter Poyner	10	1		
14	To Mr. William Bell	45	4	10	
19	To Thomas Davis	30	3		
21	To Richard Thorp	10	1		
23	To John Etherige	5		10	
23	To Mr. William Swann	20	2		
24	To Mr. Joseph Wicker	10	1		
24	To Mr. Thomas Vandermulen	10	1		
24	To Mr. Joseph Sanderson	5		10	
Aug:					
13	To Abraham Adams	5		10	
30	To Thomas Miller	4		8	
Septr.					
1	To John Ives	5		10	
Octbr					
10	To Coll. William Reed	33	3	7	
10	To Edward Jones	1		2	
10	To William Powell	1		2	
10	To Mermeduck Caple	2		4	
10	To Luke White	1		2	

A List of Coratuk Tithables Taken for the year 1716 pr ye Constable

William Bright	1	Temethie Royall	1	Benjemen Bennet	1
Henry Bright Sr.	1	Daniell Glasco Sr.	1	Edward Stafford	2
Richard Bright Sr.	1	Daniell Glasco Jur.	1	George Solsbery	1
John Bright	1	Thos. Muncref	1	Richard Bright Jur.	1
Henry Bright Jur.	1	William Muncref	1	John Kitte	2
John Haris	1	Thos: Cox	1	Richard Bright S. to H	.1
William Stafford	1	Adam Pavey	1	James Bright	1
Cristophr. Lonsdeall	1	Robert Williams	1	Thos: Warren	1
Andrew Etherige	3	Charles Linqua	1	Henry Laly	1
Edward Cox	1	Joseph Bennet	1	Robert Smith	1
William Luffman	4	Marmeduk Caple	3	Samuell Renger	1
Saml: Miller	1	George Thomson	1	Henry Etherige	1

Moses Linton	1	Thos: Tayler Jur.	2	James Mertin	1
William Etherige	1	Thos: Tayler Ser.	5	John Ives	1
Wm: Etherige Jur.	1	Saml: Burger	1	Wm: Davis	2
Nicolas Marshall	1	Saml: Poyner	1	Benjn: Beesly	1
John Warren	1	Wm: Poyner	1	Thos: Williamson	1
William Linton	1	John Mills	1		
Edward Jones	1	Joseph Church	8	Tithables not taken by	
Mertin Bowlen	1	Foster Jervis	5	the Constable	
Thos: Miller	5	Malleke Winter	1	Benjn: Brickhouse	1
Richard Linton	1	Jeremiah Smith	1	Wm: Powell	1
Saml: Jones	2	Mioall Oneall Jur.	1	John Ives Ser.	1
Wm: Scotte	1	Wm Bell	3	Mermek: Etherige Ser.	3
Obedya Rich	2	James Duglas	1	John Northen	3
Thos: Davis	1	Abraham Bome	1	Thos: Fansher Ser.	3
James Brown	3	Henry Woodhouse	2	John Fansher	1
Charles Brunt	1	Isaac Jones	1	Thos: Fansher Jur.	1
John Brunt	1	John Jones Ser.	3	Frans: Jervis	1
Thos: Brunt	1	Coll: Wm: Reed	10	Robert Tucker	2
Robert Heath	1	John Jones Jur.	1	John Liggitt	1
Thos: Jonston	1	John Whitbee	1	Southd: Danbe	1
Joseph Coper	2	Thos: Williams	4	John Pirkens	1
John Pirkens	1	Richard Etherige	2	Danl: Savill	1
John Barber	1	Wm: Rusell	1	Richd. Selvester	1
Charles Barber	1	Petter Dauge	1	Saml: Simmons	1
Petter Parker	1	John Caron	1	Moses Ramsey	1
Richard Dauge	1	James Caron	1	George Span	1
Joseph Poyner	1	John Man	2	David Liggitt	1
Thos: Poyner	1	George Scarborow	1	John Chant	1
Petter Poyner	1	Thos: Commander	3	Joseph Wicker	1
ye Widow Poyner	2	Capt. Richd. Sanderson	2	Thos: Swann	1
Wm: Williams	2	Wm: Tillett	1	Wm: Willson	1
Walis Bray	2	Wm: Johnson	1	Richd: Sanderson Esqr.	2
Joseph Wicker	2	Moses Bino	1	John Woodhouse	1
Wm: Swann	4	Ralph Mathom	1	Joseph Sanderson	4
Thos: Vandermulon	4	Ralph Doe	1	Lionell Reeding	4
Andrew Consall	1	Danl: Linsay	1	William Lerry	2
James Poyner	1	John Evans	1	Asricom Parker	3
John Swindall	1	Wm: Hamton	1	John Smith negro	1
Wm: Parker	1	Thos: Spencer	1	Richard Ballence	1
Aron Prescot	1	John Cape	1	John Oneall	1
Moses Prescot	1	Christ: Buskens	1	Wm: Wells	1
Even Miller	1	Wm: Stevens	1	John Lewist	1
Saml: Baker	1	Adolfus Hauson	1	Henry Gibs	1
Thos: Vince	2	Ambros Mackay	2	David Jones Ser.	1
Humphry Vince	6	Richd: Smith	2	David Jones Jur.	1
Luke White	1	Thos: Johnson	1	Richard Jonston	1
Michall Oneall	1	Joseph: Beckly	1	John Robertson	1
John Conner	1	Archbell Hartly	1	Frances Farow	1
Wm: Nickallson	1	John Bailes	2	Henry Davis	1
Wm: Rose	1	John Mason	2	John Mecuing	1
John Penny	1	Christ: Bailes	1	Thos: Spencer SB	2
Thos: Simmons	1	Ralph Love	1	Bryan Callehan	1

CURRITUCK COUNTY TAX AND MILITIA LISTS

Tithables not taken by the Constable

John Callehan	1	Edward Bonny	1	Mathew Hanna	1

Levies not paid in ye year 1716

Samuell Miller Insoll	1	John Conner Insoll	1	Richard Smith	2
Timothey Royall Insoll	1	Samuell Poyner Insoll	1	Thos: Jonston	1
Edward Stafford Insoll	1	Robert Williams Insoll	1	Capt. Richd Sanderson	2
Moses Ramsey Refuses to		William Rose Insoll	1	John Bales	2
pay pretending ye		John Evens Insoll	1	Thos: Commander	3
privilige of two years	1	William Hamton Insoll	1	Wm: Tillitt	1
David Liggit cames ye		Samll Burges	1	Thos: Williams	1
same privige:	1	John Chant	1	John Whittbe	1
				Wm Rusell	1

Consealed tith:in 1716

John Oneall	1	John Robertson	1	John Macusing	1
Wm Wells	1	Frans: Farow	1	Thos: Spencer So Ba	1
Henry Gibs	1	Henry Davis	1	Bryan Callehan	1
Richd. Jonston	1			John Callehan	1

In all 39 tithbls that has not paid

Levies Recd.	258	193:20:0
Land Taxes Recd. 187 tracts 45180 akers		056:12:3
		250:02:3
To thirty bushels of Rotten Corn at 6d pr bull		0:15:0
		250:17:3
To my Sollry		7:10:0
		243:07:3
To Wm: Williams and Thos: Taylor		2:05:0
		241:02:3
one levie paid for Luke Whit by Mr. Tayler		000:15:0
Novr: 7th 1717 Due to the Publick		241:17:3
A list of Coratuck tithbls: for ye year 1716		Jas: Browne

Land taxes Recd. in Coratuck for ye year 1716

	tracts	akers	£	S	D		tracts	akers	£	S	D
Luke White	2	270		6	9	William Luffman	1	300		7	6
Obedya Rich	1	160		4		Henry Etherige	1	100		2	6
Thomas Miller	4	900	1	2	6	Samuell Ballence	1	150		3	9
Joseph Bennett	2	200		5		John Waring	1	200		5	
Henry Bright	2	340		8		Moses Linton	1	100		2	6
William Stafford	2	780		19	6	Daniell Mackay	1	150		3	6
Andrew Etherige	2	320		8		Mertin Bowlin	1	100		2	6
George Solsbery	1	300		7	6	Charles Sinqua	1	150		3	6
Nickeolus Mershall	1	100		2	6	Richard Bright	2	700		17	6
Andrew Mackferson	1	300		7	6	Edward Cox	1	640		16	
Daniell West	1	130		3	3	Thomas Muncref	1	160		4	
Daniell Mackferson	1	150		3	9	Robert Heath	1	450		11	3
John Monke	1	100		2	6	Thomas Brunt	2	300		7	6
Benjemen Bennett	6	600		15		Mermeduk Etherige	2	360		9	
James Warding	1	450		11	3	John Northen	2	450		11	3

CURRITUCK COUNTY TAX AND MILITIA LISTS

	tracts	akers	£	S	D		tracts	akers	£	S	D
Petter Parker	2	290		7	3	John Jones Ser.	2	750		18	9
Richard Eyland	1	100		2	6	Col. William Reed	7	3180	3	19	6
John Barber	1	080		2		John Jones Jur.	1	240		6	
Charles Barber	1	080		2		Petter Dauge	1	490		12	3
Thomas Stonhouse	1	300		7	6	James Dauge	1	530		13	3
Thomas Fanshaw	2	970		14	3	Thomas Williams	3	900	1	2	6
Joseph Poyner	1	100		2	6	Richard Etherige	2	660		16	6
Southwood Danby	1	150		3	9	James Carron	1	200		5	
John Liggitt	1	140		3	6	David Jones Ser.	1	400		10	
David Liggitt	1	140		3	6	Thomas Evens	1	300		7	6
Francis Jervis	1	100		2	6	Humpry Vince	1	450		11	3
Charles Brunt	1	200		5		Thomas Vince	1	400		10	
Samuell Jones	3	400		10		Benjemen Tull	1	400		10	
William Davis	1	250		6	3	John Pirkens Ser.	1	150		3	9
Thomas Davis	2	540		13	6	John Pirkens Jur.	1	050		1	3
William Muncref	1	080		2		Daniell Savaill	1	050		1	3
Daniel Glasco Ser.	1	200		5		Robert Tuker	1	050		1	3
Daniel Glasco Jur.	1	080		2		William Linton Ser. for					
William Williams	3	900	1	2	6	ye year 1715	1	150		3	9
Walis Bray	1	260		6	6	William Linton Ser.	1	150		3	9
Joseph Wicker	2	400		10		Thomas Cox	1	100		2	6
Joseph Wicker for ye						Mermeduk Caple	1	250		6	3
New England Compe:	1	580		14	6	Daniell Linsay	1	160		4	
Richard Ballence	1	300		7	6	Moses Ryno	1	100		2	6
Aron Prescott	1	160		4		Andrew Consall	1	020			6
Mr. Thos: Vandermulen	1	400		10		John Penny	2	600		15	
Mr. William Bell	2	900	1	2	6	James Mertin	1	200		5	
Mr. Thos: Tayler Ser.	7	1250	1	11	3	John Lewist	1	200		5	
Thomas Tayler Jur.	3	400		10		John Mason	1	460		11	6
James Duglas	1	050		1	3	Thomas Spencer ye					
Michall Oneal	4	600		15		No. Banks	1	100		2	6
John Walker	1	200		5		Ralph Love	1	150		3	9
Henry Woodhouse	1	400		10		Petter Poyner	1	100		2	6
William Willson	1	300		7	6	John Pell	1	250		6	3
Richard Sanderson Esqr	3	1200	1	10		Mr. William Swann	9	2800	3	10	
John Woodhouse	1	250		6	3	Docter Hunter for					
Jeremya Smith	1	100		2	6	ye year 1715	1	550		13	9
William Poyner	2	100		2	6	Docter Hunter	1	550		13	9
Joseph Sanderson	4	1100	1	7	6	William Parker	1	070		1	9
William Lerry	2	850	1	1	3	Capt. William Nickalls	2	400		10	
Mathew Hanna	1	060		1	6	Even Miller	1	090		2	3
Asricom Parker	2	650		16	3	Richard Linton	1	050		1	3
Foster Jervis	3	888		1	2	Moses Ramsay	1	050		1	3
Joseph Church	2	1100	1	7	6	Thos: Elkes	1	150		3	9
John Ives	3	800	1			Joseph Beatman	1	150		3	9
John Smith free Negro	1	300		7	6	Samuell Simmons	1	200		5	
Isaac Jones	1	240		6		Thomas Sheperd	1	100		2	6

Levies Recd. in Coratuk for ye year 1716

	tithble	£	S		tithble	£	S
Joseph Beckly	1		15	Luke White	1		15

Lovies Roc.ᵈ in Coraluk for yᵉ year 1716		£	s	d
Joseph Bockly	1	—	15	—
Luke White	1	—	15	—
Thoᵐ: Jouston	1	—	15	—
Obediah Rich	2	1	10	—
Thoˢ Miller	5	3	15	—
Joseph Bennet	1	—	15	—
Henry Bright Soᵉ	1	—	15	—
Henry Bright Juᵉ	1	—	15	—
William Stafford	1	—	15	—
Andrew Etherige	3	2	5	—
Richard Bright Son to Henry Bright	1	—	15	—
George Solsbery	1	—	15	—
Nickolas Marshall	1	—	15	—
John Bright	1	—	15	—
Benjamen Bennet	1	—	15	—
William Luffman	4	3	—	—
The Widow Poyner	2	1	10	—
Henry Etherige	1	—	15	—
Thomas Waring	1	—	15	—
John Waring	1	—	15	—
Moses Linton	1	—	15	—
Martin Bewlin	1	—	15	—
Charles Jukqua	1	—	15	—
Adam Pavoy	1	—	15	—
Christopher Lonsdall	1	—	15	—
Richard Bright Juᵉ	1	—	15	—
George Thomson	1	—	15	—
Richard Bright Soᵉ	1	—	15	—
James Bright	1	—	15	—
William Bright	1	—	15	—
Henry Lawly	1	—	15	—
	42	31	10	—

Plate VIII

29

Name	tithble	£	S	Name	tithble	£	S
Thos; Jonston	1		15	John Liggitt	1		15
Obediah Rich	2	1	10	Frances Jervis	1		15
Thos: Miller	5	3	15	Charles Brunt	1		15
Joseph Bennet	1		15	Samuel Jones	2	1	10
Henry Bright Ser	1		15	William Scote	1		15
Henry Bright Jur.	1		15	Benjemen Brickhouse	1		15
William Stafford	1		15	Thomas Davis	1		15
Andrew Etherige	3	2	5	William Moncref	1		15
Richard Bright Son to Henry Bright	1		15	Daniel Glasco Ser.	1		15
George Solsbery	1		15	Daniel Glasco Jur.	1		15
Nickcolas Mershall	1		15	William Williams	2	1	10
John Bright	1		15	Walis Bray	2	1	10
Benjemen Bennet	1		15	Joseph Wicker	3	2	5
William Luffman	4	3		Richard Ballence	1		15
The Widow Poyner	2	1	10	John Swendall	1		15
Henry Etherige	1		15	Samuel Backer	1		15
Thomas Waring	1		15	Aron Prescot	2	1	10
John Waring	1		15	Mr. Thomas Vandermulen	4	3	
Moses Linton	1		15	Mr. William Bell	3	2	5
Mertin Bowlin	1		15	Thomas Tayler Jur.	2	1	10
Charles Linqua	1		15	James Duglas	1		15
Adam Pavey	1		15	Mr. Thomas Tayler Ser.	5	3	15
Christopher Lonsdeall	1		15	Michall Oneall Ser.	1		15
Richard Bright Jur.	1		15	Michall Oneall Jur.	1		15
George Thomson	1		15	Thomas Simmons	1		15
Richard Bright Ser.	1		15	Mallykay Winter	1		15
James Bright	1		15	Henry Woodhouse	2	1	10
William Bright	1		15	William Willson	1		15
Henry Lawly	1		15	Richard Sanderson Esqr.	9	6	15
Edward Cox	1		15	John Woodhouse	1		15
Thomas Muncref	1		15	Jerimyah Smith	1		15
Robert Heath	1		15	William Poyner	1		15
John Brunt	1		15	Abraham Boome	1		15
Thomas Brunt	1		15	Joseph Sanderson	4	3	
Mermeduk Etherige	3	2	5	William Lerry	2	1	10
John Northen	3	2	5	Mathew Hanna	1		15
John Ives Ser.	1		15	Asricum Parker	3	2	5
Richard Dauge	1		15	Foster Jervis	5	3	15
Eward Bonny	1		15	Joseph Church	8	6	
Petter Parker	1		15	John Ives Jur.	1		15
John Barber	1		15	John Smith free Negro	1		15
Charles Barber	1		15	Isaac Jones	1		15
Richard Selvester	1		15	John Jones Ser	3	2	5
Petter Poyner	1		15	John Jones Jur.	1		15
Thomas Fanshaw Ser	3	2	5	Coll: William Reed	10	7	10
Thomas Fanshaw Jur	1		15	Petter Dauge	1		15
John Fanshaw	1		15	Christopher Boskens	1		15
Joseph Copper	1		15	Thomas Williams	4	3	
Joseph Poyner	1		15	William Stevens	1		15
Southerd Danbee	1		15	Richard Etherige	2	2	10
				James Carron Ser	1		15

CURRITUCK COUNTY TAX AND MILITIA LISTS

	tithble	£	S		tithble	£	S
John Carron	1		15	William Powell	1		15
David Jones Ser.	1		15	William Davis	1		15
Ralph Mathon	1		15	Mr. William Swann	4	3	
David Jones Jur.	1		15	Benjemen Beasly	1		15
Humphry Vince	6	4	10	James Poyner	1		15
Thomas Vince	2	1	10	Lionel Reading	4	3	
John Mills	1		15	William Parker	1		15
John Pirkens Ser.	1		15	Ambros Mackay for			
John Pirkens Jur.	1		15	ye year 1715	1		15
Daniell Sevill	1		15	Ambros Maokay	2	1	10
Robert Tuker Ser.	2	1	10	Capt. William Nickallson	1		15
John Kitte	2	1	10	Even Miller	1		15
Thomas Cox	1		15	Richard Linton	1		15
William Linton for 1715	1		15	James Browne	3	2	5
William Linton	1		15	William Etherige for			
Edward Jones	2	1	10	ye year 1715	1		15
Mermeduk Caple	3	2	5	William Etherige	1		15
Ralph Doe	1		15	William Etherige Jur	1		15
Daniell Linsay	1		15	Moses Ryno	1		15
Samuell Renger	1		15	George Spain	1		15
John Man	3	2	5	Luke Whit	1		15
George Scarborow	1		15	Christopher Beals	1		15
Andrew Consall	1		15	Thomas Poyner	1		15
John Penny	1		15	Samuell Simmons	1		15
James Mertin	1		15	John Harris	1		15
Robert Sdmith	1		15	Ralph Love	1		15
John Lewist	1		15	John Cape	1		15
John Mason	2	1	10	William Jonston	1		15
Adelffus Hanson	1		15	Archebald Hartly	1		15
Archebald Hartly for				Thomas Spencer of ye No. Bank	1		15
ye year 1715	1		15				

to Mr. Wm Williams on wolfs killed in pitt
to Mr. Willm: Williams 5 ditto kill by gon
to Mr. Thos: Tayler four wild Catt's heads

An account [torn]salvant pepel Such as [torn] upon virgany pattend Lan[d a]nd Such as are disurtars o[f t]his govarment and Such a[s] are none poor and Such as ar[e] gone into other presincs

Daniel Makefason	2	[Torn]n Linton Senr	[Torn]
Rogar Hogis	3	[Torn]s Riordin	[Torn]
Danil Maccoy	1	[Torn]mas Robinson	[Torn]
John Barinton	1	[Torn]neser White	[Torn]
Richd Hogis	1	[Torn]hn Page	[Torn]
Wm Ballons	1	[Torn]gh Jones	[Torn]
Andrew Makefason	1	[Torn]ge Barns	[Torn]
Disartars of our govarman		[Torn]ccount of poor pep	[Torn]
Thomas Waril	1	[Torn]nary Perkins	[Torn]
Robard Barfoot	1	Briant Callehan	1
[Torn]tofur Crafts	[Torn]	Thomas Unarwood	1
[Torn]he Gallap	[Torn]	Hanary Pirkins Senr.	1

CURRITUCK COUNTY TAX AND MILITIA LISTS

Nicklas Bruston	1	[Torn]n Backlo	6
Rd Linton	1	Hancock and Ashlo	3 4
Thomas James	1	[Torn]n Mackuin	10
Edward Golf	6		

[on reverse side]

[Torn] Kalse & Son	
[Torn]ohn Jones	2
[Torn] Dowies	1
Nuton - Son	
[Torn] Willm	2
[Torn] Ball & 2 Sons	3
[Torn]s Beale	1
[Torn]Commiskee	1
[Torn]ed Bolt	1
[Torn]as Hastings	1
[Torn] Moore	1
[Torn]as Elliott	1
[Torn]Carteret	1
[Torn]Kemp	1
[Torn]Ffairecloth	1
[Torn]Jooler	4
[Torn]t Parsoll	1
[Torn]ight	1
[Torn] Raymond	1
[Torn] Harrison	1
[Torn]rbush & [Torn] Billy	2
[Torn][illegible]	
[Torn]Brown	1
[Torn]ghan	1
[Torn]rharey	1
[Torn]awkins	6
[Torn]regin	7
[Torn]Hayman	1
[Torn]Hayman	1
[Torn]Bray & Son George	2
[Torn] Bray	1
[Torn]riffin	1
[Torn]llor & Negroes	
[Torn]Norton & Hardin	2
[Torn]Jones	1
[Torn]in Blisk	1

A List of Coratuk Tithables for ye year 1717

Mermeduk Caple	1	Richard Bright Ser.	3	Samuel Rencher	1
George Thomson	1	John Waring	1	Joseph Beatman	1
Henry Bright Ser.	1	Thomas Waring	1	Mermeduke Etherige	
John Bright	1	Richard Linton	1	Ser.	2
Henry Bright Jur.	1	John Linton	1	John Etherige	1
George Solsbery	1	Moses Linton	1	Andrew Etherige	1
John Eks	1	Henry Etherige	1	Luke Etherige	1
Edward Cox	1	Henry Laley	1	William Luffman	3

32

Name		Name		Name	
Lidya Miller	3	Charles Barber	1	Jos: Smith negro	
Robert Poyner	1	John Barber	1	levie free	1
William Luffman Jur.	1	Edward Bonny	2	Robert Borros	1
William Poyner Ser.	1	Petter Parker	1	Capt: Richd. Sanderson	5
William Poyner, Jur.	1	Thomas Poyner	1	William Lerry	3
Thomas Cox, Jur.	1	George Spann	1	Joseph Sanderson	5
Joseph Bennett	1	Richard Dauge	2	Richd. Sanderson Esqr.	8
Benjemen Bennett	1	Joseph Poyner	1	John Wodhouse	2
Merin Bowlin	1	Petter Poyner	1	John Ives	1
Richard Bright, Jur.	1	James Poyner	1	Azricom Parker	3
Thomas Elks	1	Richard Selvester	1	John Jones Ser.	5
William Stafford	2	William Williams	3	John Man	3
John Kitts	2	Thomas Liggett	1	George Scarbrough	1
Charles Linque	1	Joseph Church	8	William Tillitt	1
Nicolus Mershall	1	Foster Jervis	5	William Jonston	1
James Rickets	1	Jerimyah Smith	1	Moses Ryno	1
Daniell Glasco Ser.	1	Maleca Winter	1	Ralph Mathon	1
Daniell Glasco Jur.	1	Thomas Tayler Ser.	5	Daniell Linsey	1
Thomas Muncref	1	William Bell	4	John Evens	1
William Muncref	1	John Pell	1	Thomas Spencer	1
Thomas Jonston	1	Michall Oneal Ser.	1	John Cape	1
Moris Jonston	1	Michall Oneal Jur.	1	Christopher Buskens	1
Webly Payne	3	James Duglas	1	William Stevens	1
Samuell Jones	2	Thomas Simmons	1	Adolphus Hanson	1
William Scote	1	William Nicallson	1	Ambros Makey	2
Benjemen Brickhouse	1	Thomas Taylor, Jur.	2	Archebald Hartley	1
Thomas Davis	2	Samuell Burges	1	John Beals	2
Charles Brunt	1	Luke Whitte	2	John Mason	2
John Brunt	1	Humphry Vince	5	Christopher Beals	1
Thomas Brunt	1	Thomas Vince	2	Ralph Love	1
Robert Heath	1	William Parker	2	James Mertin	1
John Northen	4	Aron Prescot	1	William Davis	1
Robert Smith	1	Even Miller	1	Benjemen Beesly	1
Thomas Fanshaw, Ser.	1	Thos: Vandermulen	4	Thos: Williamson	1
Richard Fanshaw	1	Andrew Consall	2	John Whittbe	1
John Fanshaw	1	William Swann	4	Alixander Makey	1
Thomas Fanshaw Jur.	1	Joseph Wicker	3	John Oneall	1
Robert Tuker Ser	1	Wallis Bray	1	William Wells	1
Robert Tuker, Jur.	1	Benjemen Tull	1	John Lewist	1
Moses Ramsey	1	Richard Ballence	1	David Jones Ser.	1
Samuell Simmons	1	Richard Etheridge	2	David Jones Jur.	1
John Liggett	1	William Russell	1	Richard Jonston	1
David Liggett	1	James Carone Ser.	1	Frances Farow	1
David Ambros	1	James Carone Jur.	1	Henry Davis	1
John Pirkens Ser.	1	John Carone	1	Thos: Spencer	
Daniell Savells	1	Petter Dauge	1	So: Banks	2
Thomas Swann	1	Coll: Wm: Reed	10	John Beckly	1
Frances Jervis	1	Thomas Williams	4	Thomas Evens	1
Wm Powell levie free	1	Isaac Jones	1	John Kirke	1
Emanuell Elks	1	Henry Wodhouse	3	John Scarborow	2
Joseph Caper	1	Abraham Boome	1	Henry Gibson	1
John Pirkens Jur.	1	William Wilson	1	Patrick Kallehan	1

CURRITUCK COUNTY TAX AND MILITIA LISTS

Henry Gibs	1	John Jones Jur.	1	Levie free		2
Constables for		Joseph Beckly	1	Constables		4
Coratuk in 1717		Tithables in all for the		taken out of		286
Richard Bright Jur.	1	year 1717 is	286	Remains		274
Wallis Bray	1	Tithbl: Insolvist	6			

Coratuk Levies Recd. for the year 1717

	tith	£	S		tith	£	S
Petter Parker	1		15	Azricom Parker	3	2	5
Mr. Joseph Wicker	3	2	5	Mr. Joseph Church	8	6	
William Scote	1		15	Michall Oneall Jur.	1		15
Mr. William Poyner Ser.	1		15	James Duglas	1		15
Mrs. Lydia Miller	3	2	5	Mr. William Bell	4	3	
William Luffman Ser.	3	2	5	John Penny	1		15
William Luffman Jur.	1		15	Michall Oneall Ser.	1		15
Andrew Etheridge	1		15	Mr. Thomas Tayler	5	3	15
Luke Etheridge	1		15	Even Miller	1		15
Capt: William Stafford	2	1	10	Aron Prescoat	1		15
Edward Cox	1		15	James Poyner	1		15
Richard Bright Ser.	3	2	5	Wm: Davis for Emanuell Elks	1		15
Benjemen Bennet	1		15	John Pirkens Jur.	1		15
Nicolus Mershall	1		15	Thomas Fanshaw Ser.	2	1	10
John Waring	1		15	Richard Fanshaw	1		15
Thomas Cox	1		15	John Fanshaw	1		15
Joseph Beatman	1		15	Thomas Fanshaw Jur.	1		15
Moris Jonston	1		15	Moses Ramsey	1		15
George Thomson	1		15	Frances Jervis	1		15
Joseph Bennett	1		15	John Northen	4	3	
Henry Bright Ser.	1		15	Mermeduke Etheridge	2	1	10
Richard Bright Jur.	1		15	John Etheridge	1		15
Henry Bright Jur.	1		15	Robert Heath	1		15
Daniell Glasco Ser.	1		15	Henry Lawly	1		15
Daniell Glasco Jur.	1		15	Richard Dauge	2	1	10
Charles Brunt	1		15	Richard Sellvester	1		15
Benjemen Brickhouse	1		15	James Carone Ser.	1		15
Thomas Muncref	1		15	James Carone Jur.	1		15
William Muncref	1		15	John Carone	1		15
Mr. William Williams	1		15	Samuell Jones	2	1	10
Wallis Bray	1		15	Thomas Williams	4	3	
Petter Dauge	1		15	Petter Poyner	1		15
Mr. Thomas Vandermulen	4	3		Thomas Davis	2	1	10
Richard Ballence	1		15	Moses Linton	1		15
Luke White	2	1	10	Richard Linton	1		15
Mr. John Woodhouse	2	1	10	Henry Etheridge	1		15
Richard Sanderson Esqr.	8	6		Charles Barber	1		15
William Lerry	3	2	5	Thomas Poyner	1		15
Henry Woodhouse	3	2	5	Robert Poyner	1		15
Abraham Boome	1		15	Isaac Jones	1		15
Coll: William Reed	12	9		Thomas Brunt	1		15
Richard Etheridge	2	1	10	John Pell	1		15
William Willson	1		15	Thomas Tayler Jur.	2	1	10
Mr. Joseph Sanderson	5	3	15	Malecay Winter	1		15

CURRITUCK COUNTY TAX AND MILITIA LISTS

Name	tith	£	S	Name	tith	£	S
Ralph Love	1		15	John Brunt	1		15
Daniell Savell	1		15	Ralph Mathon	1		15
Joseph Cupper	1		15	William Poyner Jur.	1		15
William Stevens	1		15	Robert Tuker Ser.	1		15
Mr. Thomas Swann	1		15	Robert Tuker Jur.	1		15
David Liggett	1		15	Jerimya Smith	1		15
Edward Bonny	2	1	10	John Barber	1		15
George Spann	1		15	Samuell Simons	1		15
Joseph Poyner	1		15	John Linton	1		15
William Russell	1		16	Patriok Kallehan for : 1716:			
Thomas Liggett	1		15	1717	2	1	10
John Liggett	1		15	Capt. Richard Sanderson	5	3	15
Mr. Foster Jervis	5	3	15	Andrew Consall	2	1	10
Mermeduk Caple	1		15	Henry Davis for ye year:			
John Elks	1		15	1716: 1717	2	1	10
Thomas Evens	1		15	Capt. Richard Sanderson			
John Mason	1		15	for ye year 1716	2	1	10
John Beales for ye year 1716				Richard Smith for ye year 1716	2	1	10
& 1717	4	3		Thos: Jonston for ye year 1716	1		15
James Mertin	1		15	John Norton	1		15
Samuell Burges for ye year				Benjemen Tull	1		15
1716 & 1717	2	1	10	Samuell Wrensher	1		15
John Beckly	1		15	John Pirkens Ser.	1		15
Alixander Mckay	1		15	Mr. Humphry Vince	5	3	15
Ambros Mckay	2	1	10	Mr. Thomas Vince	2	1	10
Christopher Buskens	1		15	William Parker	2	1	10
John Cape	1		15	Thomas Spencer So. Banks.			
Mr. John Jones Ser.	5	3	15	1716:1717	4	3	
Robert Borows	1		15	John Kirke	1		15
William Jonston	1		15	Charles Sinquea	1		15
Adolphus Hanson	1		15	Thos: Spencer No. Banks	1		15
Archebald Hartly	1		15	David Jones Ser.	1		15
Moses Ryno	1		15	Benjemen Beasly	1		15
Daniell Linsey	1		15	Robert Smith	1		15
John Oneall for ye year 1716				John Bright	1		15
& 1717	2	1	10	Thos: Jonston	1		15
Nathaniel Grea for ye year				George Solsbery	1		15
1715:1716:1717	3	2	5	Capt: Wm: Nickallson	1		15
Henry Gibs	1		15	Mr. Wm: Swann	4	3	
Frances Farow for ye year				Thomas Waring	1		15
1716:1717	2	1	10	Thomas Simons	1		15
David Jones Jur.	1		15	John Ives	1		15
Richard Jonston for ye year				Webly Payve	3	2	5
1716:1717	2	1	10	David Ambros	1		15
John Man	3	2	5	James Rickets	1		15
George Scarborrow	1		15	John Whittbee for ye year			
William Tillitt	1		15	1716:1717	2	1	10
John Scarborrow	2	1	10	John Kitte	2	1	10
Mertin Bowlin	1		15				

Land Taxes Recd. in Coratuck for ye year 1717

	tra	acres	£	S	D
Petter Parker	2	200		5	
Mr. Joseph Wicker	2	450		11	3
William Scote	1	50		1	3
William Poyner Ser.	4	1000	1		5
William Luffman Ser.	1	350		8	9
Wm: Luffman for his wifes plantation	1	100		2	6
Samuell Balence	1	150		3	9
Daniell West	1	120		3	
Nickolus Mershall	1	100		2	6
Daniell McFerson	1	150		3	9
John Waring	1	200		5	
Thomas Cox	1	100		2	6
Joseph Beatman	1	140		3	6
Joseph Bennett	2	250		6	3
John Assey	1	120		3	
Widow Harris	1	150		3	9
Henry Bright	2	350		8	9
Daniell Glasco Ser.	1	250		6	3
Daniell Glasco Jur.	1	080		2	
Charles Brunt	1	150		3	9
William Davis	1	250		6	3
Thomas Muncref	2	200		5	
William Muncref	2	120		3	
Mr. William Williams	4	1000	1		5
Walls Bray	2	350		8	9
Petter Dauge	2	1000	1		5
Mr. Thomas Vandermulen	1	400		10	
Capt. John Webster	2	750		18	6
Richard Balence	2	500		12	6
Luke White	2	300		7	6
Richard Sanderson Esqr.	6	2400	3		
William Lerry	2	900	1	2	6
John Smith negro	1	300		7	6
Henry Woodhouse	1	400		10	
Abraham Boome	1	150		3	9
Coll: William Reed	2	1500	1	17	6
Richard Etheridge	2	650		16	3
William Wilson	1	300		7	6
Mr. Joseph Sanderson	7	1900	2	7	6
Ralph Love	1	300		7	6
Azricum Parker	2	650		16	3
Mr. Joseph Church	2	1100	1	7	6
James Dugles	1	050		1	3
Michall Oneall Ser.	4	600		15	
William Bell	2	900	1	2	
John Penny	1	070		1	9
Mr. Thomas Tayler	3	930	1	3	3
Andrew Etheridge	2	325		8	
Isabell Beatman	1	100		2	6
Capt. William Stafford	2	700		17	6
Edward Cox	1	640		16	
Benjemen Bennet	5	600		15	
Richard Bright Ser.	2	750		18	9
Even Miller	1	150		3	9
Aron Prescoat	1	150		3	9
James Poyner	1	070		1	8
John Pirkens Ser.	1	150		3	9
Moses Ramsey	1	050		1	3
Frances Jervis	1	100		2	6
John Northen	3	600		15	
Mermeduk Etheridg	2	350		8	9
Robert Heath	1	450		11	3
Richard Jones	1	100		2	6
James Warding	1	450		11	3
Richard Selvester	1	300		7	6
James Carone Jur.	2	350		8	9
Mr. Robert Paton for Judy Scofild	1	150		3	9
Samuel Jones	3	550		13	9
John Pirkens Jur.	1	050		1	3
Thomas Williams	5	900	1	2	6
Mr. John Woodhouse	1	250		6	3
Thomas Davis	3	750		18	9
Daniell Savell	1	050		1	3
John Chrisp	1	300		7	6
John Penny	1	200		5	
Moses Linton	1	100		2	6
Richard Linton	1	050		1	3
John Nash	1	100		2	6
Henry Etheridg	1	100		2	6
Charles Barber	1	080		2	
Thomas Poyner	1	100		2	6
Isaac Jones	1	240		6	
John Walker	1	120		3	
Thomas Brunt	2	300		7	6
John Pell	1	250		6	3
Andrew McFerson	1	350		8	9
Thomas Taylor Jur.	1	300		7	6
Malecay Winter	1	200		5	
John Brunt	1	050		1	3
Daniell McKay	1	150		3	9
Joseph Cupper ye halfe of ye Ridge planta:	1	160		4	
Mr. Thomas Swann	1	200		5	
David Liggett	1	140		3	6
Thomas Sheperd	1	100		2	6
Joseph Poyner	1	100		2	6

CURRITUCK COUNTY TAX AND MILITIA LISTS

	tra	acres	£	S	D		tra	acres	£	S	D
[Torn] Poyner	1	100		2	6	Mr. William Hunter	1	550		13	9
John Liggett	1	140		3	6	Benjemen Tull	1	400		10	
Mr. Foster Jervis	3	800	1			Henry Davis	1	400		10	
Mermed Caple	1	240		6		Capt. John Norton	3	640		16	
Thomas Evens	1	300		7	6	Thomas Spencer So.					
John Mason	1	400		10		Banks: 1716: 1717	1	050		2	6
John Beales	1	160		4		John Kirke	1	180		4	6
James Merten	1	200		5		Charles Sinkquea	1	150		3	9
John Cape	1	400		10		Capt: William					
Daniell Linsey	1	160		4		Nickallson	2	500		12	6
Moses Ryno	1	100		2	6	Thos: Spencer					
Archebald Hartly	1	400		10		No: Banks	1	050		1	3
Capt. John Oneall	1	350		8	9	David Jones Ser.	1	480		12	
Henry Gibs	2	860	1	1	6	Robert Smith	1	300		7	6
Frances Farow	2	600		15		John Mank	1	120		3	
Richard Jonston	1	160		4		Denis Ryording	1	150		3	9
Jerimiah Smith	1	100		2	6	Thos: Corpeo	1	350		8	9
John Barber	1	080		2		Mr. Wm: Swann	9	2970	3	14	3
Samuel Simmons	1	200		5		Giles Randall	1	120		3	
Robert Tuker Ser.	1	050		1	3	John Ives	1	160		3	9
George Solsbery	1	300		7	6	Temothey Ives Jur.	1	160		3	9
Patrick Callehan	1	200		5		Temothey Ives Ser.	1	480		12	
Capt. Richard						David Ambros	1	150		3	9
Sanderson	5	2110	2	12	9						

Clames Wolfes & wild Catts Heads paid for in Coratuk in ye year 1717 per James Browne Trear.

To Mr. Thomas Swann	3=12=9	Capt: Benjemen West	2=10=0
To Henry Davis	2=18=6	To Wm: Parker	0=09=0
to Matheyas Towler	0=10=0	To Mermek: Caple for Thomson	0=12=0
to Caleran Callehan	0=10=0	Mr. Wm: Swann	0=15=0
to Mermeduk Etheridge		To fereges to ye assembly	
for a wolfe	0=10=0	twise	1=00=0
Andrew Etheridge for a wolfe	0=10=0	To my deyat and Horses pro-	
Thos: Williams for a wolfe	0=10=0	vender & lodging twice com-	
Thos: Brunt for a wolfe	0=10=0	ing to ye assembly	2=00=0
John Northen for a wolfe	0=10=0		
John Jones for two wolfes	0=10=0		
Robert Tuker for a wolfe	0=05=0		
Thos: Brunt for a Catt	0=02=6		
John Fenton for two Catts	0=05=0		
Mermeduk Etheridge for a wolfe	0=05=0		

A List of those persons that has not paid their Land tax In Coratuk and the Number of acres

William Wells	400	Elisabeth Williams	100
Christopher Beals	100	John Whittbe 600 orfans land	1200
John Lewist	100	William Johnston	480
John Miller	100	Ann Mecuiong	150
Eals Beatman	100	John Burton	199
William Etheridge	100	The Widow Hamton Orfans Land	600

CURRITUCK COUNTY TAX AND MILITIA LISTS

Joseph Lewin Orfans land	250	John Jones Ser. orfans Land	550
Mathew Migitt	150	Thomas Spencer No. Banks	640
John Dauge	110		

A List of Severall persons that houlds Land in Coratuk but can not find out ye Number of acres

William Waymouth	[Adolphus] Hanson	Thomas Cready Island
William Steal orfans	[Torn]nce Woodhouse	Collington Island
Nottoway Broome orfans	James Dauge	Croatan
[Torn]	Roanoke Island	Jonathon Jervis orfans

The whole acompt: of publick monys Recd. in Coratuk for the year 1717 per Jas: Browne Trear:

To 294 Levies	220:10:0
To 51975 acres of Land tax	065:00:3
The whole Sum Recd: is	285:10:3
To mony paid out	018:14:9
Remains	266:15:6
To my Salry	009:03:0
The whole sum Remaining due to ye con: is	257:12:6

The fouer Constables is Richard Bright Walis Bray John Jones Jur. Joseph Beckly in all 4
The Insolvents is Lorence Mertensen John Evens, Thomas Williamson
John [Torn] William Davis Christopher Beals   In all   6
Levie free William Powell & John Smith negro   2
Henry Gibson Extreme pore
William Wells gon in to Maryland

List of Coratuk Tithabls for the year 1718

Richard Etheridge	1	Mathew Hanna	1	Humphry Vince	6
Thomas Jones	1	Thomas Jervis	1	Thos: Vince	2
James Carone Ser.	1	Thomas Parker	1	Andrew Pecock	1
James Carone Jur.	1	Azricom Parker	1	Wm: Parker	1
John Carone	1	Joseph Sanderson	4	Sall: Baker	1
Henry Jones	1	Jerimyah Smith	1	Even Miller	1
Thomas Lewis	2	Petter Poyner	1	Aron Prescod	2
Thomas Williams	1	Henry White	2	Richard Ballence	1
Isaac Jones	1	Joseph Church	6	Shusana Thomas	2
Henry Woodhuse	2	Foster Jervis	4	Mr. Thos:Vandermulen	5
Coll: William Reed	1	Thomas Simmons	1	Mr. Wm: Swann	1
Squr: Richard Sanderson	2	Thomas Tayler Ser.	5	Joseph Wicker	2
		James Duglas	3	Petter Dauge	1
Abraham Boome	1	Mr. Wm: Bell	1	Benjemen Tulle	1
Malica Winter	1	Michall Oneal Ser.	1	Walis Bray	2
William Willson	1	Michall Oneal Jur.	1	Mr. Wm: Williams	2
William Leary	4	John Walker	1	Joseph Poyner	1
Madam Dael: Sanderson	8	Thomas Tayler Jur.	1	Richard Dauge	2
		John Chrisp	1	Thomas Poyner	1
John Woodhouse	2	Cpt: Wm: Nickallson	1	Thomas Shipard	1
John Ives	1	Luke White	1	Petter Parker	1

CURRITUCK COUNTY TAX AND MILITIA LISTS

John Barber	1	Henry Bright Jur.	1	Archebald Hartly	1
George Span	1	Benjemen Bennet	1	Ralph Mathon	1
Charles Barber [illegible]		John Munk	1	Daniell Linsey	1
John Perkins Ser.	1	Charles Sinqua Negro	1	William Jonston	1
Thomas James	1	Richard Selvester	1	Adolphus Hanson	1
JamesPoyner	1	Thomas Cox Jur.	1	John Ears	1
John Fenton	1	Antony Sammons	1	John Caps	1
William Poyner	4	Joseph Bateman	1	Christopher Bales	1
William Luffman	3	Daniell Glasco Ser.	1	Christopher Busken	1
Andrew Etheridge	1	Morris Johnston	1	John Whidby	1
Luke Etheridge	1	Danieel Glasco Jur.	1	Ambros McKay	1
William Luffman Jur.	1	Thomas Muncref	1	Alixander McKay	1
Edward Cox	1	William Muncref	1	William McKay	1
Richard Bright Ser.	1	Charles Brunt	1	John Beckly	1
Richard Bright Jur.	1	William Scott	1	Capt. John Norton	1
George Thomson	1	Benjemen Brickhouse	1	Samuel Burges	1
Thomas Eks	1	Robert Heath	1	John Bales	1
Merten Bowlin	1	John Brunt	1	James Mertin	1
Thomas Gotherd	1	Thomas Brunt	1	Mathins Fowler	1
Robert Smith	1	Henry Lawly	1	Ralph Love	1
Jacob Marsh	1	Joseph Bennett	2	Timothey Ives	1
Moses Linton	1	Samuell Jones	2	William Ives	1
Richard Linton	1	Thomas Fanshaw	2	William Davis	1
Henery Etheridge	1	Thomas Fanshaw Jur.	1	John Peny	1
James Man	1	John Fanshaw	1	Henry Gibson	1
William Etheridge	1	Richard Fanshaw	1	George Stiring	1
Nickolus Mershall	1	Robert Tuker Ser.	1	Mr. Robert Peyton	8
John Warill	1	Robert Tuker Jur.	1	Andrew Consaul	2
Henry Bright Ser.	2	Moses Ramsey	1	John Oneal	1
Edward Bright	1	Daniell Phillips	6	John Cirk	1
Capt: Wm: Stafford	2	Frances Jervis	1	William Wells	1
Thomas Davis	2	John Legatt	1	David Jones Ser.	1
William Davis	2	David Legatt	1	David Jones Jur.	1
Mermeduk Etheridge		Samuell Simmons	1	John Macuing	1
Ser.	2	Denis Riordane	1	John Macuing	1
John Etheridge	1	Mr. Thos: Swann	1	Daniell Guthree	1
Jacob Barber	1	Thomas Haman	1	Henry Gibe	1
John Chance	1	Joseph Bowren	7	Henry Davis	1
Mermeduk Etheridge		John Perkins Jur.	1	William Jonston	1
Jur. [illegible]		Daniell Savell	1	Frances Farow	1
John Northen	2	John Man	3	John Lewis	1
Webly Peavey	3	George Scarbrough	1	Thomas Spencer	1
George Solsbery	1	William Tillitt	1	Robert Paumer	1
Richard Bright waver	1	Moses Rynard	1	Foster Jervis Jur.	1
John Shippard	1				

The whole List of Tithabls for ye year 1718 is   283

Coratuk Levies Recd. for the year 1718

	ttih	£	S		ttih	£	S
Richard Etheridge	1	15		John Carone	1	15	
James Carone Ser.	1	15		Henry Jones	1	15	
James Carone Jur.	1	15		Thomas Williams	4	3	

39

CURRITUCK COUNTY TAX AND MILITIA LISTS

Name	tith	£	S	Name	ttih	£	S
Isaac Jones	1		15	Richard Bright Jur.	1		15
Henry Woodhous	2	1	10	Merin Bowlin	1		15
Coll: William Reed	1		15	Thomas Gotherd	1		15
Sqr: Richard Sanderson	2	1	10	Jacob Marsh	1		15
Abraham Boome	1		15	Moses Linton	1		15
Malica Winter	1		15	Richard Linton	1		15
William Wilson	1		15	Henry Etheridge	1		15
William Leary	4	3		Nicolas Mershall	1		15
Sqr: Richard Sanderson:				Henry Bright Ser.	2		15
ye ould Sqr. astat	10	7	10	Edward Bright	1		15
Mr. John Woodhouse	2	1	10	Capt: William Stafford	2	1	10
John Ives	1		15	Thomas Davis	2	1	10
Mathew Hanna	1		15	Mermeduk Etheridge Ser.	2	1	10
Thomas Jervis	1		15	John Etheridge	1		15
Thomas Parker	1		15	Jacob Barber	1		15
Azricom Parker	1		15	John Chance	1		15
Henry White	2	1	10	John Northen	4	3	
Joseph Church	6	4	10	George Solsbury	1		15
Foster Jervis	4	3		Henry Bright Jur.	1		15
Mr. Thomas Tayler Ser.	5	3	15	Benjemen Bennett	1		15
James Duglas	3	2	5	John Munk	1		15
Mr. William Bell	4	3		Charles Sinqua Negro	1		15
Michall Oneall Ser.	1		15	Joseph Beatman	1		15
Michall Oneall Jur.	1		15	Daniell Glasco Ser.	1		15
John Walker	1		15	Morris Jonston	1		15
Mr. Thomas Tayler Jur.	2	1	10	Daniell Glasco Jur.	1		15
Andrew McFerson	1		15	Thomas Muncref	1		15
Luke White	1		15	William Muncref	1		15
Humphry Vince	6	4	10	Charles Brunt	1		15
Thomas Vince	2	1	10	William Scoat	1		15
Andrew Peacock	1		15	Benjemen Brickhouse	1		15
William Parker	1		15	Robert Heath	1		15
Samuell Baker	1		15	Thomas Brunt	1		15
Aron Prescod	2	1	10	Joseph Bennett	2	1	10
Richard Ballence	1		15	Samuell Jonson	2	1	10
Mr. Thomas Vandermulen	5	3	10	Thomas Fanshaw Ser.	2	1	10
Joseph Wicker	2	1	10	Thomas Fanshaw Jur.	1		15
Petter Dauge	1		15	John Fanshaw	1		15
Benjemen Tulle	1		15	Richard Fanshaw	1		15
Mr. William Williams	2	1	10	Daniell Philips	6	4	10
Joseph Poyner	1		15	Frances Jervis	1		15
Richard Dauge	2	1	10	Samuell Simmons	1		15
Thomas Shippard	1		15	Denis Riording	1		15
Petter Parker	1		15	Joseph Bowron	1		15
John Fenton	1		15	John Pirkens Ser.	1		15
William Poyner	5	3	10	Daniell Savell	1		15
William Luffman	3	2	5	Moses Rynard	1		15
Andrew Etheridge	2	1	10	Daniell Linsay	1		15
William Luffman Jur.	1		15	Christopher Buskens	1		15
Edward Cox	1		15	Ralph Mathon	1		15
Richard Bright Ser.	3	2	5	Alixander McKay	1		15

CURRITUCK COUNTY TAX AND MILITIA LISTS

Name	tith	£	S		Name	ttih	£	S
Samuell Burges	1		15		Robert Burrows	1		15
Ralph Love	1		15		Thos: Jones	1		15
Temothey Ives Ser.	1		15		Mr. Joseph Sanderson	4	3	
William Ives	1		15		Thos: Simmons	1		15
John Penny	1		15		Walis Bray	2	1	10
Mr. Robert Peyton	8	6			Moses Ramsey	1		15
Henry Gibs	1		15		John Legett	1		15
Frances Farow	1		15		David Legett	1		15
Robert Paumer	1		15		Mr. Thomas Swann	1		15
Andrew Consaul	2	1	10		Thomas Haman	1		15
John Linton	1		15		John Man	3	2	5
Robert Poyner	1		15		George Scarbrough	1		15

Land Taxes Recd. in Coratuk for the year 1718

Name	number tract	acres	£	S	D		Name	number tract	acres	£	S	D
Richard Etheridge	2	660		16	6		Richard Ballence	2	550		13	9
James Carone Jur.	1	350		8	9		Joseph Wicker	3	460		11	6
John Carone	1	200		5			Petter Dauge	1	490		12	3
Thomas Williams	4	1500	1	17	6		Benjemen Tulle	2	480		12	
Henry Woodhouse	1	400		10			Mr. Wiliam Wiliams	2	1000	1	5	
Coll: William Reed	3	1500	1	17	6		Joseph Poyner	1	100		2	6
Sqr. Richard Sanderson	5	2100	2	12	6		Thomas Shippard	1	100		2	6
Malicay Winter	1	200		5			Petter Parker	1	200		5	
William Wilson	1	300		7	6		William Poyner	4	900	1	2	6
William Leary	2	900	1	2	6		William Luffman	1	350		8	9
Sqr. Rich: Sanderson ye ould Sqr. asteat	9	2140	2	13	6		Andrew Etheridge	2	325		8	
Mr. John Woodhouse	1	250		6	3		Edward Cox	1	640		16	
John Ives	1	160		4			Richard Bright Ser.	2	720		18	
Mathew Hanna	1	080		2			Mertin Bowlin	1	180		4	6
Thomas Jervis	1	320		8			Moses Linton	1	100		2	6
Azricom Parker	2	680		17	6		Richard Linton	1	050		1	3
Henry White	1	400		12	6		Henry Etheridg	1	100		2	6
Joseph Curth	2	700	1	3	6		Nickoles Mershall	1	100		2	6
Foster Jervis	2	500		15	9		Henry Bright Ser.	2	350		8	9
Mr. Thomas Tayler Ser.	3	940	3				Capt: William Stafford	2	780		19	6
James Dauglas	1	050		7	6		Thomas Davis	2	380		9	
Mr. William Bell	2	906	1	2	6		Mermeduk Etheridge Ser.	2	360		8	6
Michall Oneall	4	630		15	9		John Northen	2	600		15	
John Walker	1	120		3			George Solsbery	1	300		7	6
Thomas Tayler Jur.	2	300		7	6		Benjemen Bennett	5	600		15	
John Pell	1	250		6	3		John Munk	1	120		3	
Luke White	2	320		8			Joseph Beatman	1	140		3	6
Humphry Vince	1	400		10			Daniell Glasco Jur.	1	080		2	
Thomas Vince	1	400		10			Thomas Muncref	1	200		5	
William Parker belonging to Jon: Evens	2	400		10			William Muncref	1	080		2	
Aron Prescod	1	160		4			Charles Brunt	1	150		3	9
Mr. Thomas Vandermulen	1	400		10			William Scote	1	050		1	3
							Robert Heath	1	400		11	3
							Thomas Brunt	2	300		7	6

CURRITUCK COUNTY TAX AND MILITIA LISTS

	number tract	acres	£	S	D		number tract	acres	£	S	D
Joseph Bennett	2	250		6	3	Giles Randall	1	120		3	
Samuel Jones	3	500		12	6	John Relph	1	250		6	3
Thomas Fansha Ser.	1	500		12	6	Mary Harris	1	150		3	9
Thos: Fansha Ser. for						Mr. Thos: Dent	1	200		5	
ye year 1717	1	500		12	6	John Smith Negro	1	300		7	6
Daniell Phillips	2	370		9	3	Thomas Nash	1	100		2	6
Frances Jervis	2	120		3		Robert Stuard	2	350		8	9
Samuell Simmons	1	200		5		Richard Ballence Shoar					
Denis Riording	1	100		2	6	Land	1	300		7	6
Joseph Bowring	1	150		3	9	Samuell Ballence	1	150		3	9
John Pirkens	1	100		2	6	Daniell McFerson	1	500		12	6
Daniell Savell	1	100		2	6	Daniell West	1	120		3	
Mermeduk Etheridge Jur.	1	450		11	3	John Jones Jur.	1	400		10	
Thomas Evens	1	300		7	6	Andrew McFerson	1	500		12	6
Moses Rynard	1	100		2	6	Richard Island	1	100		2	6
Ralph Mathon	1	150		3	9	Mr. Joseph Sanderson	7	1900	2	7	6
Daniell Linsey	1	150		3	9	Walis Bray	2	350		8	9
Ralph Love	1	200		5		Moses Ramsey	1	100		2	6
Temothey Ives Ser.	1	480		12		John Legett	1	130		3	3
John Penny	5	900	1	2	6	David Legett	1	140		3	6
Mr. Robert Peyton	2	340		8	6	Mr. Thos: Swann	1	200		5	
Henry Gibs	2	860	1	1	6	Temothey Ives Jur.	1	150		3	9
Frances Farow	1	300		7	6	John Burton 1715: 1716:					
Robert Poyner	1	100		2	6	1717: 1718	1	190		19	
Robert Burros	1	100		2	6	Mr. Thos: Swann -					
Abraham Boome	1	150		3	9	1717: 1718	2	230		11	6
Wm: Parker for ye year:						Walis Bray 1715: 1716:					
1715: 1716:1717	1	250		18	9	1717: 1718	1	100		2	6
George Solsbery for the						James Warding	1	450		11	3
year 1717	1	300		7	6	John Miller	1	100		2	6

A List of Those that has not paid their Levie Nor Land Tax in Coratuk for ye yr. 1718

	No. of Tithbl.	No. of acres		No. of Tithbl.	No. of acres
Thos: Lewis	2		George Thomson	1	
Jerimiah Smith	1	100	Thos: Elks	1	
Petter Poyner	1		Robert Smith	1	300
John Chrisp	1		James Man	1	
Wm: Nickallson	1	500	William Etheridge	1	200
Even Miller	1	150	John Waring	1	200
Shusana Thomas	2	300	William Davis	2	
Mr. Wm: Swann	1	2970	Webly Payve	3	
Thos: Poyner	1	100	Richard Bright Waver	1	
John Barber	1	080	Richard Selvester	1	
George Spann	1		Thomas Cox Jur.	1	
Charles Barber	1	080	Antony Sammons	1	
John Pirkens Jur.	1	050	John Brunt	1	050
Thos: James	1		Henry Lawly	1	100
James Poyner	1	170	Robert Tuker Ser.	1	
John Shiperd	1		Robert Tuker Jur.	1	

CURRITUCK COUNTY TAX AND MILITIA LISTS

Mermeduk Etheridge Jur.	1		Luke Etheridg	1	
Patrick Kalehan	1	200	Henry Gibson	1	
William Tillett	1		George Stearing	1	
Wm: Jonston	1		Archebald Hartly	1	400
Adolphus Hanson	1		John Oneal	1	350
John Ears	1		John Kirk	1	180
John Cape	1	400	Wm: Wells	1	440
Christopher Beals	1	100	David Jones Ser.	1	480
John Whittbe	1	1200	John Mecuing	1	
Ambros McKey	1		Daniel Gutthry	1	
William McKey	1		Henry Davis	1	900
John Norton	1	640	John Beckly	1	
John Beals	1		Richard Jonston	1	
James Mertin	1	200	John Lewis	1	200
Matheyas Forober	1		Thos: Spencer	1	050
William Davis	1		Foster Jervis Jur.	1	
Thos: Waring	1		David Jones Jur.	1	

Tithl: 74 - - 11090
Land from ye last 4640 Lease
     15730

Monys paid ove the publick a compt for Wolfes and Catts heads & one panter

Thos: Williams one Catte head	William Stafford two wolfes heads
John Palmer one Catte head	Benjemen Bennett one wolfes head
Andrew Etheridge one Wolfes head	Edward Bright one wolfes head
Isaiah Fanshaw three Wolfes heads	Richard Bright one wolfes head
John Northen one Wolfes head	Mr. Thos: Tayler Ser. one wolfes head
Thos: Muncref one painters head	John Fenton one Catts head
John Northen one Wolfes head	Robert Heath one Catts head
Edward Cox one Wolfes head	John Ligett two wolfes heads
Andrew Etheridge one wolfes head	Even Miller one Catts head

The whole a Compt of publick monys In Coratuk for the year 1718 pr. Jas: Browne Trear

To 220 levies	169=00=0
To 45652 acres of Land tax	59=01=3
The whole Sum Recd. is	224=01=3
to monys paid out	6=07=6
Remains	217=13=9
to my Solry	6=17=0
to my charges and fereges in Coming and going to ye Assembly	1=10=0
The whole Sume Remaining due to the Contry is	209=06=3

A List of Sum Virginia people and others yt. houlds land and has not paid for ye yr. 1718

	No. of acres		No. of acres		No. of acres
John Asey	120	Wm: Hunter	550	John Jones Ser:	550
Robert Bell	250	Henry Halstead	180	Ann Mecuing	150
Richard Jones	1[torn]	Eals Beatman	100	Thos: Spencer	640
Andrew McFerson	3[torn]	Isabel Beatman	100	Mathew Miggett	100
Daniel McKey	150	Wm: Rose	130	The widow Hampton	640
Joseph Cuper	320	Elizabeth Williams	100	John Dauge	110

Wm: Waymouth
Joseph Lewing
Thos: Williamson
Cread: Island
Collington Island
Rownocke Island
Croatan

A List of Tithables in ye Prisct. Of Coratuck for ye Year 1718 Taken By ye Severall Constables
whos: Names Are _____ written Vizt

Name	Tithables	Name	Tithables	Name	Tithables
Richd: Etheridge	1	John Walker	1	Luke Etheridge	1
Thos: Jones	1	Thos: Tayler Jur.	2	Wm: Luffman Jur.	1
James Caron Ser.	1	John Crisp	1	Edwd. Cox	1
James Caron Jur.	1	Wm: Nickolson	1	Richd. Bright Ser.	8
John Caron	1	Luke White	1	Richd. Bright Jur.	1
Heny: Jones	1	Humphry Vince	6	Geo Thompson	1
Thos: Lewis	2	Thos: Vince	2	Thos Elk	1
Thos: Williams	4	Andw: Peacock	1	Martin Bolen	1
Isaac Jones	9	Wm: Parker	1	Thos Godord	1
Heny: Woodhouse	2	Saml. Baker	1	Robt. Smith	1
Conll: Wm: Reed	1	Even Miller	1	Jacob Marsh	1
Capt. Richd: Sanderson	2	Araon Prescod	2	Moses Linton	1
Abraham Boom	1	Richd. Ballance	1	Richd. Linton	1
John Smith free neg:	1	Susannah Thomas	2	Heny: Etheridge	1
Mallica Winter	1	Thos: Vandermulen	2	James _____	1
William Wilson	1	Wm: Swann	4	Wm: Etheridge	1
William Leary	4	Jas. Wicker	2	Nicho: Mershall	1
Dameris Sanderson	8	Peter Dauge	1	John Warin	1
John Woodhouse	2	Benja: Tulle	1	Heny: Bright Jur.	2
John Ives	1	Walls Bray	2	Edwd. Bright	1
John Ronnalls	1	Wm: Williams	2	Wm: Stafford	2
Mathew Hannah	1	Jas. Poyner	1	Thomas Davis	2
Thos: Jervis	1	Richd: Dauge	1	Wm: Davis	2
Thos: Parker	1	Thos: Poyner	1	Marmeduke	
Azricom Parker	1	Thos: Shippard	1	Etheridge Ser.	2
Joseph Sanderson	4	John Shippard	1	John Etheridge	1
Jeremiah Smith	1	Peter Parker	1	Jacob Barber	1
Peter Poyner	1	John Barber	1	John Chance	1
		Geo: Spann	1	Mermeduke	
		Charles Barber	1	Etheridge Ser.	1
Taken By John Jones		John Pirkins Ser	1	John Northen	2
Constable of Powells Point		Thos: Davis	1	Webly Peavey	3
Heny: White	2	James Poyner	1	Geo Shlasberry	1
Jos: Church	6	John Fenton	1	Richds. Bright Weaver	1
Ffoster Jervis	4			Heny: Bright Jur.	1
Thomas Simmons	1			Benja. Bennit	1
Thomas Tayler	5	Taken by John Pell		John Munk	1
James Duglis	3	Constable		Chas. Sinqua negr.	1
Wm: Bell	4	William Poyner	4	Richd. Silvester	1
Michl: Oneal	1	William Luffman	3	Thos: Cox Jur.	1
Michl: Oneal Jur	1	Andw. Etheridge	1	_____ Simmons	1

CURRITUCK COUNTY TAX AND MILITIA LISTS

Jos. Bateman	1	Moses Ramsey	1	Danl. Linsey	1
Danl: Glasco	1	Danl: Phillips	6	Wm Johnson	1
Morris Johnson	1	Frances Jervis	1	Adolphus Hanson	1
Daniel Glasco Jur.	1	John Loyall	1	John Ears	1
Thos: Muncref	1	David Loyall	1	John Cope	1
Wm: Muncref	1	Saml: Simmons	1	Christ Bales	1
Chas. Brent	1	Denis Riordan	1	Christ Buskin	1
Wm: Scott	1	Thos: Swann	1	John Whidby	1
Benja. Brickhouse	1	Thos: Haman	1	Ambros M_____	1
Robt. Heath	1	Jos. Bouren	1	Alexdr. M_____	1
John Brent	1	John Perkins Jur.	1	Will M_____	1
Thos: Brent	1	Danl. Savill	1	John Beckly	1
Henr: Lawly	1			John Norton	1
Jos. Bennit	1			Samon Burgis	1
_____	2	The Nor West List		John Bales	1
Thos: Ffansow	1	John Man	[torn]	James Merten	1
Thos: Fansow Jr.	1	Geo Scarbrough	[torn]	Mathias Fowler	1
John Fansow	1	Wm: Tillitt	[torn]	Ralph Love	1
Richd. Fansow	1	Moses Rynard	[torn]	Timo: Ives	1
Robt. Tucker Ser.	1	Archd: Hartly	1	Wm: Ives	1
Robt. Tucker Jur.	1	Ralph_____	[torn]	Wm. Davis	1

Arears of Levies and Land tax Recd. in Coratuk for the year 1718

Robert Tuker Ser.	1	00:15:0			
Mermeduk Etheridge Jur.	1	00:15:0	Rovings charged		
William Tillitt	1	00:15:0	by the Constable		
Christopher Beals	1	00:15:0			
John Beals	1	00:15:0	1	160	00:04:0
Matheyas Towler	1	00:15:0			
Foster Jervis Jur.	1	00:15:0			
George Spann	1	00:15:0			
William Jonston	1	00:15:0			
John Mason	1	00:15:0	1	450	00:10:0
Thomas Williams Jur.	1	00:15:0			
Jerimiah Smith	1	00:15:0			
Petter Poyner	1	00:15:0			
Capt: William Nickallson	1	00:15:0	2	400	00:10:0
Even Miller	1	00:15:0	1	150	00:03:9
Shusana Thomas	2	01:10:0	1	300	00:07:6
William Swann	4	03:00:0	9	2690	03:07:3
John Barber	1	00:15:0	1	080	00:02:0
Charles Barber	1	00:15:0	1	080	00:02:0
John Pirkens Hickry	1	00:15:0	1	050	00:01:3
Thomas James	1	00:15:0			
James Poyner	1	00:15:0	1	070	00:01:9
Luke Etheridge	1	00:15:0			
Webly Payve	3	02:05:0			
Richard Bright waver	1	00:15:0			
Richard Selvester	1	00:15:0			
Thomas Cox Jur.	1	00:15:0			
John Brunt	1	00:15:0	1	050	00:01:3

Years of Levies and Land Recoved in Corratuck the year 1718	Tythable	Sums of Leavos for Levies	Tra: of Land	Number of Acres	for
Enrolld for ye year 1718 & 1717					
Los Lewis	1				
Wm Cheise	1				
Los: Baynor	1		1	100	
John Sigardo	1				
George Thomson	1				
Thomas Ellis	1				
Robert Smith	1		1	300	
James Man	1				
Antony Sammoux	1				
Thomas Waring	1				
Adollphus Hanson	1				
John Ears	1				
Ambros McCay	1				
William Davis	1				
Henry Gibson	1				
George Stearing	1				
John Stearing	1				
Richard Jonston	1				
John Lewis	1				
Thomas Spencer	1				
John Whitbee	1		2	1000	
William Elbridge	1				
	22				
petter Lux	1				

Plate IX

46

CURRITUCK COUNTY TAX AND MILITIA LISTS

Henry Lawly	1	00:15:0	1	100	00:02:6
Archebald Hartly	1	00:15:0			

William Tiler	1	Antony Seall	1	Richard Jonston	1
Charles Thomas	1	John Burton	1	John Macuing	1
Mary Willes Love	1				

Arears of Levies and Land tax Receved in Coratuk for the year 1718

John Caps	1	00:15:0	1	400	00:10:0
Robert Tuker Jur.	1	00:15:0	1	050	00:01:3
William McCay	1	00:15:0			
John Norton	1	00:15:0	3	744	00:11[torn]
James Merten	1	00:15:0	1	200	00:05:0
Thomas Lewis	1	00:15:0			
David Jones Jur.	1	00:15:0			
John Oneall	1	00:15:0	1	700	00:17:6
David Jones Ser.	1	00:15:0	1	400	00:10:0

Delinquints for the year 1718

John Waring	1		1	200
John Beckly	1		1	200
Patrick Kallehan	1			
Daniel Guthry	1			
Henry Davis	1		2	1000

Insolts: for ye year 1718 & 1717

Thos. Lewis	1			
[Torn]hn Crisp	1			
[Torn]hos: Poyner	1		1	100
John Shipard	1			
George Thomson	1			
Thomas Elks	1			
Robert Smith	1		1	300
James Man	1			
Anrtony Sammons	1			
Thomas Waring	1			
Adolphus Hanson	1			
John Ears	1			
Ambros McCay	1			
William Davis	1			
Henry Gibson	1			
George Stearing	1			
John Mecuing	1			
Richard Jonston	1			
John Lewis	1			
Thomas Spencer	1			
John Whittbee	1		2	1000
William Etheridge	1			
Petter Lux	1			

CURRITUCK COUNTY TAX AND MILITIA LISTS

A List of Coratuck Tythabls taken for ye year 1719

William Tuker	1	Luke Etheridge	2	Joseph Bennett	2
John Fanshaw	1	Edward Cox	1	Thomas Seagars	1
Thomas Fanshaw	1	Thomas Cox Ser.	1	Thomas Swann	2
Henry Fanshaw	1	Thomas Cox Jur.	1	Thomas Mills	1
Richard Fanshaw	1	Capt: Wm. Stafford	2	Benjemen Brickhouse	1
Frances Jervis	1	Richard Bright Ser.	2	Jacob Barber	1
John Northen	3	George Solsberry	1	John Flora	1
William Davis	1	Richard Bright Waver	1	Thomas James	1
John Etheridge	1	Edward Bright	1	John Pirkens Hukry	1
Mermeduk		Mertin Bowlen	1	Charles Barber	1
Etheridge Ser.	1	Henry Bright Ser.	2	Petter Parker	2
Robert Heath	1	John Munk	1	Thomas Shipard	1
Thomas Brunt	1	Joseph Beatman	1	Joseph Poyner	1
John Brunt	1	Jacob Mash	1	Robert Poyner	1
Thomas Williams	1	William Etheridg	1	Mr. William Williams	2
Charles Brunt	1	Robert Smith	1	Walis Bray	2
Thomas Davis	2	Daniell West	1	Daniell Phillips	7
William Scote	1	Nicolus Mershall	2	Joseph Wicker	2
Samuell Jones	2	Henry Lawly	1	Mr. William Swann	4
William Muncref	1	Charles Sinqua	1	Mr. Thos: Vandermulen	2
Daniell Glasco Ser.	1	Richard Selvester	1	Richard Ballence	2
Daniell Glasco Jur.	1	Moses Linton	1	Aron Prescoat	2
Moris Jonston	1	Richard Linton	1	Richard Dauge	2
William Poyner	6	Benjemen Bennett	1	Even Miller	1
Thomas Jonston	1	John Barington	1	William Parker	1
William Luffman Ser.	3	Henry Etheridge	1	Thomas Vince	1
William Luffman Jur.	1	Andrew McFerson	1	James Poyner	1
Andrew Etheridge	2	John Waring	1	Humphry Vince	7
Jobe Etheridge	1	John Ailer	1	Luke White	1
Thomas Parker	1	Temothey Ives	1	Benjemen Beasly	1
Capt: Wm: Nichalson	2	Abraham Boome	1	William Davis	1
John Fenton	1	Mr. Joseph Sanderson	4	John Penny	1
William Davis	2	Richard Williamson	1	George Stearing	1
Suesanna Thomas	4	Mathew Hanna	1	John Man	4
Benjemen Tull	1	James Browne	4	Robert Burros	1
Thomas Tayler Jur.	2	Malekey Winter	1	William Tillitt	1
John Pell	1	Edward Barber	1	George Scarborrow	2
Mr. William Bell	4	William Alexander	1	Charles Thomas	1
James Duglas	2	Thomas Jervis	1	Antony Seale	1
Mr. Thomas Tayler Ser.	4	Robert Peyton	7	John Burton	1
Edward Tayler	1	Moses Ryno	1	Henry Bright Jur.	1
Michall Oneall Ser.	1	Archebald Hartly	1	Webly Payve	8
Michall Oneall Jur.	1	Adolphus Hansen	3	Daniell Savell	1
John Walker	1	Ralph Mathon	2	Joseph Bowring	1
Thomas Simmons	1	William Gibs	1	John Pirkens Ser.	1
Petter Poyner	1	Daniell Linsay	1	Petter Dauge	1
Jerymiah Smith	1	William Jonston	1	George Spann	[torn]
Henry White	[torn]	Thomas Spencer	1	Denis Ryording	1
Joseph Church	[torn]	John Whidbee	1	John Liggett	1
Foster Jervis	[torn]	John Caps	1	David Liggett	1
Coll: Wm: Reed	2	Aden Beals	1	Samuell Simmons	1

CURRITUCK COUNTY TAX AND MILITIA LISTS

Henry Woodhouse	3	Christopher Bustian	1	Andrew Consall	2
John Jones	1	Samuell Burges	1	John Oneall	1
Thomas Jones	1	John Beckly	1	Patrick Kallehan	1
Richard Etheridge	1	Capt: John Norton	2	David Jones	1
Thomas Williams	5	Denis Callehan	1	Frances Farow	1
William Willson	1	Matheyas Towler	1	Daniell Gutthery	1
William Leary	4	Alixander McCay	1	Henry Davis	1
Sqr. Richd. Sanderson	12	Ralph Love	1	Henry Gibs	1
Mr. John Woodhouse	2	Petter Luge	1	James Parks	1
Azricum Parker	1	Robert Palmer	1		
John Ives	1	Temothey Ives Ser.	3	In all 301 Tythabls	

Levies & Land tax Recd. in Coratuk for the year 1719

John Fanshaw	1	00:15:0	1	540	00:12:6
Thomas Fanshaw	1	00:15:0			
Henry Fanshaw	1	00:15:0			
Richard Fanshaw	1	00:15:0			
Francis Jervis	1	00:15:0	1	075	00:01;3
John Northen	3	02:05;0	2	600	00:15:0
John Etheridge	1	00:15:0	1	150	00:03:9
Mermeduk Etheridge Ser.	1	00:15:0	1	200	00:05:0
Robert Heath	1	00:15:0	1	450	00:11:3
Thomas Brunt	1	00:15:0	2	200	00:05:0
John Brunt	1	00:15:0	1	050	00:1:3
Thomas Williams	1	00:15:0			
Charles Brunt	1	00:15:0	1	150	00:03:9
Thomas Davis	2	01:10:0	4	1000	01:05:0
Isaac Davis	1	00:15:0	1	160	00:04:0
William Scots	1	00:15:0	1	050	00:01:3
Samuell Jones	2	01:10:0	2	270	00:06:9
William Muncref	1	00:15:0	1	050	00:01:3
Daniell Glasco Jur.	1	00:15:0			
Daniell Glasco Ser.	1	00:15:0	1	250	00:06:3
William Poyner	6	04:10:0	4	900	01:02:6
Thomas Jonston	1	00:15:0			
William Luffman Ser.	3	02:05:0	1	350	00:08:9
William Luffman Jur.	1	00:15:0			
Andrew Etheridge	2	01:10:0	2	325	00:08:0
Jobe Etheridge	1	00:15:0			
Luke Etheridge	1	00:15:0			
Edward Cox	1	00:15:0	1	640	00:16:0
Thomas Cox Ser.	1	00:15:0			
Thomas Cox Jur.	1	00:15:0			
Capt: Wm: Stafford	2	01:10:0	2	750	00:18:9
Richard Bright Ser.	3	02:05:0	2	700	00:17:6
George Solsberry	1	00:15:0	1	300	00:07:6
Richrad Bright waver	1	00:15:0	1	100	00:02:6
Edward Bright	1	00:15:0	1	050	00:01:3
Mertin Bowlin	1	00:15:0	1	140	00:03:6
Henry Bright Ser.	2	01:10:0	1	150	00:03:9
John Munk	1	00:15:0	1	120	00:03:0
Joseph Beatman	1	00:15:0	1	120	00:03:0

CURRITUCK COUNTY TAX AND MILITIA LISTS

William Etheridge	1	00:15:0	1	050	00:01:3
Daniel West	1	00:15:0	1	120	00:03:6
Nicolus Mershall	2	01:10:0	1	100	00:02:6
Charles Sinqua	1	00:15:0			
Moses Linton	1	00:15:0	1	100	00:02:6
Benjemen Bennett	1	00:15:0	5	640	00:16:0
John Barington	1	00:15:0	1	150	00:03:9
Henry Etheridge	1	00:15:0	1	100	00:02:6
Joseph Bennett	2	01:10:0	2	220	00:05:6
Thomas Seayers	1	00:15:0			
Thomas Swann	2	01:10:0	1	430	00:10:9
Benjemen Brickhouse	1	00:15:0			
Jacob Barber	1	00:15:0	1	100	00:02:6
Thomas James	1	00:15:0			
John Pirkens Hickry	1	00:15:0			
Charles Barber	1	00:15:0	1	080	00:02:0
Petter Parker	2	01:10:0	1	200	00:05:0
Thomas Sheppard	1	00:15:0	1	100	00:02:6
Joseph Poyner	1	00:15:0	1	100	00:02:6
Robert Poyner	1	00:15:0	1	100	00:02:6
Mr. William Williams	2	01:10:0	2	1000	01:05:0
Walis Bray	2	01:10:0	1	150	00:03:9
Daniel Philips	7	05:05:0	1	260	00:06:6
Joseph Wicker	2	01:10:0	1	460	00:11:6
Mr. Thomas Vandermulen	5	03:15:0	1	400	00:10:0
Richard Ballence	2	01:10:0	1	300	00:07:6
Aron Prescoat	2	01:10:0	1	160	00:04:0
Even Miller	1	00:15:0	1	150	00:03:9
Thomas Vince	1	00:15:0	1	300	00:07:6
Humphry Vince	7	05:05:0	1	400	00:10:0
Luke White	1	00:15:0	1	320	00:08:0
Thomas Parker	1	00:15:0			
Shusana Thomas	4	03:00:0	1	300	00:07:0
Benjemen Tulle	1	00:15:0	2	700	00:17:6
Thomas Tayler Jur.	2	01:10:0	1	300	00:07:6
Capt: William Nickalson	2	01:10:0	1	120	00:03:0
John Fenton	1	00:15:0			
Mr. William Bell	4	03:00:0	1	900	01:02:6
James Duglas	2	01:10:0	1	050	00:01:3
Mr. Thomas Tayler Ser.	4	03:00:0	2	670	00:16:9
Edward Tayler	1	00:15:0			
Michal Oneall Ser.	1	00:15:0	2	500	00:12:6
Michal Oneall Jur.	1	00:15:0	1	090	00:02:3
John Walker	1	00:15:0	1	120	00:03:0
Thomas Simmons	1	00:15:0	2	170	00:04:3
Henry White	4	03:00:0	1	400	00:10:0
Joseph Church	4	03:00:0	2	700	00:17:6
Foster Jervis	4	03:00:0	2	550	00:13:3
Henry Woodhouse	3	02:05:0	1	400	00:10:0
John Jones	1	00:15:0	1	640	00:16:0
Richard Etheridge	1	00:15:0	2	640	00:16:0
Thomas Williams	5	03:15:0	4	1600	02:02:0

50

CURRITUCK COUNTY TAX AND MILITIA LISTS

William Willson	1	00:15:0	1	300	00:07:6
William Leary	4	03:00:0	2	900	01:02:6
James Carone	4	03:00:0	3	500	00:12:6
Mr. John Woodhouse	2	01:10:0	1	250	00:06:3
Azricum Parker	1	00:15:0	2	640	00:16:0
John Ives	1	00:15:0	1	150	00:03:9
Temothey Ives Jur.	1	00:15:0	1	150	00:03:9
Mr. Joseph Sanderson	4	03:00:0	4	1770	02:04:0
Mathew Hanna	1	00:15:0	1	080	00:02;)
James Browne	4	03:00:0	2	550	00:13:9
Thomas Jervis	1	00:15:0	1	300	00:07:6
Ralfe Mathon	2	01:10:0	1	150	00:03:9
William Gibs	1	00:15:0			
Christopher Bustian	1	00:15:0			
Samuell Burges	1	00:15:0			
Matheyas Towler	1	00:15:0			
Temothey Ives Ser.	3	02:05:0	1	440	00:11:0
Benjemen Beasly	1	00:15:0			
John Penny	1	00:15:0	4	800	01:00:0
Henry Bright Jur.	1	00:15:0	1	050	00:01:3
Webly Peyve	3	02:05:0			
Daniell Savill	1	00:15:0	1	080	00:02:0
Joseph Bowring	1	00:15:0	1	150	00:03:9
John Pirkens	1	00:15:0	2	250	00:06:3
George Spann	1	00:15:0			
Denis Ryording	1	00:15:0	1	100	00:02:6
John Liggett	1	00:15:0	1	140	00:03:6
David Liggett	1	00:15:0	1	140	00:03:6
James Parker	1	00:15:0			
Samuell Simmons	1	00:15:0	1	200	00:05:0
Andrew Consall	2	01:10:0			
Petter Poyner	1	00:15:0			
Jerymiah Smith	1	00:15:0			
Mr. William Swann	4	03:00:0	9	2695	03:07:6
Daniell Linsey	1	00:15:0	1	150	00:03:9
John Caps	1	00:15:0	1	400	00:10:0
John Man	4	03:00:0			
Richard Selvester	1	00:15:0			
Andrew McFerson	1	00:15:0	1	500	00:12:6
John Flora	1	00:15:0	1	100	00:02:6
Richard Dauge	2	01:10:0	1	050	00:01:3
William Parker	1	00:15:0	2	140	00:03:6
James Poyner	1	00:15:0	1	100	00:02:6
William Davis	2	01:10:0			
Abraham Boome	1	00:15:0	1	150	00:03:9
Malecay Winter	1	00:15:0	1	200	00:05:0
Thomas Spencer No. Banks	1	00:15:0			
John Norton	2	01:10:0	3	440	00:11:0
Allixander McCay	1	00:15:0			
William McCay	1	00:15:0			
George Scarborow	2	01:10:0			
Robert Borows	1	00:15:0	1	100	00:02:6

CURRITUCK COUNTY TAX AND MILITIA LISTS

Robert Palmer	1	00:15:0			
Henry Lawly	1	00:15:0	1	100	00:02:6
Richard Sanderson Esqr.	12	09:00:0		3000	04:15:0
Coll: Wm: Reed	2	01:10:0	3	1510	01:17:9
Archebald Hartly	1	00:15:0	1	400	00:10:0
Petter Dauge	1	00:15:0	2	900	01:02:6
John Oneall	1	00:15:0	1	700	00:17:6
David Jones	1	00:15:0	1	400	00:10:0
Robert Peyton	7	05:05:0	2	550	00:13:9

Delinquints for ye year 1719

William Tuker	1			
Richard Williamson	1			
William Alixander	1			
John Beckly	1			
Ralph Love	1		1	200
Patrick Callehan	1		1	200
Daniell Guthery	1			
Frances Farow	1		1	300
James Jonston	1			
Henry Davis	1		2	1000
Henry Gibs	1		2	800
John Waring	1			

Insoll: for the year 1719

William Davis	1			
Morris Jonston	1			
Robert Smith	1		1	300
Richard Linton	1			
Thomas Waring	1			
John Ails	1			
Thos: Mills	1			
Thomas Jones	1			
Henry Gibson	1			
Edward Barber	1			
Moses Ryno	1			100
Adollphus Hanson	1			
John Whittbe	1			1000
Aden Beals	1			
Denis Callehan	2			
Petter Lux	1			
John Pallmer	1			
William Davis	1			
George Stearing	1			

Monys Paid ove the Publick A Compt in ye yr. 1719 in Coratuk

	£	S	d
To Andrew Barber for a Clame of 141 days & alowed	7	1	
To Andrew Etheridge for a wolfe Catched in a pitt		10	
to John Northen for a wolf Catched in a pitt		10	
To John Ives for a wild Catt		02	6

William Buffell for a wild Catt		02	6
[Torn] Joseph Sanderson for a wild Catt		02	6
Mr. Joseph Sanderson for two wild Catts		05	
To Mr. Joseph Sanderson for a wild Catt		02	6
To Moses Prescoat for a wild Catt		02	6
To Mr. Wm: Williams for a wild Catt		02	6
To Henry Fanshaw for a wolfe Killed wth: a gun		05	
To John Fanshaw for a wolf Killed with a gun		05	
To John Liggett for a Painter		10	
To Andrew Etheridge for a wolfe catched in a pitt		10	
To Benjemen Bennett for a wild Catt		02	6
[Torn] Robert Heath for a wolfe taken in a pitt		10	
To John Northen for a wolfe taken in a pitt		10	
To Foster Jervis for a painter		10	
To moses Prescoat for a painter		10	
To Aron Prescoat for a painter		10	
To Even Miller for two painters	1		
To Wm: Buffell for a painter & a wild Catt		12	6
Luke Etheridge for a wolfe taken in a pitt		10	
Petter Dauge for two wolfes Killed wth: a gun		10	

Land Taxes Recd: in Coratuk for ye year 1718 & 1719 of those yt. is not tythabls.

Henry Edey	1	1	150	00:03:9
Thomas Muncref	1	1	160	00:09:0
Sarah Barber	1	1	080	00:02:0
Richard Eyland	1	1	100	00:02;6
Mary Harris	1	1	150	00:03:9
Robert Stuard	1	2	390	00:09:9
Samuell Ballence	1	1	150	00:03:9
Richard Ballence in machepunga	1	1	200	00:05:0
Daniel McFerson	1	1	150	00:03:9
Daniell McKay	1	1	150	00:03:9
Rebecka Ramsey	1	1	100	00:02:6
John Dauge	1	1	140	00:03:6
Mermeduk Etheridge Jur.	1	1	050	00:01:3
John Smith free Negrow	1	1	300	00:07:6
The Widow Hunter	2	1	500	01:00:0
Isabella Beatman	2	1	100	00:05:0
Robert Bell	2	1	250	00:06:3
James Warding	1	1	450	00:11:3
Richard Ballence Stoars Land	1	1	320	00:08:0
The Widow Merten	1	1	200	00:05:0
Richard Sanderson for Rowneoake	2	1	1000	02:10:0

Publick Monys Recd: in Coratuk for the year 1718:1719 pr Jas. Browne Treasr.

	£	S	d
[Torn] ye Tythabls Recd: for ye yr: 1718	33	15	00
[Torn] ye land tax of 7054 acres of land	08	16	03
[Torn] 68 tythbl: Recd: for ye yr. 1719	201	00	00
[Torn] land tax of 45825 acres of Land	057	02	09
[Torn] land tax of 05090 acres of land	008	[torn]	

CURRITUCK COUNTY TAX AND MILITIA LISTS

	£	S	d
	308	19	03
paid out ove ye publick aCompt	015	05	00
	293	03	03
To my Sollry	009	15	00
	283	08	03
To my Expences to asembly	001	10	00
Remains due to the Contry	281	18	03

An Acct. of Tithables from Roanok [torn] Inlet May the 25th 1719

Name	Tith	Name	Tith
Moses Rignnow & Arched: Hartly	2	Ralph Love	1
Dolphus Hanson & Willm: Baker	2	The Dutchman living on	
Ralph Mathum & Joseph Lewis	2	Capt. __oeres planta.	1
Willm: Gibbs	1	John Palmer & Robert his son	2
Danll: Linsay	1	Timothy Ives & his son & 1 Negros	3
Willm: Jonson & John Airs	2	Benjamin Beasley	1
Thos: Spencer	1	Willm: Davis & Geo: Blackwell	2
John Whitbee	1	John Penney	1
John Capes & Aden Bales &		George Stering	1
Christ Bales	2	John Man	4
Christor: Bustien	1	Robert Burrow	1
Saml: Burges	1	Mr: Tillit	1
Jno: Beckley	1	Mr: Scarborow & his Son all Roanoak	2
Jno: Norton	2	Charles Thomas	1
Dennis Callehan	2	John Burton	1
Matthias Towler	1	The Widdow Weonses Son	1
Alexr: Maccoy Ambros Maccoy &		[Illegible]	1
Wm: Maccoy	3		

North Caro [torn] uk Pricinct

The Land list and list of Tithables for the Aforesaid Precinct for ye year 1720 Which Orderly Follows

Tith	Names	tracts	where	acres	
2	Rich: Etheridg	2	Powells	560	Patin
	son: Richd.		Point	100	Dito
2	Jam: Caron Sen	3	not named	515	Patin
	Jam: Caron Jun			200	Dito
				115	Dito
1	Mth: Howard				
5	Tho: Williams	7		630	Patin
	tony: negr. m			578	Dito
	tom: Ditto			350	Dito
	bety: Dito. w			125	Deed
	filis: Dito: w			100	Dito
				208	Dito
				160	Dito
4	Hen: Woodhouse	1		450	Deed
	Bada: negr. m				
	sara: Dito: w				

54

N: Ck Cur[roll]... ... ... MILL

The Land list and list of Tithables for the
aforsaid Precinct for yr year 17[?] on Which
Order[ly] follow

[Tithables] Names	Hands	Where	Ms	No of Tithables
2 Rich: Etheridge		Powells	5 60 Patin	6 Jos: Sanderson
ron: Richt	2	Point	100 Ditto	Ja: Edwards
				white man
2 Jam: Caroh sen	3	not nomin	515 Patin	Jack: neg: m
Jam: Caroh jun			200 Ditto	squa: Ditto
			115 Ditto	Tom: Ditto
				hanah Ditto w
1 mth: Howard				2 Ino: woodhous
5 Tho: williams	7		630 Patin	sara: neg: w
tony: neg: m			578 Ditto	1 Tho: Jarvis
Tom: Ditto			550 Ditto	1 Jin: Ives Jun
bety Ditto w			125 Deed	1 Ino: Ives
flis: Ditto w			100 Ditto	mth: Hunter
			208 Ditto	of: virginia
			160 Ditto	1 mth: Hanah
4 Hen: woodhous				1 Tho: Parker
Bada: neg: m	1		450 Deed	2 aux: Parker
raru: Ditto w				son: John:
seny: Ditto w				
1 abr: Boun	1		150 Deed	5 wm: williams
1 tom: willson	1		300 Deed	ron Stephen
1 mth: winter	1		218 Deed	Jac: neg: m
1 Hen: Gibson				begs: Ditto w
2 Ric: Sanderson Esq				riie: Ind: w
will: neg: m				5 som: grant
woman: Ditt				Jem: ha: man
6 wm: Lerrey				Lewis: ind: m
tho: Lertey				cro: neg: m
Jac: neg: m	3		400 Patin	nan: neg: w
nan: neg: w			630 Ditto	
fran: Ditto			200 Ditto	
sare: Ditto				2 Ric: Knage
3 Ja: Brown				Pet: neg: m
sam: neg: m				
seny: Ditto w				2 Tho: Shepard
John: Smith				John: Shepard
				E.w: Dugles

Plate X

55

	jeny: Dito: w			
1	Abr: Boom	1	450	Deed
1	Tom: Willson	1	300	Deed
1	Mck: Winter	1	218	Deed
1	Hen: Gibson			
2	Ric: Sanderson Esq.			
	will: negr. m			
	woman: Ditt			
6	Wm: Lerrey	3	400	Patin
	Tho: Lerrey		630	Dito
	Jac: negr. m		200	Dito
	nan: negr. w			
	Fran: Ditto			
	Sare: Dito			
3	Ja: Brown			
	sam: negr. m			
	jeny: Dito. w			
	John: Smith			

[Torn]

6	Jos: Sanderson	7	2589	Patin
	Ja: Edwards			
	white man			
	Jack. negr: m			
	Sqas. Ditto			
	Tom. Ditto			
	hanah. Ditto. w			
2	Jno: Woodhouse	2	150	Patin
	Sara: negr. w		050	Deed
1	Tho: Jarvis			
1	Tim: Ives: Jur.	1	116	Deed
1	Jno: Ives	1	116	Deed
	Margt: Hunter	1	515	Deed
	of Virginia			
1	Mth: Hanah	1	088	Deed
1	Tho: Parker			
2	Azr: Parker	2	530	Patin
	son: John		150	Survey
5	Wm: Williams	4	264	Deed
	son: Stephen		150	Patin
	Jac: negr. m		519	Dito
	Bess: Ditto. w		102	Patin
	Sue: Ind. w			
5	Wm: Swann	9	400	Patin
	Tom: Hall: mallt.		400	Dito
	Lewis: Ind. m		316	Dito
	Cro: neg. m		055	Dito
	Nan: neg. w		053	Dito
			295	Survey
			150	Deed
			475	Survey
			640	Dito

56

2	Ric: Dauge	2		050	Deed
	Petr: negr. m			533	Patin
2	Tho: Shepard	1		100	Deed
	John: Shepard				
[torn]	Jas: Duglas	1		050	Deed
1	Pet[er Par]ker	2	head of	125	Patin
			Tulls Creek	070	Ditto
1	Geo: Spann				
1	Charles: Barber	1	Dito	080	Deed
2	Wall: Bray	1	Dito	100	Deed
	Sepeo: negr. m				
1	Mo: Ceaton	1	Dito	025	Deed
	Jas: Barber	1	Dito	080	Deed
1	Tho: James				
2	Andw: Consaul				
	Wm: Bursill				
2	Wbly: Pavey				
	negr: man				
2	Mard: Etheridg	2	Dito	360	Deeds
	son: Tim.				
	Ja: Nichols	1		300	Patin
	of: Virginia				
1	Robt Tucker				
1	Jo: Bouren				
1	Wm: Bell				
1	Jno: Perkins	2	Dito	169	Deeds
1	Dan: Savell	2	Dito	170	Patin
	Wm: Tucker	1	Dito	050	Deed
1	Den: Riordan	1		100	Deed
1	David Legat	1		156	Patin
1	Jno: Legat	2		140	Deed
1	Sa: Simons	1		200	Deed
1	Jos: Poyner	1			
1	Robt: Dito				
1	Mo: Prescot				
1	Evn: Miller	1		150	Patin
1	Sam Baker				
1	Jno: Fenton				
	Tho: Co[torn]			376	Deed
	of V[irginia]				
			[Currituck] Shoar		
1	Wm: Parker	2	Dito	073	Survey
				090	Dito
1	Ja: Poyner	2	Dito	100	Deed
				071	Patin
1	Tho: Vince	1	Dito	330	Patin
	Jac: negr. m				
6	Hum: Vince	1	Dito	406	Patin
	Fran: Gamige				
	Ishim: negr. m				
	Pete: Ditto: m				

57

	Tom: Ditto. m				
	Jeny: negr. w				
1	Lu: White	2	Dito	143	Deed
				170	Patin
2	Wm: Nicholson	2	Dito	300	Patin
				130	Dito
1	Jno: Crabb				
1	Petr: Poyner	2		200	Deed
	125 Patin				
2	Sil: Thomas	1		330	Deed
	Tom: negr. m				
	Cris: Dito. w				
3	Tho: Tayler	2		250	Patin
	Gilb: Portwood			047	Deed
	Jase: negr. m				
1	Jno. Bell	1		250	Patin
6	Wm: Bell	2		511	Patin
	son: Wm			396	Dito
	Guy: negr. m				
	York: Dito. m				
	Kate: Negr. w				
	Jeny: Dito. w				
1	Jno: Eden				
4	Tho: Tayler Sen.	2		350	Patin
	Lery: negr. m			320	Dito
	Phill: Dito. m				
	Bes: negr. w				
1	Edw: Tayler				
1	Mi: Oneal	3		[torn]	
			Covinjock		
1	Mi: Oneal Jun.	1	Dito	091	Deed
2	Jno: Walker	1		075	Patin
	Jas. Parker	1		050	Deed
1	Hen: Eden	1		500	Deed
1	Tho: Simons	2		050	Deed
				100	Dito
4	Fos: Jarvis	2		305	Patin
	Jac: negr. m			320	Dito
	Davy: Indian				
	Jac: negr. m				
4	Jos: Church	1		730	Patin
	Tony: negr. m				
	Juda: negr. w				
	Hana: negr. w				
3	Hen: White				
	Dic: negr. m				
	Hana: Ditto. w				
2	Esb: Prescot	2		160	Survey
	Aron: Dito			053	Dito
	Jno: Ditto				
2	Jos: Wicker	3		359	Patin
	Bess: negr. w			102	Dito

				095	Dito
	Margt: Barott	1		025	Deed
3	Wm: Davis				
	Manu: Elks				
	Wm: Philips				
1	Benj: Tull				
			No. West River		
1	Jno: Barenton				
1	Jams: Bateman	1	Dito	140	
	Tho: Miller of Virginia	1	Dito	100	
1	Jac: Mash				
1	Jno: Flowrey	1		100	Deed
1	Mo: Linton				
[torn]	Hen: Etheridg	1		112	Deed
	[torn]n: Etheridg	1		050	Deed
	[torn Haris	1		150	Deed
1	Tho: Waran	1		285	Deed
1	Dan: West	1		130	Patin
2	Nic: Marshall	1		100	Deed
	Ric: Bradley				
1	Jno: Mounk	1		129	Patin
1	Benj: Benett	2		650	Patin
				056	Survey
1	Jam: Warden				
2	Hen: Lauley				
	Jam: Parmac				
1	Robt: Williams				
2	Andw: Etheridg	2		300	Patin
	son: Andw.			025	Dito
1	Ja: Barber				
1	Job: Etheridg	1		080	Deed
3	Ric: Bright	2		175	Patin
	son: Wm.			550	Dito
	son: James				
1	Jam: Rickets				
1	Wm: Ives				
2	Hen: Bright	1		156	Patin
	son: Adam				
1	Hen: Bright Jur.				
1	Martn: Bowlen	1		180	Patin
1	Edw: Bright				
1	Ric: Bright Jur.				
1	Wm: Staford	2		640	Patin
				114	Dito
1	Jno: Pricket				
1	Tho: Cox				
1	Tho: Cox Jur.				
1	Edw. Cox	1		640	Patin
1	Cha: Kite				
1	Lu: Etheridg				

1	Benj: Bric[khouse]				
	Saml: Went[worth]				
	and Compa:				
1	Samsn: negr: mn:				
	of: H; Halsteads				
2	Wm: Luffman	1	Ditto	270	Patin
1	Wm. Luffman Jun.				
2	Tho: Swann	2		394	Deeds
	Jeny: negr. w				
1	Jno: Eley				
2	Jo: Benne	2		151	Patin
	son: Jo.			080	Dito
1	Tho: Shears				
1	Geo: Shroesbery				
1	Cha: Sinqua				
7	Wm: Poyner	6		325	Patin
	Edw: Dito			315	Dito
	Ketur: negr. m			100	Deed
	Sam: Dito. m			160	Patin
	Fran: Dito. w			250	Dito
	Sara: negr. [w]			325	Deed
	John Will[torn]				
1	Wm: Poyner				
1	Tho: Nash				
1	Dan: Glas[co]				
1	Tho: Munc[ref]	1		160	Deed
1	Isa: Dav[is]	1		160	Deed
1	Wm: Mun[cref]	1		053	Deed
3	Sam: Jon[es}	1		270	
	son: Sam				
	son: Tho:				
1	Wm: Scot	1		050	Deed
7	Dan: Philips	1		260	Patin
	Tom: negr. m				
	Park: negr. m				
	Oring: Ditt. m				
	Grace: negr. w				
	Deb: Dito. w				
	Sara: Ditto. w				
2	Tho: Davis	3	Dito	615	Patin
	Phil: negr. w			085	Dito
				300	Dito
1	Cha: Brunt	1		350	Patin
1	Jno: Ditto				
1	Robt: Heth				
1	Tho: Brunt	2		200	Patin
				100	Deed
2	Mard: Etheridg	2		361	Patins
	son: John				
4	Jno: Northern	3		150	Deed
	Samsn: negr. m			220	Patin
	Ja: free negr. m			330	Deed

	Dina: negr. w.				
1	Jno: Fancher	1		540	Patin
1	Ric: Fancher				
1	Thos: [Di]to				
1	H[en]: Fancher				
1	Fran: Jarvis	2		100	Patin
				053	Deed
1	Tho: Williams				
1	Petr: Dauge	3		493	Patin
				200	Dito
				200	Deed
			Sand Banks		
1	Wm: Gibs				
1	Wm: Keito				
1	B[torn]athern	1		050	Survey
1	[Tho:] Spencer				
1	[Torn] Jonston				
	[torn] Heirs				
	[torn] Bailes				
	[torn] Clark				
	[torn]	1		500	Patin
	[torn]			150	Deed
	[torn]			160	Patin
	[torn]				Patin
1	Jno: Whittby	1		440	Patin
1	Wm: Macoy	1		065	Patin
1	Jno: Beckley				
1	Saml: Burgis				
2	Wm: Gray				
1	Den: Calehoun				
1	Jno: Evans				
1	Patk: Toler			300	Patin
1	Jno: Burton	1		190	Patin
1	[R]a: Love				
1	Jno: Penny	2		404	
				260	
2	Jno: Paumer				
	son: Robt.				
1	Geo: Stiring				
1	[Smeared]man	1	quarter: of: Ronak Island		
1	[Torn] Buris	1	[torn]		
1	[Torn] Willey				
2	[Torn] Ives	1		480	Deed
8	[Rob]t Peyton	4		120	Patin
				053	
				268	Patin
				150	Deed
L[torn] Hed: Owners Living: In: Virginia					
	[Torn] Eiland	2		150	Deed
				100	Dito
	[Torn] Balance	1		150	Patin

CURRITUCK COUNTY TAX AND MILITIA LISTS

[Torn] Linton	1	150	Deed
[Torn] Baronton	1	150	D[torn]
[Torn] Mounk	1	129	[torn
Ann: Makefason	1	250	[torn]
Wbl: Merchant	1	26[torn]	
Dan: Macoy	1	[torn]	
Mo: Etheridg	1	[torn	
Dan: Makefason	1	[torn]	
Corn: Jenes	1	[torn]	
Wm: Dauge	1	[torn]	
Jno: Dauge		[torn	

Tythables in Currytuck Precinct Jan 1720/21

Sand·à Banks List

Wm. Gibbs Mulatt	1	Jenney do woman	3
Wm. Healo	1	Hen. Woodhouse, Bada a negro	
Ralph Mathew	1	man Sarah & Jenney negro	
Tho. Spencer	1	woman	4
Wm. P__d_____, J____	1	Wm Lurry, Tho. Lurry his son	
Jno. Ears	1	Jack negro man Sarah, Nanny	
Chi. Bayles	1	& Frank negro woman	6
Jno. Clark	1	Jos. Sanderson Jams ____ over-	
Jno. Copps	1	seer Jack, Squash, Tom negro	
Jo. Whidbee	1	man, Hannah negro woman	6
Wm. McCoy	1	Jno. Woodhouse: Sarah Nego w	2
Jno. Beckley	1	Fos. Jarvis	1
Simon Burges	1	Jno. Ives	1
Wm. Gray	2	Tim. Ives	1
Den. Calyhan	1	Matt. Hannah	1
Jas. Eades	1	_____ Parker	1
Matt. Towler	1	Edw. Parker & son John	2
Jno. Burton	1		40
Ralph Love	1		
Jno. Penny, Jno. Palmer R __	3	Thos. Vince List Currytuck Shore	
Jno. Mann	1	Wm. Williams son Stephen	
Robt. Burrus	1	Jack a Negro man Bess Negro	
Jno. Wilee	1	woman, son Jno.	5
Timo. Ives	1	Wm. Swann, James mulatto man	
Rt. Peyton	8	Lewis Ind. man Eron Negr man	
Archd. Hartley Constable	40	Nan a negro woman	9
		Rd. Dauge & Petter Negro	2
John Jones's List from Powells Point &		Tho. Sheppard	1
Azricum Parker's		Jno. Sheppard	1
Rd. Esorid & son Richard	2	Petr. Parker	1
James Caron & son James	2	Geo. Spann D___	1
Matt. Howard & Robt. Seegin	2	Cha. Barber	1
Abrhm. Boom, Malachia Mershal	2	Wallis Bray & Scipio Neg.	2
Wm. Wilson, Hen. Gespeno	2	Moses Ceaton	1
Rd. Sanderson Esq., Willee Neg.		Tho. Jarvis	1
man Maria do woman	2	Andw. Consale & _ a mulatto	2
Jams Brown, Sampson Negr man		Webley Peavy, Sandfer Neg.	2

62

CURRITUCK COUNTY TAX AND MILITIA LISTS

Mermeduk Etheridg son Peter &		Benj. Tulle	1
Wm Tucker	2		95
Robt. Tucker	1		
Jos. Bowrens	1	N W River List Taken by Geo: Powers	
Jno. Perkins	1	Jno. Barrington	1
Den. Reyordin	1	Jas. Bateman	1
Davd. Legitt	1	Rd. Marsh	1
Jno. Legitt	1	_____	1
Saml. Simons	1	[Mos]es Linton	1
Jos. Poyner Dead	1	Hen: Etheridge	1
Pet. Poyner	1	Jno. Warren	1
Mos. Prescott	1	Danl. West	1
Evan Miller	1	Nickl. Marshall, Rd. Bradley	2
Saml. Baker	1	Jno. Monk	1
Jno. ____ton Jur.	1	Benj. Bennett	1
Wm. Parker	1	Jams. Worden	1
Jams. Poyner	1	Hen: Bright, Jams. _____	2
Thos: Vince & Jack negro man	1	Jas. Williams	1
Hump Vince Fra. Gomage		Andw. Etheridge ____ _____	2
_____ negr man Peter neg man		Jno Barber	1
Tom Do Jenney neg woman	6	Rd. Bright Son John & James	3
Luke White	1	Jams. Picketts	1
Wm. Nickelson & son Wm	2	Wm Ives	1
Jno. Crabb	1	Hen: Bright & son Adam	2
Susan Thomas Tom negro man		Hen: Bright Jur.	
Cris negro woman	2	Martin Bowlen	1
Thos. Taylor Jur. one apprent-		Edwd. Bright	1
ice Jeffrey negro man	3	Rd. Bright son of Henry	1
Jno Pell	1	Wm. Stafford	1
Wm Bell son Wm, Guy &		Jno. Bickett	1
Jak neg. man Kate &		Thos. Cox Jur.	1
Jenney negro woman	6	Thos. Cox Senr.	1
Jno. Eden	1	Edwd. Cox	1
Thos: Taylor Ser., Tony		Chas. Kite mulatto free	1
Philip negro man Bess woman	4	Luke Etheridge	1
[Torn] Taylor	1	Benj. Brickhouse	1
[Mi]chll. Oneel Ser.	1	Hen: Nal_____ free negro	1
[Mi]chll. Oneel Jur.	1	Wm Luffman, son, slave	3
[Torn] Parker	1	Thos: Swann Jenney negr wom.	2
_____	1	Jno. Ciely	1
_____ Simons	1	Thos. Sears	1
_____son, Jack &		Geo. _____berry	1
[torn]ck negro man D___ Ind.	4	Chas. Sinquer free negro	1
[Jos} Church Folls negro man		Wm Poyner Jno. Wilson Keah	
Judy & Hannah woman	4	Frank Sam negro men Sarah	
Henry White, Dick negro man		negro woman	6
Hannah negro woman	3	Wm Poyner Junr.	1
_____, J. Prescott	2	Thos: Nash	1
[Tron]bole Jno & Aron	2	Danll. Glasco	1
[Jos] Wicker Bess negr woman	2	Tho. Muncrief	1
Wm Davis _____ & Wm		Isa: Davis	1
Phillips	3	Wm Muncrief	1

63

Saml Jones & son Saml	2	Tho. Brunt	1
Thos. Jones	1	Marmkd Etheridge & son Jno.	2
Wm Scott	1	Jno Northen Sampson & Jeffrey	
Danl Philip Tom Parker Mingo		neg. man Dynah a woman	4
James negro man Grace Deb &		Jno Fanshere _____	1
Sarah	7	Rd. Fanshere	1
Tho Daow Philis negro	2	Tho. Fanshere	1
Chas. Brunt	1	Tho. Williams	1
Jno. Brunt	1	Fra. Jarvis	1
Robt. Heath	1	Pet. Dauge	1
			92
			95
			80
		Total	267

North Carolina
Corotuck Prect.

The Land List And List of Tithables
For ye afore Said Prect. for ye year
1721 which Orderly Followeth

Tiths	Names	tracts	Acres	How
2	Richd. Etheridge			
	son Richard			
2	Jas. Caron			
	son James			
1	Chs. Buskin			
1	Mat. Howard			
3	Coll.: Wm. Reed			
	2 Negr.			
6	Tho: Williams	8	587	Patten
	Jno: Herly Wt: M:		630	Do.
	Tony Negr. M:		350	Do.
	Tom Do: M:		212	Do.
	Betty Do M		100	Deed
	Hilly Do. W:		160	Do.
			200	Do.
1	Wm. Wilson			
1	Adam Segio			
4	Henry Woodhouse	1	[Torn]	Deed
	Bada Negr Man			
	[Torn]			
	Jenny Do W			
2	Richd: Sanderson Esq.			
	Wile Negr. Man			
	Marrose Do W			
1	Abr. Boom			
1	Mat: Winter			
5	Tho: Lerry			
	Jack negr: Man			
	Ffrank Do. W:			
	Nan Do. W:			
	Sarah Do. W;			
2	Mary Brown			

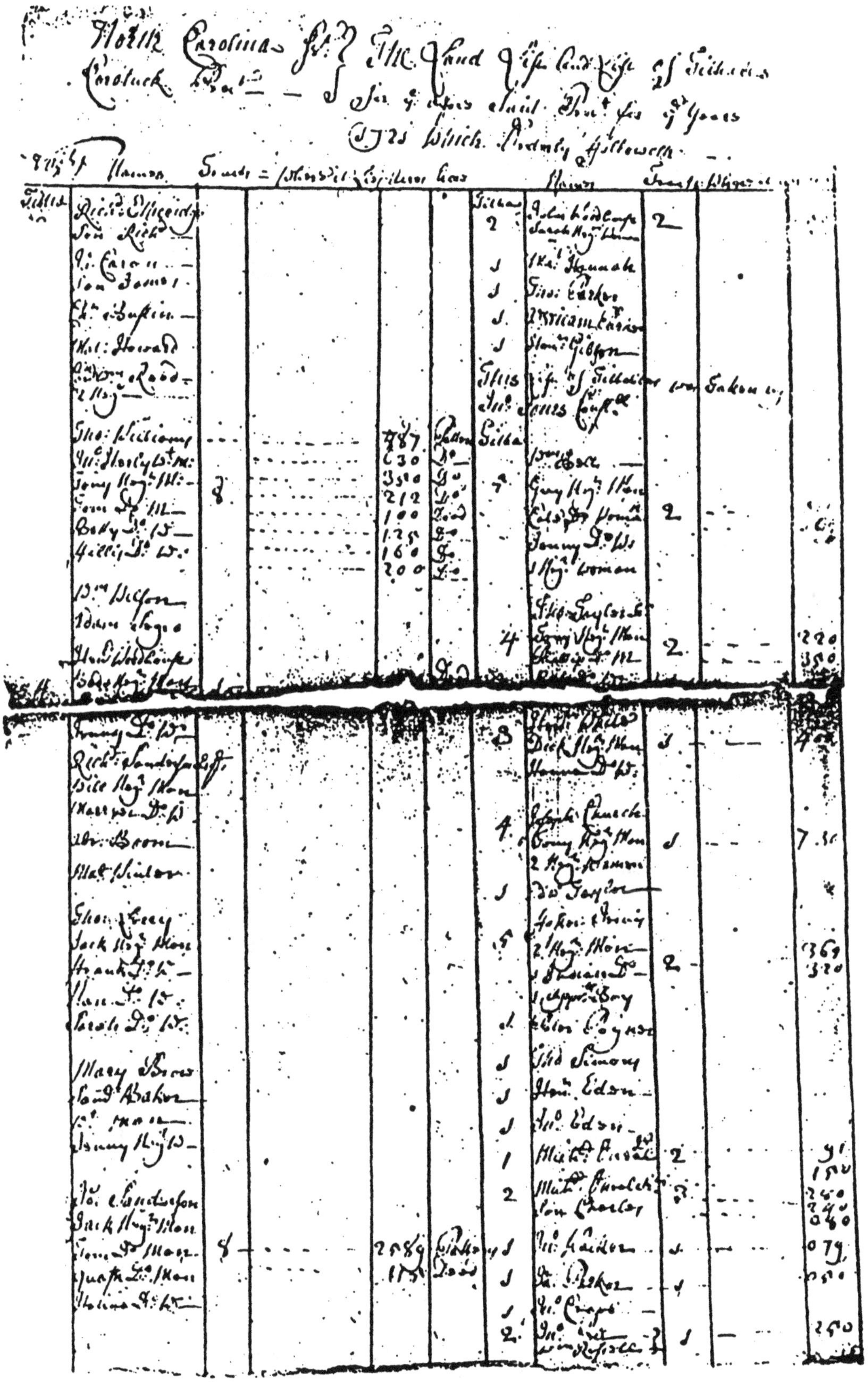

Plate XI

	Saml. Baker			
	Wt. Man			
	Jenny Negr. W.			
5	Jos. Sanderson	8	2589	Pattens
	Jack Negr. Man		115	Deed
	Tom Do. Man			
	Quash Do. Man			
	Hanna Do. W.			
2	John Woodhouse	2	250	Patten
	Sarah Negr. Woman		050	Deed
1	Mat: Hannah			
1	Tho: Parker			
1	Azricum Parker			
1	Henr: Gibson			

This List of Tithables was Taken by Jno. Jones Constbl.

5	Wm Bell	2	511	Patten
	Guy Negr. Man		395	Do.
	Cate Do. Woman			
	Jenny Do. W:			
	1 Negr. Woman			
4	Tho: Tayler Ser.	2	220	Patten
	Tony Negr Man		350	
	Do.			
	Phillip Do. M:			
	Bess Do. W.			
3	Henr: White	1	400	Deed
	Dick Negr. Man			
	Hanna Do. W:			
4	Joseph Church	1	730	Patten
	Tony Negr. Man			
	2 Negr. Woman			
1	Edwd. Tayler			
5	Ffoster Jarvis	2	369	Patten
	2 Negr. Men		320	Do.
	1 Indian Do.			
	1 Apprt. Boy			
1	Peter Poyner			
1	Tho: Simons			
1	Henr. Eden			
1	Jno. Eden			
1	Michl: Oneal Jur.	2	091	Deed
			150	Do.
2	Michl: Oneal Ser.	3	280	Deed
	son Charles		240	Do.
			080	Patin
1	Jno: Walker	1	079	Deed
1	Jas. Parker	1	050	Deed
1	Jno: Crabb			
2	Jno: Pell	1	250	Deed
	Wm: Russell			
2	Webly Peavy	1	240	Deed

CURRITUCK COUNTY TAX AND MILITIA LISTS

	1 Negr. Man			
2	Andw: Consaul			
	Wm: Bursill			
3	Marmdk: Etheridge	2	310	Deed
	2 sons		050	Deed
1	David Savell	2	050	Deed
			035	Pattin
1	Wm Bell			
1	Jos. Bouren	1	105	Patten
1	Jno: Perkins	2	119	Deed
			170	Patten
1	Denis Riordan	1	100	Deed
1	David Legatt	1	156	Patten
1	Jno. Legatt	2	140	Deed
			095	Patten
1	Saml: Simon	1	200	Deed
1	Tho: Jarvis			
2	Walis Bray	1	100	Deed
	Sippias Negr. M:			
1	Moses Ceaton	1	025	Deed
1	Cha: Barber			
1	Peter Parker	2	195	Patten
			070	Do.
1	Tho: _____	1	100	
2	Richd: Dauge			
	____ Negr. man			
1	Robt. Poyner	1	100	
1	Moses Prescot			
1	Aron Prescot			
1	Jno: Prescot			
3	Wm: Nickalson			
	2 sons			
1	Luke White			
6	Hump Vince	1	405	Patten
	Fran: Gomage			
	3 Negr. Men			
	2 woman Do.			
2	Tho: Vince			
	Jack negr. Man			
1	James Poyner			
1	Evan Miller	1	150	Deed
2	Wm: Bell Jur.			
	Jack Negr. Man			
1	Jno: Fenton Jur.			
2	Jno: Fenton Ser.			
	son Richd.			
1	Wm: Baker	2	073	Survey
			096	Do.
6	Wm. Swann	9	400	Patten
	Tom Mat: Man		400	Do.
	Lewis Indian Do.		316	Do.
	Eano Negr. Do.		055	Do.

67

	Nan Do. woman		053	Do.
	Jenny Do. W.		295	Survey
			750	Deed
			475	Survey
			640	Do.
2	Jos. Wicker	3	359	Patten
	Bess Neg. W.		102	Do.
			095	Do.
2	Wm: Davis	1	053	Deed
	Prentis Boy			
2	Benj. Tulle			
	Sarah Negr. W.			
5	Wm. Williams			
	Son Stephen			
	Jack Negr. Man			
	1 Negr. Woman			
	1 Indian Do.			
3	Susanna Thomas			
	Son George			
	Criss Negr. W.			
	Tom Do. M.			
3	Tho: Fenton Ser.	3	259	Patten
	Prentis Boy		040	Deed
	Jeffrey Negr. M.		177	Do.
	Widow Duglas	1	050	Deed

This List of Tithables was taken By Tho: Tayler Jur. Constbl.

2	Tho: Williams			
	Jeremy Negr.			
5	David Phillips			
	Tom Negr. Man			
	Parker Do. M.			
	Deb: Do. W			
	Son: David			
1	Robt. Heath	1	445	Patten
1	Cha: Brent	1	350	Patten
1	Jno: Brent			
1	Tho: Brent	2	100	Patten
			100	Lease
2	Tho: Davis	3	615	Patten
	Fillis Negr. W.		086	Do.
			300	Do.
1	Peter Dauge			
2	Saml. Jones			
	Son Saml.			
1	Wm. Scott			
1	Ean Elks			
1	Isa Davis			
1	Wm. Moncrief			
1	Tho: Moncrief			
1	Daniel Glasco			
1	Tho: Mash			

9	Wm. Poyner	6	325	Patten
	Edwd. Poyner		325	Do.
	Keto Negr. Man		160	Do.
	Sam Do. Man		100	Deed
	Sarah Do. W.		250	Patten
			325	Do.
2	Wm. Luffman	1	270	Deed
	Moll Negr. W.			
1	Wm. Luffman			
2	Jos. Bennit			
	Son Joseph			
1	Tho: Shoors			
1	Cha: Sinqua			
1	Geo: Shrosberry			
2	Tho: Swann			
	Jeny Negr. W.			
1	Andw. Etheridge	2	394	Pattens
1	Job: Etheridge	1	080	Deed
2	Andw. Etheridge Jur.			
	Jacob Barber			
2	Luke Etheridge			
	Wm. Poyner			
3	Richd. Bright	2	185	Patten
	Son James		500	Do.
	Son W.			
1	Jas. Rickets			
1	Wm. Ives			
1	Edwd. Cox	1	640	Patten
1	Tho: Cox			
1	Tho: Cox Jur.			
1	Wm: Stafford	1	780	Patten
1	Jno. Bright			
1	Benja. Brickhouse			
1	Richd. Bright Jur.			
2	Hen: Bright	2	156	Patten
	Son Adam		185	Do.
1	Marten Bolen	1	180	Patten
1	Tho: Godord			
1	John Bright			
1	Jas: Carmack			
1	Wm. Bateman			
1	Jno. Munk	1	129	Patten
1	Jas. Bateman	1	140	Patten
1	Jacob Mash			
	[Illegible]			
1	Moses Linton	1	100	Deed
1	Ben Etheridge	1	050	Deed
1	Hen: Etheridge	1	112	Deed
1	Jno. FFluery	1	100	Deed
1	Nick. Mershal	1	100	Deed
1	Richd. Bradley			
1	Danll. West	1	130	Patten

1	Jno. Barington	1	380	Patten
1	Dan. Alcock			
1	Benja. Bennit	2	650	Patten
			050	Survey
1	John Ele			
1	James Warden			
1	Richd. Johnson			
1	Hen: Halstead			
	negr. Samson			
1	Cha: Kite			
5	Jno. Northern	3	400	Deed
	4 Negr.		220	Patten
			070	Do.
	Wido Jarvis	2	100	Deed
			050	Do.
1	Jno. Etheridge	1	150	Patten
1	Hen: Etheridge	1	211	Patten
1	Paul Rigby			
	Geo. Powers	1	100	Deed
3	Tho: Ffanshaw	1	540	Patten
	Richd. Ffanshaw			
	Hen. Ffanshaw			

This List of Tithables Taken by Geo. Powers Constbl.

The Sand Banks

1	Wm. Gibbs			
1	Wm. Keito			
1	Ralph Mathew			
1	Tho: Spencer			
1	Jno. Eares			
1	Chr. Bailes			
1	Jno. Clark			
1	Jas. Cope			
1	Archd. Heartley			
1	Jno. Whidbee			
1	Jno. Beckley			
1	Samon Burgis			
2	Wm. Gray			
1	Matt. Towler			
1	Jno. Burton			
1	Ralph Love			
1	Jno. Penny			
1	Jno. Paumer			
1	Geo: Stering			
4	Jno. Man			
1	Robt. Burros			
1	Jno. Willy			
2	Timo. Ives			
8	Robt. Peyton	5	130	
			057	
			120	
			150	

440

The Following Lands Hold by Sevr. Gent. In Virga:

Corn. Jones	1	200	Deed
Andw. Makefation	1	210	
Richd. Ballance	2	180	Deed
		110	Patten
Jno. Nosay	1	132	Deed
Giles Roirdors	1	122	Do.
Wm. Tucker	1	053	Deed
Wm. Linton	1	150	Deed
_____ Balance	1	150	Deed
Dan Makefation	1	150	Deed
Danll: Macoy	1	100	Patten
Moses Etheridge	1	050	Deed
Robt. Stuart	2	250	Patten
		247	Deed
_____ Etheridge	1	150	Deed
Richd. Linton	1	150	Do.
How. Holsted	3	100	Deed
		100	Survey
		080	Patten
James Wilson	1	030	Patten
Witt. Merchant	1	260	Patten
Jas. Nicholis	1	300	Patten
Jno. Miller	1	100	Deed
Moses Boule	1	020	Deed

[This list, while undated, is for 1722. The list is given in the following order: Name, Tithables, Tax for Tithables, Acres in No. of Tracts, Tax for Land. The document is badly damaged.]

[Torn]Nickolson	2	Delinquent			
[Torn]k White	1	0=10=0			
Hum Vince	6	3=00=0	406	in 1	0=06=9
Tho: Vince	1	0=10=0	330	in 1	0=05=6
Jams Pinor	[Torn]				
Even Miller	1	0=10=0	150	in 1	0=02=6
Will Bell Junr	2	1=00=0			
Jno. Fenton	1	0=10=0			
Jno. Fenton Senr	2	1=00=0			
Will Parker	1	0=10=0	169	in 2	0=02=10
Will Swan	6	3=00=0	2784	in 9	2=06=4
Joseph Wicker	2	1=00=0	556	in 3	0=09=3
Will Davis	2	1=00=0	53	in 1	0=00=10 1/2
Benj Tull	2	1=00=0			
Will Williams	5	2=10=0	1035		0=17=3
[Torn]	2	1=00=0			
Thos: [Torn] Junr.	2	1=00=0	486	in 3	0=08=1
Foster Duglis			50	in 1	0=00=10
Tho: Williams	2	1=00=0			
Danll Phillops	5	2=10=0	260	in 1	0=04=4
Charles Brunt	1	0=10=0	350	in 1	0=05=10

nicholas	2					
A White	1	0=	=0			
m Vince	6	3=0		406	m:1	0= 06=9
Tho: Vince	1			3.30	m:1	0= 0.n=6
Jam's Pinor						
Euon mile	1					1 0=02=6
Will: Bell jun	2					
Jno fenton jun	1	0=				
Jno fenton son	2	1=0=0				
Will: Parker	1	0=10=0		369	m:2	0= 02=10
Will: Sloan	6	3=00=0		2 784	m:9	2= 06=4
Joseph Wishon	2	1=00=0		506	m:3	0= 09=3
Will: Davis	2	1=00=0		053	m:1	0= 00=10½
Bon'y Hill	2	1=0				
Will: Williams	2	2=10		1035		0= 17= 3
	2	1=00				
Tho: ___ jun	2	1=0		4.86	m:3	0= 08= 8
Hosfor Dugles				050	m:1	0= 00=14
Tho: williams	2	1=0				
Dan Phillips	2	2=1=0		260	m:	0= ___
Charles Brunt	1	0=10=0		3no	m:1	0= 0n=10
Jno Brunt	1	0=10=0				
Rob Heath	1	0=10=0		448	m:1	0= 07=n
Tho Brunt	1	0=10=0			m:2	0= 02=4
Tho: Davis	2	1=0		01	m:3	0= 16-8
Pob Jor						
		10=2				
		0				
		0		1.60	m:1	0= 02=7
		1=0				

Plate XII

Jno. Brunt	1	0=10=0			
Robd. Heath	1	0=10=0	445	in 1	0=07=5
Tho: Brunt	2	1=00=0	200	in 2	0=03=4
Tho: Davis	2	1=00=0	1001	in 3	0=16=8
Peter Dau[ge]					
			270	in 1	0=04=6
[Torn]		10=0			
		Not to be found			
		=0			
		=0	160	in 1	0=02=7
	3	1=10=0			
	1	0=10=0			
[Torn] Ives	1	0=10=0			
[Ed]w Cox	1	0=10=0			
Tho: Cox Senr	1	0=10=0		[Torn]	0=03[torn]
Tho: Cox Junr	1	0=10=0			
Will Stafford	1	0=10=0	780	in 4	0=13=0
Henr Brighte	[Torn]				
Jno. Brighte	[Torn]				
Benj Brickhouse	1	0=10=0			
Richard Brighte	1	0=10=0			
Henr Bright	2	1=00=0	341	in 2	0=05=8
Marten Bollon	1	0=10=0	180	in 1	0=03=0
Tho: Godord	1	Delinquent			
Jno. Brighte	1	Not to be found			
Jams Cormack	1	Delinquent			
Jno. Monk	1	0=10=0	129	in 1	0=02=1 1/2
Joseph Bateman	1	0=10=0	140	in 1	0=02=4
Jacob Mash	1	0=10=0			
Moeses Lenton	1	0=10=0	112	in 1	0=01=10
Will Ethirigh	1	0=10=0	50	in 1	0=00=10
Henr Ethirigh	1	0=10=0	112	in 1	0=01=10
Will Bateman	1	0=10=0			
Jno. Florey	1	0=10=0	100	in 1	0=01=8
Nick Marshall	1	0=10=0	100	in 1	0=01=8
Richd Bradley	1	0=10=0			
Dan West	1	0=10=0	130	in 1	0=02=2
Jno Barrington	1	0=10=0			
Danll Alcock	1	[Torn]			
Benj Bone[r]	1	[Torn]			
Jno. McCoy	1	[Torn]			
Jams Worden	1	[Torn]			
Richd Jonson	1	0=10=0	[Torn]		
Henr Holstead	1	0=10=0	[Torn]		
[Torn]	1	0=10=0	[Torn]		
[Torn]	5	2=10=0	[Torn]		
[Torn]	1	0=10=0			
[Hen]r: Woodhouse	4	2=00=0	450	in 1	[Torn]
Rich.] Sanderson	2	1=00=0			

Abra Boone	1	0=10=0	150	in1	0=02=6
Maliy Winter	1	0=10=0			
Thos Leary	[Torn]		[1230]	[Torn]	1=00=6
Mary Browne	[Torn]				
Joseph Sanderson	[Torn]		[Torn]89	in 7	2=02=4
Jno. Woodhouse	2	1=00=0	300	in 2	0=05=0
Mathw Hannah	1	0=10=0	080	in 1	0=01=4
Tho: Parker	1	0=10=0			
Azaricom Parker	1	0=10=0	580	in 2	0=11=4
Henr Gibson	1	0=10=0			
Jno. Ives	1	0=10=0			
Will Bell Senr	5	2=10=0	817	in 2	0=13=7
Thos: Taler Senr	4	2=00=0	670	in 2	0=11=2
Henr White	3	1=10=0	400	in 1	0=06=8
Josep Church	4	2=00=0	730	in [Torn]	[Torn]
Foster Jarvis	5	2=10=0	870	in [Torn]	[Torn]
Edw Taler	1	0=10=0			
Peter Pinor	1	0=10=0	320	in 2	0=05=4
Thos. Simons	1	0=10=0			
Henr Eden	1	0=10=0	150	in 1	0=02=6
Jno Eden	1	0=10=0			
Micall Oneal Senr	2	1=00=0	600	in 3	0=10=0
Micall Oneal Junr	1	0=10=0	241	in 2	0=04=0
Jno Walker	1	0=10=0	079	in 1	0=01=3
Jams Parker	1	0=10=0	050	in 1	0=00=10
Jno Crab	[Torn]				
Jno Bell	2	[Torn]			
Webly Pavey	2	1=00=0	[Torn]		0=04=2
Andw Consall	2	1=00=0	[Torn]		[Torn]
Mard: Either4ige	2	1=00=0	[Torn]		
Danll Silvels	1	0=10=0	[Torn]		
[Torn]	1	0=10=0	[Tron]		
[Torn]	1	0=10=0	[Torn]		
[Torn]	[Torn]	0=10=0	[Torn]		
[Torn]	[Torn]	0=10=0	[Torn]		
[Torn] Whed[bee]	[Torn]	[Torn]	440	in 1	0=07=5
Jno Beckly	[Torn]	[Torn]0			
Samll Burgis	[Torn]		[Torn]		
Will Gray	[Torn]				
Mathw Toler	[Torn]				
Jno Burlon	1	0=10=0	190	in 1	0=03=2
Relph Love	1	0=10=0			
Jno Peney	1	0=10=0	660	in 2	0=11=0
Jno Palmor	1	Dead			
Gorg Styring	1	Delinquent			
Jno Man	4	2=00=0	4000	in 1	3=06=8
Robd Burous	1	0=10=0	100	in 1	0=01=8
Jno Willey	1	0=10=0			
[Torn]	1	0=10=0			
[Torn]	8	4=00=0	897	in 5	0=14=11

CURRITUCK COUNTY TAX AND MILITIA LISTS

Land Owners Living in Virginia

Jams Worden	480	in 1	0=08=0
Cornelas Jones	200	in 1	
Andr. McFashtion	210	in 1	0=03=6
Richd Ballance	255	in 2	0=09=11
Jno. Noesay	132	in 1	0=02=2
Gales Randall	132	in 1	0=02=2
Will Tucke	050	in 1	
Will Lenton	150	in 1	0=02=6
Saml Ballance	150	in 1	0=02=6
Danll [McFashtion]	150	in 1	0=02=6
[Torn]	050	in 1	0=00=10
[Torn]	100	in 1	0=01=8
[Torn]	497	in 2	0=08=4
[Torn]	150	in 1	0=02=6
[Torn]	150	in 1	0=02=6
[Torn]	280	in 1	0=04=8
[Torn]	130	in [Torn]	
[Torn]	260	[Torn]	

List of Jurymen In Curratuck
[1723]

Richard Etheridge	1	James Poyner	23	Thomas Moncreef	44
Thomas Lurley	2	Thomas Poyner	24	Andrew Etheridge	45
Joseph Sanderson	3	William Davis	25	William Lufman	46
Thomas Jarvis	4	Richard Doger	26	Edward Cox	47
Thomas Parker	5	Richard Bright Junr	27	William Bright	48
Fostor Jarvis	6	Daniel Savell	28	James Bright	49
Isza Parker	7	Peter Dowger	29	Benjamin Bennett	50
Richard Church	8	Wallis Bray	30	John Muncke	51
Peter Peyner	9	Edward Taylor	31	Moses Linton	52
Thomas Simons	10	Samuel Simons	32	John Linton	53
Henery Caden	11	John Legett	33	Henery Brightt	54
Thomas Taylor Senr	12	David Legett	34	Daniel Getree	55
Thomas Taylor Junr	13	Dennes Riordan	35	Henery Gibbs	56
William Bell	14	John Perkins	36	David Jones	57
John Bell	15	Joseph Bowren	37	Ralph Matham	58
John Crabb	16	Richard Fanshaw	38	William Patason	59
Luke White	17	Robert Heath	39	Thomas Spencer	60
John Wallker	18	John Brent	40	John Burton	61
Evan Miller	19	Thomas Davis	41	John Man	62
Robert Patern	20	Thomas Brent	42	George Powers	63
William Parker	21	Charles Brent	43	John Penny	64
Samuel Parker	22				

North Carolina

Accompt of the Receipt of one half of the arrears of His Majesty's Quitrents for Albemarle County Viz. from the 20th of September 1729 to March 1732 Computed at the difference of Sevenfor one pound Sterling in the currency of the Province.

Currituck Precinct

By Whom Paid	Acres of Land	Quitrents	By Whom Paid	Acres of Land	Quitrents
Baker Samuel	100	1=15=0	Nicholson Josiah	304	5=06=5 1/4
Bray Wallace	320	9=-2=1 3/4	Pyner William (Minor)	250	4=07=6
Barret Margaret	020	0=07=3 1/4	Parker William		
Bennet Benjamin	938	16=08=1 1/2	(his widow)	105	1=16=10 3/4
Baun Peter	256	4=09=8	Pyner Peter	438	7=04=0
Curron John	306	6=08=4	Pell John	050	4=15=1
Deal Joshua	089 1/2	1=11=6	Ditto for his wife	240	
Dadley Thomas	421	7=09=11	Parker John	100	1=15=0
Duke Andrew	180	3=03=0	Parker William	110	1=18=9 1/4
Dauge Peter	050	0=17=6	Parker Azariah	480	2=09=0
Etheridge John	770	13=09=9 1/2	Parker Peter	110	1=18=9 1/4
Etheridge Marmadke	050	0=17=6	Parker Wiker	070	1=04=9 1/2
Etheridge Henry	162	2=16=10 1/2	Parkins John	119	2=01=6 3/4
Etheridge Andrew Junr.	150	2=12=6	Parr William	050	0=17=6
Etheridge Christian	150	1=00=0	Powers George	425	7=08=9
Ervin Robert	134	2=07=1 1/4	Pyner James	100	1=15=0
Ferreby John	030	0=10=6	Sanderson Thomas	375	6=11=3
Gregroy Richard	366	6=08=4	Simmons Samuel	532	9=02=0
Hodges Richard	320	5=12=3 1/4	Slake Nicholas		
Heath Nathaniel	150	3=00=0	(whole amt)	490	20=12=1 1/4
Jervis Jonathon	256	4=09=8 1/4	Stevans John	100	1=15=0
Jervis Samuel	100	1=15=0	Sanderson Joseph	2498	43=13=6 1/4
Jervis Foster in part	721	5=07=6	Scott William	050	0=17=6
Lowther Thomas	586	10=04=10 3/4	Stafford William	500	8=15=0
Legat David	100	1=15=0	Shappord Sampson	110	1=18=7 3/4
Lenton Moses	062	1=01=1 3/4	Sanderson Richard &		
Lee Samuel	175	3=01=3	Tully Williams	1750	30=14=8 1/4
Moncrief Thomas	213	3=13=6	Swindel Parker	200	3=10=0
Miller Evan	150	2=12=6	Taylor Thomas	492	8=12=1
Mercer John	050	0=17=6	Taylor Thomas Junr.	487	8=10=7 1/4
Mash Ralph	149	2=12=6	Ditto for 2 years	150	2=02=0
Mereday Thomas	350	6=02=6	Vince Humphry	410	7=05=10
Mereday Thomas	350	6=02=6	Walker John	073	1=09=9
Marshall Nicholas	200	3=10=0	Write Luke	340	3=19=0
Norton John	480	8=04=0	Williams Stephen	166	2=18=4
Northen Philip	315	5=10=4 3/4	Williams Samuel	904	15=16=10 1/4
			Williams Thomas	420	7=07=3 1/2

Resolved that the following Lists of Jurymen now produced to this House be added to the former List: Viz!

Currituck List of Jurymen

Jos. Sanderson	Edwd. Litchfield	Jos. Lewing
Timothy Ives	Jona. Jarvis	Warmaduke Savil
Thomas Lurry	Sampsn Etheridge	Jas. Towler

CURRITUCK COUNTY TAX AND MILITIA LISTS

Benja. Beasley	Jno. Etheridge	Benja. Bennet
Evan Jones	Saml. Lee	Lemuel Britt
Bullock Symons	Richd. O'Dowdy	Owen Dockelee
Robt. Symons	Robert Overton	George Powers
Benone Heath	John West	Lewis Jenkins
Richardson Mors	Jno. Armstrong	Waitman Emery
Wm. Rowlinson	Danll. Docklee	Saml. Slow
Zekiah Fremon	Richd. Bradley	Thoms. Robb
John Neal	Willobey Merchant	Wm. Glaseno
Thomas Parker	James Baker	Peter Parker
John Woodhouse	David Jones	Wm. Firrell
Jos. Sanderson Jr.	Jos. Persons	Wallis Bray
Peter Boom	Joshua Creason	Thos. Moncrief
Henry Jarvis	Richd. Fenton	David Legatt
Adam Etheridge	John Perkins	Timothy Ives
George Paul	John Crabb	Luke White
Robt. Paul	John Pell	Josias Nicholson
Math. Towler	Richard Fanshaw	James Parker
Wm. O'Dowdy	John Caroon	Evan Miller
Patrick Jones	Thos. Parker	Robt. Bell
Richard Jones	Wm. Scott	Thoms. Lowther
Cor: Jones	Thomas Davis	Wm. Lurry
John Heath	Nehemiah Heath	Jacob Caroon
George Turner	Wm. Williamson	Jer: Stephens
John Whittbey	Saml. Britt	Saml. Symons
Jacob Farrow	Saml. Berry	Caleb Merchant
Hanson Brile	Thomas Cox	Jos. Bowrin
Michll. O'Neal	Moses Linton	Benja. Cowell
Thos. Sanderson	Parker Swindell	Stephn. Williams
Peter Luts	John Buckner	Jas. Poyner
Heny. Woodhouse	Henry Gibbs	Richd. Gregory
Thos. Russell	Stephen Emerey	Jer: Moscer
Jos. Applestole	Saml. Silbey	Andrew Privatt
John Tillet	James Phillips	Soloman Bennett
Robt Paul Junr	Peter Dange	John Hughs
Danll. O'Dowdy	Wm. Parker	Edwd. Taylor
Wm. McKoy	Wm. Parr	Gilbert Parker
Thos. Dudley	Moses Fanshaw	Otho Holland
Thos. Legatt	Saml. Jarvis	James Meteer
Richd. Whicker	Richd. Jarvis	Solo. Jervis
Dennis Caps	Willm. White	Solo. Etheridge
Wm Pawlings	John Willimas	Cadar Merchant
Job Carr	Danll. Phillips	Willis Miller
Thos. Neal	Danll. Lee	John Linton
Thos. Moncrief	Chas. Brunt	Wm. Lee
Isaac Davis	Jas. Nichols	

[c1748]

A True List of the Soldiers belonging to the Company under my Command Viz.   William Bray

Joshua White Lieutenant	Absalom Legett Ensign	Lemuel Halstead Serjeant
Gideon Whitehurst Serjeant	Benjamin Daudge Serjeant	Willis Etheridge Corporal
William Ferebee Corporal	Willoughby Daudge Corporal	John Simmons Drummer

77

The names of the Tytheables I received Middle Tax from for the year 17__

Name		Brought over	72	Brought over	157
John Fisher	1	John Ballance	1	Rice Evens	1
John Answer	7	John Burton	1	Adam Etherage	1
Thomas Allen	1	John Barrow	1	Benjamin Evens	1
Thomas Austin Sr.	1	James Burnham	2	Sampson Etherage	1
Thomas Austin	1	Thomas Burges	5	Joseph Evens	1
John Armstrong	4	John Bennet	3	Thomas Evens	1
Solomon Bright	1	William Blunt	2	Elinor Etherage	5
Joseph Bowring	1	Henry Bright	1	William Etherage Jr.	1
Benj. Brickhou	1	Joseph Burns	1	Paul Edison	1
Edmond Beacham	1	Bennet Chittum	1	Lucy Etherage	1
Dam Bawm	1	John Chittum	1	Richard Etherage	1
John Bawm	1	James Chittum	1	Samuel Etherage	2
Moris Bawm	1	John Cooper	1	Willis Etherage	2
William Brock	1	Isles Cooper	1	William Etherage	2
William Beasley	1	Alice Caron	4	Micheal Ettison	1
John Beasley	1	Elias Cornish	1	Wm Etherage son of wm	1
Elizabeth Beasley	1	William Case	1	Mathew Etherage	1
Comfort Berry	1	Benjamin Crowel	6	Amos Etherage	1
John Barber	1	Joshua Campbell	2	Richard Fanshaw	3
Rich. Barret	1	Joseph Cooper	1	Richard Fenton	2
Free Jeney Blackwoman	1	Job Carr Esqr	2	Robert Fletcher	3
Robert Bell	1	John Chaplin	1	Wm Ferby	1
James Begg	1	Robert Chamberlain	1	Moses Hawkins	1
Samuel Barnit	4	Henry Clark	1	John Ferby	1
James Brant	1	Nathaniel Cain	4	Joseph Ferby	2
Peter Bawm	2	Jacob Caron	6	Hezekiah Farrow	1
Wallis Bray	3	William Chaple	1	Jacob Farrow	3
Will. Bogus	2	Thomas Davis	4	Caleb Fenton	1
Wm Blook	1	William Dudley	1	Lazarous Finey	1
Stephen Brook	1	James Duglass	1	James Garrett	2
John Brady	1	Peter Dauge	5	Jacob Goodmon	1
Solomon Burges	1	James Dauge	1	Rich. Gregory	1
Solomon Baker	1	Morrill Dibbs	4	Thomas Glasses	1
Stephen Banks	2	Ann Dibbs	3	Griffeth Gregory	1
Isaac Beasley	1	Thomas Dudley Jnr	1	Thomas Glasses Sr	1
John Burges	1	Thomas Dudley Snr	2	Elinor Gaskins	1
William Brickhous	1	George Davis	1	Henry Gipson	1
Samuel Bright	3	Cornelius Davis	1	John Gipson	1
John Bright	1	Benjamin Dauge	1	Stephen Gibons	1
Solomon Bennett	2	William Daniel	2	Wm Gilbert	1
Nehemiah Bennett	1	Christopher Dickson	3	Daniel Glasses	1
Edmond Bowring	2	Henry Evens	1	Daniel Glasses Jr	1
Robert Brooks	1	Jacob Ellygood	2	George Howard	1
William Bray	1	Willis Etherage	1	Joseph Hill	1
		Job Etherage Jr.	1	John Heath	1
		John Edy	1	Samuel Hallstead	1
Carryed over	72	Carryed over	157	Carryed over	215

Plate XIII

78

Samuel _____ Seignior
Grifoth C_____ory
Caleb C_____
William _____Junior
J_____
W_____
Henry _____
_____ Parker
Samuel _____ Seignior
_____
John _____
Moses _____
Mames Joh _____
James Biggs
Amos Etheridge
John Ba_____
Caleb Etheridge
Caleb Bell

William Lee
Thomas Perkins
Robert Brooks
William Muncreef
Samuel Jones
Thomas Fenton
Thomas Glasgow
Phillips Caps
Samuel Barnard Junior
Caleb Glasgow
Cornelius Grigory
Peter Moriset
Thomas Hutchins
Peter Daudge Junior
Solomon Baker
Jonathan Whitehurst
Silvester Varden
Jeremiah Tom _____

Josiah Lee
John Be _____
John Etheridge
Samuel Lee
Solomon Etheridge
Joseph Poyner
Robert Heath
Thomas Haword
Joshua Taylor
Asa Simmons
Thomas Ferebee
Malachi Lee
Peter Ferebee
Luke Barnard
John Ellis
John Hughs
Willoughby Muncreef

The names of the Tytheables I Received the Pole Tax from for the year 1751

Name	No.	Name	No.	Name	No.
John Fisher	1	Soloman Burges	1	Joseph Cooper	1
John Answell	7	Soloman Baker	1	Job Carr Esqr	2
Thomas Allen	1	Stephin Banks	2	John Chaplin	1
Thomas Austin Ser.	1	Isaac Beasley	1	Robert Chamberling	1
Thomas Austin Jr.	1	John Burgin	1	Henry Clark	1
John Armstrong	1	William Brickhous	1	Nathaniel Cain	1
Solomon Bright	1	Samuel Bright	3	Jacob Caron	5
Joseph Bowring	1	John Bright	1	William Dudley	1
Benjn. Brickhouse	1	Soloman Bennett	2	James Duglass	1
Edmond Beacham	1	Nehemiah Bennett	1	Peter Dauge	5
Adam Bawm	1	Edmond Bowing	2	James Dauge	1
John Bawm	1	Robert Brooks	1	Morrill Dibbs	4
Moris Bawm	1	William Bray	1	Ann Dibbs	3
William Brock	1	John Ballance	1	Thomas Dudley Jnr.	1
William Beasley	1	John Burton	1	Thomas Dudley Snr.	2
John Beasley	1	John Barns	1	George Daw	1
Elizabeth Beasley	1	James Burnham	2	Cornealus Davis	1
Comfort Berry	1	Thomas Burges	5	Benjamin Dauge	1
John Barber	1	John Bennet	2	William Daniel	2
Richd. Barret	1	William Blunt	2	Christopher Dickens	3
Free Jiney black-woman	1	Henry Bright	1	Heny Evens	1
Robert Bell	1	Joseph Barns	1	Jacob Elligood	2
James Biggs	1	Bennet Chittum	1	Willis Etherage	1
Samuel Barnit	4	John Chittum	1	Job Etherage	1
James Brant	1	James Chittum	1	John Edy	1
Peter Bawm	2	John Cooper	1	Rice Evens	1
Wallis Bray	3	Isles Cooper	1	Adam Etherage	1
Willm Bogus	2	Alice Caron	4	Benjamin Etherage	1
Willm Brooks	1	Elias Cornish	1	Samson Etherage	1
Stephen Brooks	1	William Case	1	Joseph Evens	1
John Brady	1	Benjamin Cowell	6	Elinor Etherage	5
		Joshua Campbell	2	William Etherage 3d	1

CURRITUCK COUNTY TAX AND MILITIA LISTS

Name		Name		Name	
Paul Edison	1	Samuel Jarvis	2	William Mackie	5
Lucy Etherage	1	Martin Jarvis	1	Willis Miller	4
Richard Etherage	1	Wm Jarvis Jarvis	1	John Morse	1
Samuel Etherage	1	Jonathon Jarvis	3	Thomas Morriss	1
Willis Etherage	2	Timothy Ives Snr.	1	John Makefurshon	1
William Etherage	2	Timothy Ives	1	Hunch Nicholson	3
Wm Etherage son of Wm	1	Savel Jones	1	Richard Nickens	3
		Richd Jones	2	Phillip Northen	4
Matthew Etherage	1	Jabey Jennit	2	Micheal Oneal	1
Amos Etherage	1	Jonathon Jarvis	1	William Odowdy	1
Richard Fanshaw	3	Mary Jarvis	1	Richard Odowdy	2
Rishard Fenton	2	George Jones	1	Robert Overington	1
Robert Fletcher	3	Solomon Jarvis	1	Christopher Oneal	3
Wm Ferby	1	Patrick Jones	2	John Oneal	1
Moses Fanshaw	1	John Kelley	1	Daniel Odowdy	1
John Ferby	1	Henry Kensey	1	Joel Piner	1
Joseph Ferby	2	Joseph Lewin	1	Daniel Phillips	2
Hezekiah Farrow	1	Nicholas Lynn	1	Robert Palmer	1
Jacob Farrow	3	Abner Legit	1	Peter Padrick	2
Caleb Fenton	1	David Legit	1	Benjamin Padrick	1
Lazarous Florey	1	Absolom Legit	2	James Parker	2
James Garrett	2	Thomas Love	1	Humpry Piner	1
Jacob Goodman	1	Edward Leechfield	1	Thomas Parker	2
Richd Gregory	1	Benjamin Linsey	1	Jonathon Piner	1
Thomas Glasco	1	Jacob Lutts	2	Charles Presscoat	1
Griffeth Gregory	1	Joseph Linsey	1	Robert Piner	1
Thomas Glasco Snr	1	Ann Linsey	1	James Piner	2
Elinor Gaskins	1	Daniel Lee	1	Peter Piner	1
Henry Gibson	1	Moses Linton	3	William Pirkens	1
John Gibson	1	William Lee	1	Pames Phillips	3
John Gibson	1	Thomas Miller	1	William Parr	1
Wm Gilbert	1	Kedor	2	Henry Pirkens	2
Daniel Glasco	1	Caleb Merchant	3	Moses Pirkens	1
Daniel Glasco Snr.	1	Gideon Merchant	2	John Pirkens Jnr.	1
George Howard	1	Willoughby Merchant	5	Benjamin Prescoat	2
Joseph Hill	1	William Mann	2	Gilbert Parkwood	2
John Heath	1	William McCoy	2	Willis Piner	2
Lemuel Halsteed	1	Richard Mors	2	Thomas Pane	3
Otha. Holland	1	Jeremiah Mercer	1	William Popowell	1
Henry Ham	1	James Mercer	1	Sarah Piner	1
John Hains	1	Thomas Mercer	1	Peter Piner	3
Mathew Hanah	1	John Muncreef	1	William Powers	1
Robert Harriss	1	Salley Mason	1	George Powers	1
Robert Heath	1	William Muncreef	1	Azerikam Parker	3
Thomas Hutchens	1	Joseph Midget	4	Joseph Piner	1
Joseph Hayman	1	Thomas Midget	2	John Pell	2
Sanuel Jones	1	William Meckings	2	John Poberts	1
Wm Ives	1	Wileam Marshall	1	Thomas Robb	1
Elizabeth Islands	2	Nicholas Marshall	1	William Robinson	2
Even Jones	1	James Miller	1	Robert Rolins	2
James Jenkens	1	Even Miller	2	Richard Stanley	2
Elizabeth Jones	1	Richard McClure	4	Benjamen Sickes	1

80

CURRITUCK COUNTY TAX AND MILITIA LISTS

Duke Sewills	3	Patience Smith	1	John Woodhouse Esq	4
Robert Hill	1	Joseph Sanderson	6	John Woods	3
Abel Sickes	1	Menus Smith	2	Micheal Waterfield	2
John Savel	2	Peter Stewart	1	Wm Williamson	1
William Simson	1	Clesbe Scarbrough	3	Hillary White Esq	3
Robert Simmons	2	Baker Swindal	1	Stephen Williams Esq	7
John Simsons	1	Levy Shoart	3	John Wheatley	1
James Simsons	1	William Scott Snr	2	John Whitehurst	1
Henry Simmons	3	Simon Shewcraft	3	Gideon Whitehurst	1
John Simmons	1	Major Wm Shergold	2	Charles Williams	3
James Simmons	1	Caleb Sicks	1	Wm White	2
Even Stanley	1	Thomas Turton	1	Henry White Esq	12
Samuel Simmons	2	John Tillitt Snr.	1	Wm Phillips	1
Jeremiah Stephans	1	James Towler	2	Thomas Williams	1
Thomas Simmons	3	Thomas Tatum	1	John Walker Junr	1
Benjamin Sanderson	1	Ebenezer Taylor	1	Joseph Williams	1
Samuel Salyer	1	John Thompson	1	James Wahab	2
Peter Spratling	1	Benjamin Taylor	1	John Whidbey	1
John Scarbrough Snr	1	Thomas Taylor	2	Hezekiah Woodhouse	10
George Scarbrough	1	Daniel Towler	1	Patrick White	6
William Scarbrough	1	William Thompson	1	Thomas Williams Esq	5
Augustin Scarbrough	1	Henry Valentine	1	Soloman Wilson	6
Julian Sanderson	9	Luke White	5	Caleb Wilson Esq	22
Thomas Sanderson Es	11			Total	601

The Names of The Tythables Received ye 12d Pole Tax for the Year 1752

Thomas Austin	2	Stephen Banks	2	Benjamin Crabb	1
John Armstrong	2	Solomon Baker	1	Isles Cooper	1
Thomas Allin	1	Sarah Burges	1	Hezier Cammel	1
Cornealus Osten	1	Isaac Beasley	2	Alice Caron	4
John Answell	7	Wallis Bray	4	Caleb Church	4
John Ballance	1	William Bogus	2	Nathaniel Cain	1
John Burton	1	Willoughby Bartlit	1	Benjamin Cowell	6
Robert Bell	1	Joseph Bowring	2	James Chettem	1
William Bray	1	Joseph Burnet	1	Bennet Chettem	1
John Barber	1	Thomas Burges	4	Job Kemp	2
James Biggs	1	Benjamin Brickhouse	1	Elijah Cox	1
John Barns	1	Robert Brooks	1	Elias Cornish	1
William Brickhouse	1	Samuel Bright	3	William Chapele	1
John Bowring	1	Henry Bright	3	William Case	1
John Bright	1	James Burnham	2	Moses Capps	1
Richard Bradley	2	Nehemiah Bennet	1	John Chaplim	1
John Bennett	2	Edmond Bowring	2	Robert Chamberlin	1
Soloman Bennett	2	William Brooks	1	Marmaduke Cox	1
Richard Barret	1	Stephen Brooks	1	Henry Clark	1
Adam Baun	1	Peter Baum	1	Job Carr	2
John Baum	1	Comfort Berry	1	Joshua Campbell	1
Edmund Beachum	1	Joseph Cooper	1	Morril Dibbs	6
John Burgis	1	Absolom Cox	1	Peter Dauge	5
William Brock	1	George Connor	1	Benjamin Dauge	1
John Beasley	1	Richard Cammel	1	James Dauge	1
Jacob Beasley	1	Walter Carter	2	Cornealus Davis	1

Ann Dibbs	2	Stephen Gibons	1	Daniel Linsey	1
Thomas Davis	4	John Gipson	1	Jacob Lutts	2
James Duglass	1	Wm. Gibert	1	Ann Linsey	1
George Doe	1	James Grant	1	Benjamin Linsey	1
William Daniel	3	Daniel Glasco	1	Moses Linton	2
Thomas Dudley Junr.	2	James Garret	3	John Merchant	2
Thomas Dudley	2	Daniel Glasco Junr.	1	John Moncreef	1
William Dudley	1	Thomas Glasco Senr.	1	Thomas Miller Jr.	1
George Davis	1	Jabe Jennet	2	Wm. Muncreef	1
Willis Etherage	1	John Hues	1	Thomas Mercer	3
Amos Etherage	1	Elizebeth Heath	1	Salley Mason	1
Michael Ellison	1	Thomas Hutchens	1	Thomas Miller	1
Timothy Etherage	4	Robert Heath	1	Willoughby Merchant	4
William Etherage	1	Lemuel Holstied	1	Gedian Merchant	2
Elinor Etherage	5	Joseph Hill	1	Kader Merchant	2
Richard Etherage	1	John Hannah	2	Wm. Marshall	1
John Etherage	1	Thomas Harriss	1	Nicholas Marshall	1
Luci Etherage	1	Joseph Haymon	1	Thomas Midget	2
Samuel Etherage	1	George Howard	1	Wm. Man	2
Willis Etherage	1	John Harris	1	Peter Macduel	1
Samuel Etherage	1	Otha Holland	1	John Moris	1
William Etherage	1	William Heath	1	Richardson Moris	2
Joshua Etherage	1	Patrick Jones	1	Caleb Merchant	4
Mathias Etherage	1	Samuel Jones	1	Even Miller	2
Adam Etherage	2	John Jones	1	Wm. Mackie Esq.	4
Samson Etherage	1	James Jinkens	1	Jonathan Mor	1
John Edy	1	Savel Jones	1	James Mercer	1
Henry Evens	1	Martin Jarvis	1	James Miller	1
Benjamin Evens	1	Timoth Ives	1	John Makefurshon	1
Thomas Evens	1	Richard Jones	1	Daniel Makefurshon	1
Lazarous Flory	1	Jonathan Jarvis Jr.	2	Thomas Morris	1
Robert Fletcher	2	Wm. Jarvis	2	Joseph Midgett	4
Richd. Famshaw	3	Timothy Ives	1	Wm. Meekins	2
Thomas Fenton	1	Samuel Jarvis	1	Samuel Easiltob	2
Moses Fanshaw	1	Elizabeth Jones	2	Philip Northen	5
Wm. Furby	2	Even Jones	1	Richard Nickins	2
John Furby	1	Elizabeth Island	2	Hannah Nicholson	3
Joseph Furby	2	Jonathan Jarvis	7	James Odowdy	1
Richard Fenton	2	George Jones	1	Michael Oneal	1
Jacob Farrow	3	Loyed Jones	1	Daniel Odowdy	1
Hezekiah Farrow	1	Solomon Jarvis	1	Amos Overinton	1
Adam Fisher	2	John Kelley	1	Christopher Oneal	1
Thomas Fenton	1	Henry Kinsey	1	John Oneal Jr.	1
Caleb Fenton	1	Edward Love	1	James Phillips	3
Thomas Glasco	1	Daniel Lee	1	Joseph Piner	2
Jacob Goodman	1	Samuel Lee	3	Wm. Parr	2
Richard Grigory	1	Absolom Legget	2	John Purkens Senr.	3
Griffith Grigory	1	Abner Legget	1	John Purkins	1
John Garrett	2	David Legget	1	Daniel Phillips	2
Henry Gipson	1	Wm. Lee	1	George Powers	3
Levea Gaskins	1	John Lurry	2	Henry Purkins	1
Robert Gipson	1	Joseph Lewing	1	Wm. Purkens	1
Thomas Grigory	1	Edward Leichfield	3	Azarekem Parker	3

Thomas Parker	2	Benjamin Sanderson	1	Salvester Varden	1
Wm Piner	1	Samuel Salyer	1	Brian Varden	1
Peter Piner	3	Joshua Sanderson	1	Henry Valintine	1
Joel Piner	1	Joseph Sanderson	1	John Wheatley	2
James Parker	2	Thomas Sanderson Es.	1	John Whitehurst	1
Benjamin Padrick	3	Benjamin Sicks	10	Look White	6
John Padrick	1	Duke Sivels	3	Col. Stephen Williams	8
Peter Padrick	2	Abel Sicks	1	Thomas Williams	5
Jonathan Poiner	1	Robert Simmons	2	John West	1
Stephen Pell	1	Wm. Simson	1	Solomon Wilson	5
John Pell	1	John Simson	2	John Walker Jr.	2
Wm. Popowell	1	James Simson	1	Wm. White	3
Thomas Pane	2	Laben Sickes	1	John Williams	1
Willis Piner	1	Wm. Scott	2	Thomas Williams	1
James Piner	2	Henry Simmons	1	John Woods	3
John Piner	1	Clesbe Scarbrough	2	Wm. Williams	2
Gilbert Portwood	1	John Scarbrough	2	Wm. White	2
Robert Piner	1	Peter Stewart	1	Col. Henry White	13
Benjamin Presscoat	2	Austen Scarbrough	1	Michael Waterfield	2
Thomas Russill	2	George Scarbrough	1	John Williams	2
Henry Oright	1	Wm. Shergold	5	Charles Williams	3
Robert Roling	1	Means Smith	2	Hillary White	2
Thomas Robb Esq.	1	Patience Smith	1	Patrick White	3
Wm. Rolinson	2	Thomas Williams	1	Hezekiah Woodhouse	14
John Robison	1	John Tomson	1	John Woodhouse	4
John Simmons	1	Thomas Turton	1	Col. Caleb Wilson	27
Nathaniel Spencer	1	Ebenezer Taylor	1	John Whidbey	1
Simon Shewcraft	3	Thomas Taylor	1	Joseph Williams	2
Richard Stanlay	2	Benjamin Taylor	2	Joshua Wells	1
Even Stanley	1	John Taylor	1	James Williams	1
Jeremiah Stephans	1	John Tillitt Snr.	1	James Wahab	2
Parker Swindal	1	James Towler	1	Gedion Whitehurst	1
Thomas Simmons	5	Thomas Tatum	1	Total	522

[1754]
A List of the Officers of the Regiment of Curratuck
Captains

John Lorry	Job Carr	Hillary White

Lieutenants

James Phillop	Thomas Burges	Jacob Farrow	Willaim Mackey

Ensigns

Samuel Jarvis	John Pell	William Williams
John Woods		Joshua White

Sergants

Joseph Sanderson	Benjamin Prescot	Samuel Simons
Daniel Duke	Joshua Brint	Clesbie Scarborough
Chrisr: O Neal		Charles Williams

Corporals

Jonathan Pyner	William Bray	John Barnes
James Dudge	Willm. Robinson	Francis Peel
John O Neal	Martin Jarvis	Evan Jones
Patrick Jones		William Jarvis

CURRITUCK COUNTY TAX AND MILITIA LISTS

Drummers

Jeremiah Stevens   John Simmons   Jonathan Whaly   Moses Caps

Officers Dead out of saiid Regiment

Collo. Caleb Wilson

Lieut. Collo. Henry White

Capt. Thomas Davis   Thomas Burges in Capt. Davis room   Capt. Jacob Caron

[on reverse]

Colo. William Shergold   Lt. Colo. Stephen Williams   Major Robert Whitehall

Capt. Thomas Burges in Room of Capt. Davis deceased

Capt. John Woodhouse in Room of Capt Jacob Caron deceased

Capt. Jacob Farrow in Room of Capt. Job Carr

[1754?]

A list of Men Belonging to Capt. Jacob Farrows Company Viz.

Jacob Farrow Capn:	Hezekian Farrow	oges
John Woods Lieutenant	John Farrow	Baum
Nicholas Lunn Ensign	Jabesh Gennet	Paddrick
Adam Baum Serjiant	Isaac Farrow	nson Doe
Christopher Oneal Serjiant	Joshua Wills	man Ashbie
William Rollinson Corporal	John Dowdy	George Doe
Wioliam Taylor Clark	Jacob Meekins	Joseph Midgett
Joseph Midgett Drummer	Thomas Radwell	Wm. Daniel Jr.
Thomas Oneal	Christopher Oneal	Anthony Insel
John Oneal Jr.	Stephen Brooks	Stephen Wescote
Thomas Midgett	William Harper	John Kegley
William Meekins	Joseph Luin	John Williams
John Burris	John Baum	Wm: Mann
John Bradley	Rw. Tillett	Edwd. Mann
Francis Peel	John Tillet	Spencer Rogers
Scarborough	Thos. Tillet	Abner Brickhouse
Williams	Isaac Tillet	Jonathon Jonson
Williams	Edmond Buskin	John Wipole
William Gray	Bejamen Sikes	Elekxander Brown
James Pieo	James Garrot	James Justice
Samuel Pain	Robert Ewen	Isaac Justine
Thomas Pain	James Grant	Caleb Toller
Thomas Christine	Marmaduke Savell	John Roberts
Samuel Stow Senr.	James Toller	Luis Williams
Samuel Stow Junr.	Matthias Toller	George Gamewell
Thomas Stow	Noel Sikes	John Gamewell
George Howard	John Ives	John Paulmer
William Howard	John Robertson	Soloman Asby
Joseph McCuing	George Jones	William Daniell
John Scarborough Junr.	Joseph Martyn	John Williams
Francis Rollinson	John Williams	Stephen Wescot
George Scarborough	Thos. Williams	Saml. Midgett
John Whidbey	Phillop Williams	Thos. Edbine
Joseph Mathew	Burgess	John Kelly
George Mashew	Esdil	Morris Baum
Henry Clark	Wright	James Grant
Jacob Farrow Jr.	Kelly	George Doe
James Wahab	Sanderson	Joseph Midgett

A Lift of the Field-Officers, Captains, and Subalterns, in the Regiment of *Currituch* — with the Date of their Commiffions, and the Number of Men in each Company, including Officers; which Lift, when compleat, is to be returned to His Excellency the Governor.

Date.		No. of Men.
1755.		
January 14.	William Shergold — Col.	
14:	Stephen Williams — L. Col.	
15.	Robert Whithall ... Maj.	
27.	John Surrey —	6.
27th	James Philip — L	109
27th	Samuel Jarvis — L	
30th	John Woodhous —	6.
	James Philips — L	80
30th	John Pell —	L
31:	Jacob Farrow —	6
31	John Wood —	L 90
	Nicholas Sunn —	L
28th	Hil. White —	6
—	—	6
28th	William Mackey	L 49
28.	Joshua White —	L
29th	Thomas Burgess —	6
29th	William Williams —	L 62
29.	Thomas Davis —	L 390

Plate XIV

85

CURRITUCK COUNTY TAX AND MILITIA LISTS

Joseph Midgett	Edwd. Mann	John Wescoat
Jonathan Harper	Sampson Doe	Spencer Rogers
John Palmer	William Mann	Jacob Farrow
Anthony Savell	John Foulker	

A List of the Field-Officers, Captains, and Subalterns, in the Regiment of Currituck with the Date of their Commissions, and the Number of Men in each Company, including Officers: which List, when compleat, is to be returned to His Excellency the Governor.

Date   No. of Men
1755

January 14th	William Shergold	Col.	
14th	Stephen Williams	L. Col	
14th	Robert Whithall	Majr.	
27th	John Lurrey	C.	
27th	James Philips	L.	109
27th	Samuel Jarvis	E.	
30th	John Qoodhous	C.	
30th	James Philips	L.	80
30th	John Pell	E.	
31	Jacob Farrow	C.	
31	John Wood	L.	90
	Nicholas Lunn	E.	
28th	Hilary White	C.	
28th	William Mackey	L.	49
28th	Joshua White	E.	
29th	Thomas Burgess	C.	
29th	William Williams	L.	62
29th	Thomas Davis	E.	
			390

North Carolina
Currituck County   1756
A True Copy of the Lists of Tithables returned by the Justices for the County of Currituck for the year 1755   pr. William Shergold CC

Ansell Nathan	1	Burras Sarah	1	But Stannop	1
Ansell John	2	Baum Morris	1	Bright John	2
Ansell Mary	4	Baum Adam	1	Blunt William	2
Allen Thomas	1	Becham Edmon	1	Bright Willis	1
Armstrong Assiah	1	Banks Stephen &		Ballintine Peter	2
Ashley Soloman	1	Richard	2	Burgis Thomas	4
Austin Thomas	1	Beaseley Isaac & John	2	Bradley Richard	2
Bell Robert	1	Boueus William		Barns John	1
Beecham William	1	Constable for		Bell Caleb	1
Brickhouse Benjamin	1	Daniel Boueus	1	Bell William	1
Bray William	2	Baker Solomon	1	Beaseley William	1
Bunnil Moses	1	Banks Henry	1	Bradley William	1
Ballance John	2	Boom Peter	1	Beaseley John	1
Burns John	1	Burnham James	2	Beaseley Jacob	1
Barrat Richard	1	Brookes Robert	1	Brady John	1
Ball Joshua	2	Bright Silas	1	Baum John	1
Burnit Joseph	1	Bowring Joseph	2	Burras John	1
Bartlet Willoughby	1	Bowring Edmund	2	Bussel Wulliam	1

CURRITUCK COUNTY TAX AND MILITIA LISTS

Brucks William	1	Ellis Michal	1	Farrow Hizaciah	1
Bray Willis	3	Esdel Argile	1	Fulcar John	1
Barnard Samuel	6	Etheridge William	1	Fanshaw Richard	2
Barry Comfort	1	Everton Thomas	1	Fitzgarell William	1
Brable William	3	Evans Benjamin	1	Fanshaw Moses	1
Bright Henry	2	Evans Thomas	1	Fanshaw Thomas	1
Bright Samuel	2	Elizabeth a Free Negro	1	Ferreby Jane	1
Briggs James	1	Living at Jonathan		Ferreby John	1
Burton John	1	Jarvis		Ferreby Joseph	1
Cox Absalom	1	Etheridge Samuel	1	Ferreby William	1
Chapell William	1	Evans Joseph &		Heath Robert	1
Caron Alice Widow	4	Isaac Evans	2	Hannah John	1
Cooper John	1	Evans Benjamin	1	Hannah Joseph	1
Campbell Kiziah	1	Etheridge Henry	1	Hannah Jonathon	1
Campbell Abiah	1	Etheridge Willis Junr.	2	Howard George	1
Church Caleb Constable	3	Etheridge Willis Senr.	4	Hamond Joseph	1
Carr Job	2	Etheridge Samuel Senr.	1	Hutchins Thomas	1
Cooper Joseph	1	Etheridge Richard	1	Hughs John	1
Dickson John	1	Etheridge Sarah	1	Holsted Lamuel	1
Dudley Thomas Senr.	3	Etherodge Matthias	1	Hall Spence	1
Dudley Thomas Junr.	1	Etheridge Samuel Junr.	1	Harris Robert	1
Dudley William	1	Etheridge Timothy	4	Harris Thomas	1
Duglas James	1	Etheridge Amos	1	Howard William	1
Doughdy John	1	Evans Rice	1	Holland Otho	1
Doo George	1	Etheridge Willis	1	Harrell Gilbart	1
Collins Joshua	2	Eady John	1	Jones Elizabeth	2
Chitton William	1	Etheridge Adam	3	Jones Evans	1
Carter Walter	1	Gaskin Levin	2	Jones Samuel	1
Chitton James	1	Glasgow Daniel	1	Jarvis Samel	1
Cowell Benjamin	2	Glasgow Thomas	1	Ives Timothy Junr.	2
Cowell Solomon	2	Gilbart William	1	Jarvis Jonathan	1
Case William Molatto	2	Gibbins Stephen	1	Jones Richard	1
Clark Henry	1	Gipson Robert	1	Jones Randal	1
Campbell Joshua	1	Ginnit Jabis	3	Jones Sevel	1
Chittom John	1	Goodman Jacob	2	Jones Loyd	1
Cammil Richard	1	Glascock Lemuel	1	Jarvis William	1
Campbell Richard	1	Garrot Truman	1	Jones Davis	1
Cox Duke	1	Garrot John	1	Ives Timmothy	1
Cain Nathaniel	1	Garrot James	3	Jones John	1
Cooper Isles	2	Glasgow Thomas	1	Ives William	1
Daniel William	3	Garrot James	1	Leachfield Edward	3
Dekins John	1	Grigory Richard	3	Linsey Joseph	1
Davis Thomas	2	Grigory Griffith	2	Linsey Daniel &	
Davis George	1	Grant James	1	John Linsey	1
Denby Elizabeth	1	Gipson John	1	Linsey Benjamin	1
Denby John	1	Fisher Adam	2	Love John	1
Dauge Benjamin	1	Fenton Richard	1	Linton Lamuel	1
Dauge Peter	4	Fletcher Robert	2	Linton Catron	2
Duke Daniel	1	Flowrah Lazarus	1	Lee Samuel	2
Dicken William	1	Farrow Jacob	3	Legett Absalom	1
Duge James	2	Farrow Isaac	1	Legett Abner	1
Etheridge Elenor Widow	4	Farrow Jacob Junr.	1	Lee William	1

87

Lemmond Arthur	1	Mercer Jeremiah	1	Poiner Joell	11
Lewing Joseph	2	Parker Thomas	1	Parker James	1
Love Thomas	1	Poiner Joseph	1	Parker Azaricam	1
Lurry John	3	Poiner Peter	2	Philips James	4
Jenkins James	1	Poiner Benjamin	1	Parker Rebeckah	1
Jones George	2	Poiner Joell	1	Peugh Stephen	1
Island Elizabeth	3	Portwood Gilbart	1	Rothen William	1
Jarvis Jonathan	9	Portwood Martyn	1	Richards John	1
Ives Timothy	3	Philips Michell	1	Rowlin George	3
Johnson John Hiphaven	2	Peele Francis	1	Rowlin Robert	1
Kemp Job	1	Pain Thomas	6	Roberts William Negro	
Keaton Hillary	1	Pain Samuel	1	Ned Quash &	
Kilgoar James	1	Peddrick Peter	1	Moll	4
Kelley John	1	Pew Thomas	2	Shergold William and	
Kite Amos	1	Poiner Humphry	1	Thomas Sears Negro	
Morse John	1	Patterson William	1	Henry James	
Miller Thomas	1	Powers Isabelah	2	Doll Bridget	
Mackie William	4	Powers William	1	and a malatto	
Miller William Senr.	1	Meekins William	2	Gurl	7
McCastelton Samuel	1	McCun Joseph	1	Smith Soloman	2
Morse Richardson	2	Moncreef William	1	Smith Meanas Mallatto	2
Marchant Keader	5	Nicholson	6	Smith Jacob Mallatto	1
Mercer James	1	Noel Christopher	3	Scarborow Austin	2
Michell William	1	Noel John	1	Smith Meanas and	
McDuel Peter	1	Northern Philip	5	Sarah Molattoes	2
Midget Joseph Senr.	3	Northern Benjamin	4	Smith Soloman and	
Midget Thomas	2	Nicholson Nicholas	3	William Clarage	2
Midget Samuel	2	Norton Jonathan	1	Sikes Caleb	1
Midget Joseph Ronoak	1	Oneal Michel	2	Swindale Parker	1
Midget Joseph Junr.	1	Odowdy Joseph & John		Scoot William	2
McCoy William	1	and Malatto Jeshna	3	Sweny Daniel	11
Miller Elizabeth free		Odowdy James &		Simmons Hillary	1
Negro and her		Son Thomas	2	Rogers Samuel	1
dagter Johan-		Oneal John	2	Right Henry	1
nah	2	Pursell Edward	1	Russell Thomas	2
Miller Isaac free Negro	1	Plummer John	2	Robinson William	1
Morris Thomas	2	Parker William	1	Rob Thomas	1
McPherson John	1	Pell John	1	Rob Thomas Senr.	1
McPherson Daniel	1	Poiner Peter	1	Robertson John	1
Marshall William	1	Poiner Robert	1	Simson James	1
McPherson Andrew	1	Perkins Henry	1	Simson Sarah	2
Marchant Caleb	3	Perkins Mary	1	Simson William	1
Marchant John	2	Poiner Jonathan	2	Sanderson Joseph	5
Miller Thomas	2	Parr William	1	Stanley Richard	4
Marchant Willoughby	6	Popwith William	1	Sanderson Thomas	12
Marchant Gidian	3	Pew George	1	Simmons Thomas	4
Mercer Thomas	2	Peddrick Henry	1	Salyer Samuel	1
Muncreef William and		Palmoor Robert	1	Stevens John	1
Son Thomas	1	Peddrick John	1	Simmons John	1
Morriset Peter	1	Prescot Benjamin	2	Sears Joseph	1
Mason Sally	1	Perkins John Senr.	2	Simmons Robert	3
Miller Evan	1	Perkins John Junr	2	Sicks Abel	1

Still Robert	1	Taylor Thomas	2	Weaser James	4
Savels Marmaduke	2	Taylor Evenezer	1	White Margret	2
Scarborow John Senr.	1	Valentine Henry	1	White Luke	3
Stow Samuel	4	Vardin Bryand	1	Wicker Elizabeth	1
Scarborow George	1	Vardin Silvester	1	Waterfield Michel	2
Simmons Samuel	3	Valintine Henry	1	Williams William	4
Stephens Jeremiah	1	West Nathaniel Spence	1	Williams Philip	1
Snowden William Junr.	1	Whaley Rachel	1	Woodhouse John	3
Sickes Benjamin	1	Williams Thomas	4	Williams Joseph	1
Tatom Thomas	1	Whitehurst Gidian	1	Whidbey John	1
Tomson William	1	White Easter Widow	8	Wells Joshua	1
Taylor Benjamin	1	Williams Nicholas	2	Wahabb James	2
Thomas Jeremiah	1	Williams John	1	Woods John	3
Taylor John	1	Williams Charles	3	Whitehall Robert and	
Taylor William	1	Williams Thomas	1	Thomas Whitehall	2
Thomas free Negro Living		White William	2	Williams John	1
on Churches		White Vinson	1	Walker John	1
Island	1	White Joshua	2	White Hilary	3
Turton Thomas	1	White Henry	3	Wardin William	3
Taylor Joshua	1	Williams Thomas	1	Wilson Francis	3
Tomson John	1	Woodhouse Hezeciah	7	Wilson Sarah Widow	2
Towler James	3	Williamson William	3	White Joshua	1
Tillit John	1	Walker John	3	Wicker Richard	6
Tillit Edward	1	Williamson Stephen	9		

[c1758]

A list of the Com	Leutenant	Beniama Prescot
pany und the Comm	Samuel Jarvis	Hezekiah Woodhouse
and of Capt. John	Ensigh	Robartt Gipson
Woodhouse	Joseph Sanderson	

Jonathon Jarvis, Thomas Sanderson, Ruben Bawls - Corperals

Samuel Salyer Drumer	William McCoye	Thomas O Dowdy	Caleb Walker
Azerikem Parker, Jr.	William Mitchel	Edom Simmons	O Neal Walker
Joseph Sanderson, Jr.	Jeams Dugless	Thomas Whitehall	William Williamson
[Joel] Pyner	Beniaman Porthood	Edmond Cowel	Mathew Williamson
[Jona]than Hannah	Henry Banks	Nathan Pyner	Jeams Mercer
[Wi]liam Gilbert	Joseph Bennitt	Thomas Russell	William Sanderson Sr
John Edy	Beniaman Tayler	Beniaman Pyner	William Sanderson Jr
Ebenezer Tayler	William Muncreafe	Azrikem Parker Senr.	Willis Russel
Timothy Ives Junr.	Adam Etheridge	Benin. Linsey	Samson Etheridge
Thomas Love	Edward Capps	Joseph Cooper	Daiel O Dowdy
Thomas Tayler	Peter Leichfield	Ruben Tayler	Stephen Gibbens
Richard O Neal	John Love Junr.	Jonathan Tayler	Thomas Evins
ens	Jonathan Norton	John Robertson	Beniaman Evins
ion	John Stepens	Jeremiah Barret	Joseph Evens
Linsey	James O Dowdy	John Hannah	Henry Evens
Joseph Linsey	William Etheridge	Buhler Cowel	Richard Etheridge
John Linsey	John Walker Junr.	Joseph O Dowdy	Hilary Parker
Peter Lutts	Richard Love	Josiah Nicholson	William Hopkins
John Roberson	Thomas Jarvis	Thomas Simmons	Thomas E
Jeams Etheridge	John Gipson	Samuell Simmons	Peter P
Isack Evins	Henry Gipson	Asahel Simmons	William

Abraham Kenndy   Solaman Smith   Peter Boom   Richard Barritt
John Richards

1758
A List of The Company Under The Command Of Capt. John Woodhouse

Lieutenant Samuel Jarvis   Ensign Dead

Serjants	Corporals
Mr. Robert Gipson	Mr. Thomas Sanderson Jr.
Mr. Hezekiah Woodhouse	Mr. Jonathan Jarvis
Mr. Benjamin Presscoat	Mr. Rabin Ball
Mr. James Parker by age	
exempt and dont serve	

Name	No.	Name	No.	Name	No.
Samuel Salyer	1	Edmond Cowell	38	William Williams	76
Asahel Simmons	2	Nathan Poyner	39	Benjamin Taylor	78
Azariham Parker	3	Thomas Russell	40	William Muncrief	79
Joseph Sanderson	4	Benjamin Poyner	41	Lewis Williams	80
Joel Poyner Jne.	5	Joseph Odowdy	42	James Parker	81
Jonathan Hannay	6	Josiah Nicholson	43	Adam Poyner	82
Joshua Ball	7	Thomas Simmons	44	Caleb Simmons	83
Joseph Hannah	8	Samuel Simmons	45	Abel Dugless	84
William Gilbert	9	Caleb Walker	46	Joseph Prince	85
Ebenezer Taylor	10	Oneel Walker	47	John Taylor	86
Thomas Love	12	Mathew Williamson	49	Thomas Perry	87
Michael O'Neal	13	Uriah Angel	50	Peter Thomas	88
Daniel Linsay	14	Andrew Scrimshaw	51	Bartholomew Twifford	89
Joseph Linsay	15	William Dunoson	52	Hillary Parker	90
John Linsay	16	Alexander McCaney	53	William Hopkins	91
Peter Lutts	17	William Dabbs	54	Peter Pew	92
John Robertson Jnr.	18	Samson Simmons	55	John Richards	93
Edward Capps	19	John Odowdy	56	Solomon Smith	94
Peter Leichfield	20	Robert Chamberlain	57	Peter Bawm	95
John Love Jnr.	21	Robert Poyner	58	Richard Barrett	96
James Mercer Junr.	22	James Mercer	59	Azariham Parker Jnr.	97
Willis Walker	23	William Sanderson Jnr.	60	Benjamin Linsey	98
Henry Hannah	24	Willis Russell	61	Joseph Cooper	99
Henry Gipson Jnr.	25	Samson Etherage	62	Rubin Taylor	100
William Chaplin	26	Daniel Odowdy	63	William Odowdy Jnr.	101
Joel Poyner Jnr.	27	Stephen Gibbuns	64	Jonathan Poyner	102
John Barco	28	Thomas Evens	65	John Robertson Jnr.	103
Ezekiel Evens	29	Benjamins Evens	67	Jeremiah Barritt	104
John Stephens	30	Joseph Evens	68	Butler Cowell	105
James Odowdy	31	Isaac Evens	69	George Powers	106
John Walker Jne.	32	Henry Evens	70	Thomas Allen	107
Thomas Jarvis	33	William McCoye	71	Luke Selvester	108
John Gipson	34	James Dugless	72	Thomas Russell Jnr.	109
Henry Gipson	35	Benjamin Portwood	73	Daniel Shannan	110
Thomas Odowdy	36	Henry Banks	74	James Shannan	111
Edom Simmons	37	Joseph Burnet	75	Hezekiah Morris	112

[1763]

Dr. Sir: Inabedance to your Command and the law of our Government I have herforth Sent the
List of our Regiment of Currituck Vd: Wm Williams   59
Capt. William Bray   66

Capt. William Mackie	55
Capt. Saml: Jarvis	67
Capt. Benjamen Northren	96
Capt. Nicholus Lunn	110
	453

Sir We are under a Misfourtian of Losing of our Lieutenant Colonel Robt. Whitehall I Beg you wood be Good a nuf to Send us a Lieutenant Collonels Commission Majors and Captains Lieutenants and Insigns which will very Much ablige your Harty friend and Humble Sarvt.
November 20th Day 1763   Stephen Williams

[c1763]
A Muster Roll of the Regiment of Curratuck Under the Command of Major William Shergold

The Company of Capt. John Lorry
Officers
Samuel Gervis Ensign
Joseph Sanderson Sergant
Benjamin Prestcot Do
Samuel Simmons Do
James Parker Do
Jonathan Pyner Corporal
Comon Soldiers
Richard Campbill
Evan Miller
Evan Miller Junr.
Thomas Miller
James Chetham
John Chetham
William Chetham
Bennett Cheatham
Robert Bell
John Wheatly
John Balance
William Thompson
Petr Spratling
Thomas Thompson
Peter Pyner
Humphry Pyner
John Pyner
Adam Fisher
Thomas Thethom
John Burton
William Thompson
Thomas Parker
Azricham Parker
Azricham Parker Junr.
John Nicholson
Joseph Lindsay
John Robinson
John Lindsay
William Muncrief
William Norton

Benjamin Cowell
Jonathan Norton
Edmond Cowell
Adam Etheridge
Soloman Cowell
Adam Etheridge Jr.
Butler Cowell
Sampson Etheridge
Joshua White
Richard Etheridge
James Parker
Thomas Perry
Peter Pierce
John Walker
John Walker Junr.
Neal Walker
William Williamson
Mathew Williams
Edward Love
John Love
William Love
Martin Portwood
Charles Prescot
Joshua Taylor
Philop Caps
James Mercer
James Douglas
Thomas Simons
Sanel Simons Junr.
Jonathan Jervis
Peter McDowell
Benjamin Taylor
John Taylor
Joel Pyner
Benjamin Pyner
Peter Pyner
Henry Jepson
John Jepson
Robert Jepson
William Abington

Joseph Burnet
John Hanner
Willis Hanner
Mickel O'Neal
Timothy Ives
Timothy Ives Junr.
Samuel Sallier
Joshua Sanderson
Joseph Cooper
William O'Dowthy
William O'Dowthy Junr.
Joseph O'Dowthy
Soloman Baker
John Dixon
Christopher Dicken
John Dicken
Benjamin Dicken
Rice Evans
Thomas Evans
Peter Evans
Edward Litchfield
Edward Litchfield Junr.
Peter Litchfield
Azachia Woodhouse
Manor Smith
Stephen Banks
Peter Bawn
Stephen Gibbins
William Gibbin
Henry Evans
Daniel O'Dowthy
Daniel O'Dowthy Junr.
Thomas Russell
David Lindsay
Benjamin Lindsay

The Company of Capt. Jacob Caron Decd.
Officers
James Phillops Lieutenant

John Pell   Ensign
Daniel Duke   Sergant
Jushua Brent   Sergant
William Bray   Corporal
John Barnes   Do
James Daug   Do
Jeremiah Stearns Drummer
John Simmons   Do
          Common Soldiers
Samuel Barnard
Richard Gregory
William Ferabee
Jeremiah Mercer
John Cooper
John Whitehurst
William Parr
Henry Perkins
John Perkins Junr.
Abner Legget
Willis Etheridge
Benjamin Dauge
Samuel Lee
Moses Fanshaw
James Jenkins
Otho Holland
James Briggs
Amos Etheridge
John Barber
Caleb Etheridge
Joseph Ferabee
Joseph Pyner
Sallay Magson
Lazarus Flurry
John Muncrief
Fobert Fletcher
James Etheridge
Thomas Glasgoe
Caleb Bell
Hilery Simmons
Edward Love
Samuel Halstead
Michael Ellis
Joshua White
William Lee
Thomas Perkins
Richard Spann
Abner Etheridge
Jeremiah Thomas
William Snowden
Soloman Etheridge
Silvester Varden

Bryan Varden

The Complt of Thomas
   Davis Deceased
     Officers &c
Thomas Burgess Lt.
William Williams Ensign
Thomas Davis
Willis Etheridge
Henry Bright
Joseph Bowrin
Edmond Bowrin
William Powers
Robert Heath
Soloman Jarvis
Joseph Haman
Samuel Etheridge Senr.
Richard Etheridge
Mathias Etheridge
William Marshall
Nathaniel Cain
Parker Swindal
John Bright
Samuel Bright
Robert Rolland
Luke Bowland
George Rowland
James Garrett
Soloman Armstrong
Samuel Jones
John McFarson
Amos Kight
William Scott
Daniel Lee
Marmaduke Cox
Richard Fanshaw
Willis Bright
Samuel Etheridge Junr.
Henry Etheridge
John Hughes
William Blount
Caleb Sikes
Simon Shewcraft
Richard Nickins
George Davis
Andrew McFarson
Soloman Miller
Robert Brooks
John Garett
Richard Bright
Joshua Hall

John Hunt
Silas Bright
Joseph Garret
George Powers
Caleb Powers
Abraham Etheridge
Freeman Garret
Thomas Hutchings
Philop Northern
Daniel Swinny
Peter Balentine
Lemuel Glasgoe
Samuel Ballance
William Fitz Jarret
Absolem West
Josiah Davis
Soloman Etheridge
Caleb Bright

The Company of Captain Job
   Carr & Capt. Hillary White

Capt. Job Carr Company
   Officers
Jacob Farrow Lieutenant
John Wood   Ensign
Clesby Scarboroough Sgt.
Christr. O'Neal   Do
William Robinson Corporal
Francis Peel   Do
John O'Neal   Do
   Common Soldiers
John Scarborough Senr.
Thomas Austin Senr.
George Howard
John Scarborough
Joseph McCuen
Peter Howard
Francis Robinson
John Whidbee
George Scarborough
Joshua Walls
Henry Clark
James Wahad
Hezekiah Farrow
Joshua Campbell
James Kelly
Isaac Farrow
William Brooks
Joshua Walls Junr.
Stephen Brooks

CURRITUCK COUNTY TAX AND MILITIA LISTS

Joseph Williams
Augustine Scarborough
John G. Neal Junr.
Thomas Midget
Joseph Midget Junr.
Alexr. Curtis
Thomas Paint
Jacob Mekins
Isaack Mekins
Jadex Jennet
John Brady
Thomas O'Neal
Samuel Midget
John Palmer
Joseph Lain
William Scarborough
Thomas Walls

Capt. Hilary White
   Officers
William Mackey Lt.
Joshua White Ensign
Charles Williams Sgt
Martin Jarvis Corp.
Evan Jones   Do
Patrick Jones Do
William Jarvis Do
John Ansell Clerk

Jonathan Whaley Drum.
Moses Caps   Do
   Comon Soldiers
Elisha Cornish
Robert Simmons
William Simpson
James Simpson
Thomas Dudly Junr.
William White
William Dudly
Henry Valentine
William Chappell
John Beasley
William Beasley
John Heath
John Morris
Richardson _____
Michael Waterfield
Henry Kinsey
Richard _____
Jonathan Jarvis
Soloman Heath
Thomas Grig
Vinson White
Thomas Williams
John Williams
Leven Gaskins

Soloman Simpson
Joseph Hill
John Hailes
William Hailes
William Heath
Jacob Weasley
John Ansell Junr.
John McGee
Arthur Lemmond
Paul Elison
John Dixon
Robert Heath
Edward Joice
Richard Fenton
Tomas Fenton
Cader Marchant
Gideon Marchant
Thomas Miller
Jacob Goodmond
Caleb Fenton
George Stone
Nathaniel Spene West
William Ives
Isham Fenton
William Bradley
John Jone
Richard Beasley

Field Return of the Regiment of Militia for Currituck County at a General Muster the 1 October 1771
Commissioned Officers
John Woodhouse   Colonel
Holloway Williams   Lieut. Col.
Saml Jarvis   Major

1		5		9	
Solo. Baker	Capt.	Taylor Jones	Capt.	Henery Harrison	Capt.
Wallis Bray	Lieut.	John Simmons	Lieut.	Nathaniel West	Lieut.
Willoughby Dauge	Ensig.	John Macke	Ensig.	Caleb Limmons	Ensig.
2		6			
Nicholas Lunn	Capt.	Isaac Farrow	Capt.		
William Daniel Junr.	Lieut.	Henery Clark	Lieut.		
Morris Baum Junr.	Ensig.	Thos. Poyner	Ensig.		
3		7			
Thos. Simmons	Capt.	Thos. Taylor	Capt.		
Thos. Sanderson	Lieut.	Nathan Poyner	Lieut.		
Jesse Sanderson	Ensig.	Benj. Poyner	Ensig.		
4		8			
Asahel Simmons	Capt.	Peter Ballentine	Capt.		
Josiah Nicholson	Lieut.	John Northern	Lieut.		
Robt. Poyner	Ensig.	George Bowers	Ensig.		

93

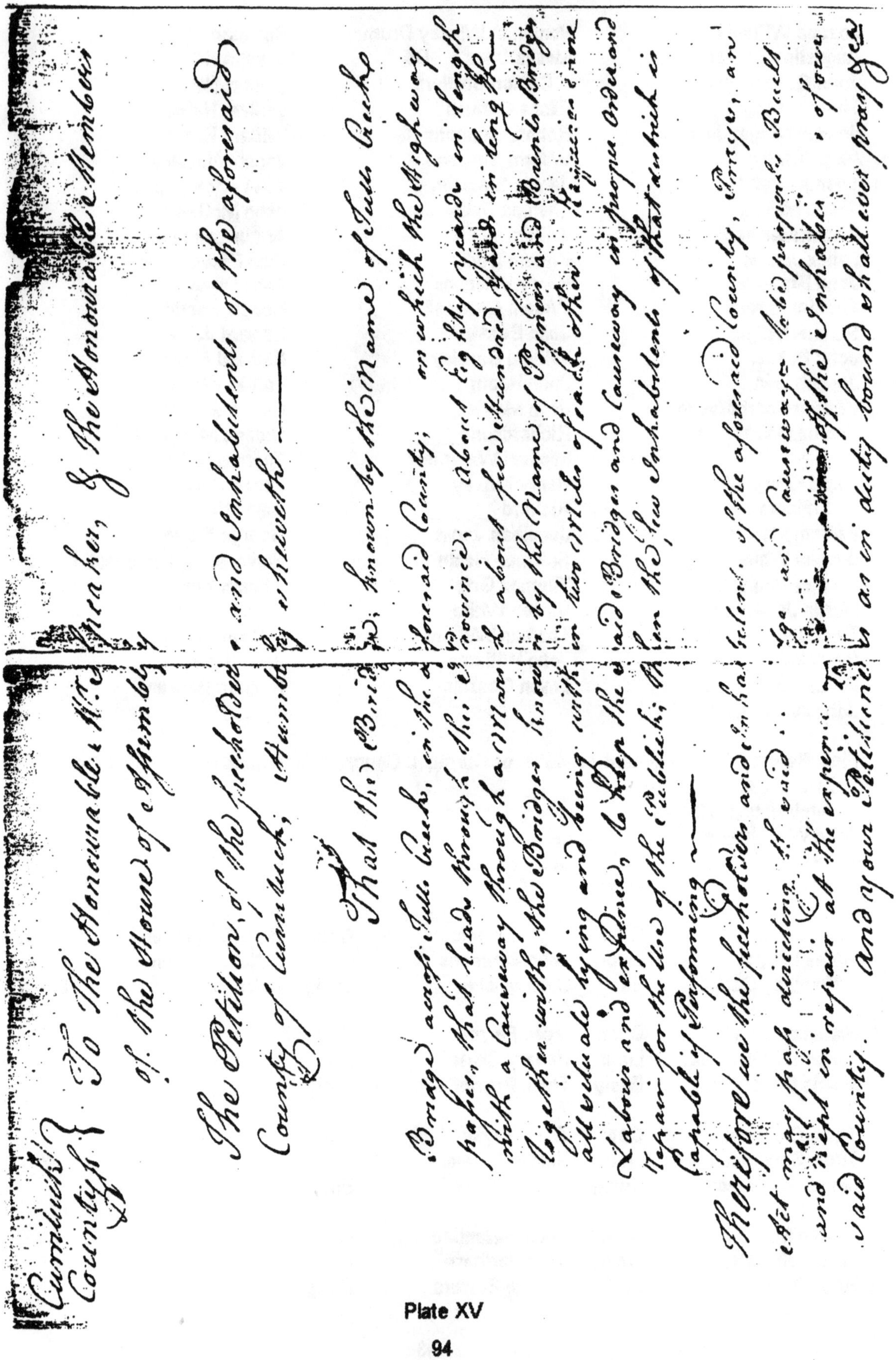

Currituck
County

To The Honourable the Speaker, & the Honourable the Members
of the House of Assembly

The Petition of the Freeholders and Inhabitants of the aforesaid
County of Currituck, Humbly Sheweth ——

That the Bridge, known by the Name of Tulls Creek
Bridge across Tulls Creek, on the General County, on which the Highway
passes that leads through this Province, about Eighty yards in length
with a Causeway through a Marsh about Five Hundred yards in length
together with the Bridge known by the Name of Synes aid Mund's Bridge
all which is lying and being within two miles of each other, However some
Labour and expence, to keep the said Bridges and Causeway in proper Order and
Repair for the use of the Publick; when the Inhabitants of that which is
Capable of performing ——

Therefore we the Freeholders and Inhabitants of the aforesaid County, pray, an
Act may that directing the said Causeways to be... proper Bridle
and kept in repair at the expence of the Inhabitants of your
said County. And your Petitioners as an in duty bound shall ever pray &c

Plate XV

94

(General Assembly Papers - 1773)

Currituck
County   To The Honourable Mr. Speaker & The Honourable
           Members of the House of Assembly

The Petition of the freeholders and Inhabitants of the aforesaid County of Currituck. Humbley sheweth -

That the Bridge known by the name of Tulls Creek Bridge across Tulls Creek. In the aforesaid County, on which the Highway passes, that leads through the Province, about Eighty yards in length with a Causeway through a Marsh about five Hundred yard in length together with the Bridges known by the Name of Poyners and Brents Bridges all situate lying and beimg wilhin two miles of each other requires more Labour and expence to keep the saild Bridges and Causeway in proper order and repair for the use of the Publick than the few inhabitants of that district is Capable of Performing -

Therefore we the freeholders and inhabitants of the aforesaid County Prays an Act may pass directing Bridges and Causeways to be properly Built and kept in repair at the expense of the Inhabitants of our said County and your Petitioners ar in duty bound shall ever pray &tc -

Hilary Simmons	Willoughby White	Thos Parker
Josias Slack	John Berry	Thos Haman
John Wyatt	William Tatum	Marmeduke Cos
Josiah Davis	John Burton	Jacob Townsend
Adam Gardner	Benjamin Daudey	Jacob Goodman
Elias Lee	John Tatum	Thomas Burgess
Daniel Lee	James Spence	Nicholis Killey
George Rowland	David Spence	Job Townsend
William Scot	Caleb Bell	John Grabes
Soloman Lurrey	Thomas Lee	Ward Nickens
Moses Fanshaw	Benjamin Crabb	Samuel Birnham
Robert Thompson	Asa Lee	Thomas Cox
James Brable	Lazarus Florah	John Garott
Evan Thompson	Thomas Wheatly	_____ Bright
James Poyner	John Wheatly	Thomas Crief
Pettit Cook	Henry Ballentine	Jesse Holstead
William Brable	John Biggs	Elias Daudge
John Brannoy	Caleb Simes	Lam Linston
John Etheridge	Chapan Jenkins	John Skinner
Nathan Lee	Charles Celly Jr.	John Curling
Robert Heath	Samuel Simmons	John Holstead
Grifith Daudge	Solo Perkins	Robert Cartwright
Laben Smith	Samuel Holstead	Thomas Shergold
Horatio Lee	Samuel Coo	Solio Etheridge
Daniel Lufman	Lemuell White Junr	_____ Celly
Willis Bright	William Perkins	William Baxter
William Northern	Richd Henley	Thompson
Daniel Phillips	Jno Northern	Cornelius Caves
Samuel Lee	Dennis Daudge	Samuel Phillips
Soliman Jarvis	Peter Morisset	Robert Fletcher
Willoughby Brooks	Joseph Poyner Sr.	Caleb Morse
Richd Fanshaw	James Poyner	Johathan Ward
Daniel Parr	Joseph Poyner Jr.	John Campbell
Wallis Bray	Dickson Morse	Joseph Bisco
Rodham Glascock Grant		Tolley Celly

CURRITUCK COUNTY TAX AND MILITIA LISTS

1779.TAX LIST

Ashbee Abel	£1894	Bell Caleb Senr	2503	Chetham Sarah	100
Ashbee Elizabeth	980	Bonney Euphon	343	Cowel Solomon	1120
Ashbee Soloman	1720	Bonney Jonathan	930	Capps Caleb	1520
Ansevel Lydia	2121	Beasley William	1330	Capps Dennis	730
Ansevel John	3766	Burrus Robert	1052	Clerk George	162
Austen William	600	Ballance William	794	Clerk Major	227
Austen Cornelius	400	Basnite Robert	632	Capps Henry	552
Austen Thomas Senr	760	Burrus John	1332	Capps Henry	164
Allen Thomas Jur	1085	Baker John	526	Duglus James	1686
Austen Thomas Jur	279	Beecham Thomas	138	Duke Andrew	2315
Austen Daniel	389	Beecham John	330	Duglus Abel	750
Ansevel Nathan	130	Beasley Jacob	397	Davis George	880
Brent Richard	1232	Berry Samuel	316	Dewe Sarah	237
Brent James	696	Bennet Edward	214	Dough Richard	2178
Barns Jonathon	3299	Berry John	143	Dough Samson	910
Baxter Joseph	1978	Beasley Caleb	103	Daniel Samuel	594
Ball Reuben	855	Burton John Senr	251	Daniel Joseph	2210
Bins Mary	1277	Barns William	168	Daniel William Jr	786
Baum Joseph	1775	Brabble Nancy	370	Daniel Beltashazer	2524
Barret Thomas	463	Burton John	235	Daniel David	904
Barnard Julian	8678	Burton Hillary	156	Daniel William Sr	2514
Baum Morris Jr	3155	Bell Lisenia	138	Dough George	313
Bernard William	3260	Bennet Moses	430	Dolby Absolem	720
Baxter John	1517	Ballance Abram	200	Dauge Angiuis	1050
Bernard Robert	5009	Brickhouse Benjamin	150	Dauge Mitchel	1012
Bernard Jesse	5009	Burket Caleb	200	Dauge James	12718
Bernard Samuel	1160	Bryant John	340	Doxey John	528
Ballance Caleb	753	Bush Frederick	300	Dauge Unas	470
Bray Wallis	4422	Brooks Isaac	178	Doughty Edward	1549
Brabble John	448	Bowen William	244	Davis Josiah	1590
Barnard Joseph	1681	Campbell Elisha Sr	1430	Dauge Tully	4275
Bell John	5663	Cowel John	670	Dauge Benjamin	1375
Bramsey Mary	1068	Capps Moses	126	Dauge Willoughby	8749
Ballance John	555	Chaplin James	1174	Dudley William Sr	500
Bates Andrew	1164	Campbell Mary	543	Dudley Thomas	2186
Bright Henry	2184	Coo___ John	1175	Duncan Thomas	3145
Bennet Jesse	2660	Callis John	2624	Dudley John	222
Bright John	970	Cook _____	1722	Eady Samuel	452
Bright Silas	2910	Curlew Courtney	2070	Easy Darah	125
Brooks Willoughby	933	Cuckton (??) John	3168	Evans Joseph	535
Ballentine Henry	4453	Cox Lewis	1059	Evans Sarah	3305
Bright Willis	1249	Chavelian Charles	423	Evans Benjamin	1235
Bradley Abel	626	Culpepper Henry	640	Everton John	1872
Bradley John	492	Cherry Josiah	330	Etheridge Sampson	2980
Bradley William	604	Cherry Luke	981	Etheridge Sampson Jr.	1637
Bowrem Maximillian	1210	Cox Thomas	3176	Etheridge Adam	840
Bennet John	1440	Cox Marmeduke	1926	Ennuls Joseph	4127
Ballentine Joseph	4075	Crab Benjamin	370	Etheridge Tart	230
Baxter James	658	Cooper Samuel	476	Etheridge James	240
Biggs John	2990	Cooper Thomas	454	Etheridge Timothy	2284
Baxter Sarah	502	Cooper John	2064	Etheridge Solomon	115

Etheridge James Sr	2465	Glasgow James	850	Jennet Joseph	397
Etheridge James Jr	320	Glasgow Thomas	560	Ives Abigail	1030
Etheridge William	240	Glasgow William	270	Jones Thomas	117
Etheridge Solomon	624	Griffith William	700	Jones Sarah	3247
Etheridge Mathew	628	Gray Thomas	590	Killam Theophilus	1220
Etheridge Abel	200	Gammet John	103	Kinnion Daniel	440
Etheridge Samuel	523	Gold Daniel	130	Knight Elisha	551
Etheridge Caleb	140	Heath Thomas	521	Kinnian John	540
Etheridge James Jr.	2300	Harrison Joshua	150	King Thomas	18539
Etheridge James Sr	3956	Hill David	145	Litchfield Abraham	1164
Etheridge Amos Sr	4231	Hall Nathan	1370	Lindsey Thomas	430
Etheridge John	430	Hall Spencer	5322	Lindsey John	1000
Etheridge Samuel	1059	Humphries John	6917	Lindsey Benjamin	2154
Etheridge John Sr	5302	Holloway William	438	Litchfield Peter	3967
Etheridge Willis	5598	Hunt Charles	420	Lungren Lawrence	299
Etheridge Richard	228	Hutchens John	477	Land Richard	328
Etheridge Jesse	110	Hutchens Nathaniel	257	Lunn Nicholas	647
Ferebee William	10991	Hutchens Richard	716	Lutts William	192
Ferebee Sarah	1148	Hutchens Thomas	690	Lurry William	4704
Fisher George	250	Hutchens Thomas Sr	837	So Orphans	2100
Fisher John	274	Holsted John	1188	Lindsey Alexander	3590
Foster Jeremiah	680	Holms James	570	Lurry Mary	2147
Fletcher Margaret	1305	Holsted John	1188	Lee Nathan	550
Flurrey Thomas	318	Haymen Thomas	1173	Lee Linton	386
Flurrey Lucy	62	Hayman John	278	Lufman Daniel	248
Ferebee James	1315	Holsted Samuel	3798	Lee Daniel	738
Flurrey William	821	Heath Robert	1004	Lee William	384
Ferebee Peter	655	Heath Ann Margaret	290	Lee Jean	120
Fanshaw Moses	700	Hill John	824	Linton Lemuel	184
Fletcher Robert	548	Haynes Elizabeth	100	Lee Josiah	820
Farrow Jacob Sr	1766	Hooper Ezekiel	190	Lee William Sr	291
Farrow Francis	1586	Mill Milborough	100	Lee Thomas	634
Farrow Jacob Jr	1766	Hayman Henry	110	Lee Asahel	1976
Farrow Hezekiah	980	Jones William	150	Litchfield Jacob	397
Farrow Thomas	613	Jarvis Thomas Col	17148	Lee Horasha	204
Farrow Vinah	270	Jarvis John	1800	Mason Josephus	640
Farrow Isaac	529	Jarvis Foster	1261	Melson William	400
Fenton Sarah	1360	Ives Timothy	2453	MacCoy John	325
Gipson Henry	403	Jarrard James	674	Morris Willoughby	721
Gipson Peter	302	Jones Randal Sr	630	Mitchell Ambrose	120
Gipson Henry Jr	181	Ives Thomas	1960	Mahorney John	522
Gamwell James	490	Jarvis Samuel Col	9900	McDaniel Joshua	1270
Gibbens Joshua	230	Jarvis Solomon	732	Midget William	1950
Gibbens Stephen	513	Jones Zadock	3131	Mann John	2060
Garden Peter	240	Jarvis James	631	Midget Samuel Jr	1620
Gibson David	520	Jenkins Elisha	130	Midget Samuel Sr	10070
Gibson Robert	810	Jarvis Maximilian	170	Mercer Jeremiah Jr	260
Gregory Griffeth Jr	470	Jones Evan Jr	2021	Mercer Jeremiah Sr	985
Gregory Cornelius	3280	Jamison George	12497	Mercer Thomas	1386
Gregory Jesse	1840	Jones Evan Sr	2561	Moreral Jeminah	743
Gregory Griffeth Sr	1220	Jesper Dorcas	2183	Matthias Matthew	350
Goodman Jacob	682	Jennet Easter	140	Moue Francis	570

Name	Amount	Name	Amount	Name	Amount
Moue Zachariah	212	Oneel Christopher	894	Rollenson William	175
Moue Richardson	830	Oakley Elizabeth	343	Rowland George	1469
Moue Elizabeth	406	Poyner Robert	5019	Robb Thomas	682
Miller William	660	Plumer George	753	Simmons Asahel	6166
Mcpharson Daniel	187	Poyner Joel	610	Simmons Sampson	1518
Miller Evan	710	Poyner Nathan	8354	Do Orphans	3757
McPherson Daniel Sr	50	Portwood Benjamin	790	Stephens Diniah	662
McPherson William	150	Poyner Adam	511	Smith William	230
Marchant Catherine	16818	Padrick Peter	348	Sanderson Thomas	11979
Mandon Epaphraditus	632	Parker Jeminah	1020	Do Orphans	2165
Marchant Malikia	2390	Parker James	1313	Sikes Benjamin	400
Do Orphans	1901	Padrick Henry	362	Simpson William	358
Muldin William	450	Padrick Peter	462	Sanderson Benjamin	4184
Marchand Willoughby	1650	Parker Thomas Jr	510	Smith Perminious	1773
May George	1190	Parker Azaricam	487	Sanderson Jesse	16684
Muncrief Heziah	410	Phillips Ann	930	Sanderson John	5106
Megg John	740	Phillips Jean	24	Do Orphans	266
Mashie John	6215	Phillips James	1207	Salyer Samuel Sr	1039
Moue Malichia	955	Do Orphans	1044	Salyer Samuel Jr	1200
Moue Reuben	463	Parker William Sr	155	Sikes Abel	351
Midget Daniel	3018	Poyner Peter	3594	Sawyers Tull	424
Miller Thomas	3134	Poyner Humphry	350	Supple Anthony	450
Midget Christopher	1027	Powers William	4197	Stanley John	1058
Midget Matthew	965	Powers Caleb Sr	271	Slaughter John	460
Midget John	937	Poyner Jonathan	130	Stanley Richard	499
Midget Richard	1031	Powers George Jr	963	Sawyer Thomas	572
McPharson Moses	255	Parker Phebe	2433	Stewart John	473
Midget Thomas	466	Parr Daniel	988	Sears Leticia	1672
Midget Joseph	281	Parr Diniah	73	Stanley Thomas	130
Meekins Roger	650	Perkins William	1503	Simmons Hilary	1189
Muncrief William	1899	Parr Jesse	330	Do Orphans	575
Mallete Lydia	50	Pew George	2079	So for Rchd Templeman	1826
Midget Thomas	574	Pew Thomas	1721	Do for Jos Poyner	51
Norton William	640	Pain Thomas Sr	3722	Shergold Thomas	810
Norton Asahel	400	Popplewell George	699	Slack Nicholas	450
Norton John	1589	Pew William	530	Swindal Parker	647
Do Orphans	901	Perkins Joshua	575	Slack Josiah	680
Nicholson Jonah	4619	Pain Thomas	425	Savan David	160
Northern William	2232	Parker Thomas	310	Sexton Jeremiah	1877
Nicholas Nichole	5652	Powers George	2192	Scott William	1115
Northen Phillip	3140	Quidley William	289	Simmons William	796
Northern John	2640	Ryan James	5835	Soles Armstead	514
Do Orphans	411	Roggers Major	270	Simmons Samuel	2238
Overton Willis	258	Rollins Ezekiel	775	Simpson James	1322
Odowdy Joseph	1103	Russel William	4109	Simmons Robert	4906
Onel Michael	2870	Robertson John Sr	120	Simpson John	942
Odowdy William	930	Robertson John Jr	190	Simpson William	1723
Olds Kedar	1378	Rale Leah	155	Simmons John	3125
Oneel Sarah	223	Reed William	800	Simmons Caleb	1740
Oneel Thomas	180	Rollenson William Sr	675	Simpson James	196
Oneel John	527	Rollenson William	188	Smith Elias	943
Oneel William	1254	Rollenson Frances	600	Smith John	3505

CURRITUCK COUNTY TAX AND MILITIA LISTS

Stow Benjamin	127	Taylor Thomas	467	Walker Oneel	130
Scarborough Austin	906	Taylor Johnathan	1025	Williams Philip	123
Scarborough John	377	Taylor Reuben	534	Wroten William	126
Scarborough John Jr	259	Taylor John	783	Walker Thomas	610
Stow Susanna	1206	Taylor Thomas Sr	3389	Whitehall Alexr. Legrand	2938
ScarboroughWilliam	416	Taylor Joseph	271	Woodhouse Hadley	2376
Scarborough Thomas	176	Thomas James	452	Williams Lewis	1932
Scarborough Edward	1182	Thomas Robert	1322	White Jamima	4976
Stow Daniel	945	Tolar Matthias	5634	Do Orphans	1366
Stow Samuel	142	Tolar James	326	Waterfield Abraham	310
Scarborough Elizabeth	444	Tillot Thomas	1327	Wahab William	1515
Simmons Jesse	1301	Thomson Mary	65	Wedbee John	114
Sanderson Richard	929	Tatem William	724	Whidbee William	653
Simmons John	1650	Tatem John	554	Williams James	162
Thomson John	1110	Thomson Evan	700	Williams Comfort	150
Taylor Ebenezer	677	Thomson William	570	Williams Jacob	176
Taylor Edward	3329	Townsend John	610	Wahab James	1542
Taylor Benjamin	1812	Turton Abner	4956	White Willoughby	4142
Taylor Joseph	810	Walker Willis	298	Wheatley Robert	320
Taylor Thomason	1184	Walker Caleb	862	Younghusband Thomas	8672

A list of the Married men in the County of Currituck that pays a Poll Tax for the Year 1779 taken from the Assessment Book

Allen Thomas	Davis Elias	Mounticue John
Ackland John	Evans Robert	Miller Thomas
Archer Armstrong	Eyellet David	Newel James
Berry John	Etheridge Josiah	Oneel Chrisopher
Barnet Samuel	Etheridge Caleb	Poyner Joel
Best William	Everton Thomas	Perry John
Barns John	Fulford Josiah	Powers Caleb
Bell Caleb Jr	Flower John	Padrick John
Bins Joseph	Gray Edward	Pell Etheridge John
Brown John	Gray Griffeth	Quidley Thomas
Bosely William	Griggs George Sr	Roggers Spencer
Brickhouse Caleb	Griggs George Jr	Rigsby James
Case Jonathon	Grinsted Roly	Robertson Thomas
Cooper Josiah	Gallop Jonah	Roberts Wrencher
Creekmoore Samuel	Gamwell John	Robertson George
Creekmoore Samuel Jr	Harrison Josiah	Shannon Daniel
Coleman Charles	Harrel John	Smith John
Case Solomon Sr	Hancock John	Spann Richard
Case Solomon Jr	Hauners Hilary	Spry James
Culplepper Peter	Harris William	Smith Elijah
Capps Enoch	Hutchens James	Simmons Willis
Capps John	Jones David	Singleton Peter
Cason John	Lemmons Arthur	Taylor Joshua
Caffee Jacob	Lemmons Henry	Thomas William
Disan Francis	Miles Moses	Thomson John
Dyar James	Mason John	Williamson William
Dough John	Morce Benjamin	Walston Jonathan
Dawley Jonathon	Marmiduke Elijah	Woodhouse William
Dauge Hezekiah	Millan Evan	Waterfield John

Waterfield Michael	Walker John	Williams Caleb
Williams Joseph	Wilkins William	Total Amount 92

A list of the Single Men that pays a Poll Tax in the County of Currituck for the Year 1779, Taken from the Assessment Book

Austin Daniel	Gamwell William	Miller Willis
Allen James	Gray Robert	Miller Caleb
Allin Richard	Gray William	Midget Joseph
Bright Aaron	Howel Sylvenious	Midget Christopher
Barnet Joseph	Holbern Adam	Midget Samuel
Braddy Thomas	Heath James	MoGown Andrew
Ball Hosea	Jones Randal	Poyner Thomas
Cavender John	Jones John	Plummer Moses
Chaplin Caleb	Jarvis Malichia	Parr Noah
Clerk Major	Jennet Job	Riggs James
Chaplin Caleb	Jennet Jessie	Shurwood James
Dauge Elias	Jennet Jabez	Smith Laban
Dudley Malichia	Jeans Thomas	Simmons Anthony
Dudley William	Ledah Edward	Stow Jeremiah
D. West George	Lee John	Scarborough Ignatious
Etheridge William	Lindsay David	Simmons Thomas
Etheridge Thoroughgood	Mercer John	Wallis Joshua
Farrow Chrostopher	Mercer Thomas	Williams John
Farrow Jacob Jr	May Joseph	Taylor Caleb
Grant ?Walter	Marchant Kedar	Townsend Jobe
Gipson William	Marchant John	Total Amount 62

NAME INDEX

It should be noted that the name may appear more than once on the page cited.

Esdil, 84
Esorid, Rd., 62
    Richard, Jr., 62
Etheridge, _____, 71
    [Torn]n, 59
    Abel, 97
    Abner 92
    Abraham 92
    Adam, 77, 79, 82, 87, 89, 91, 96
    Adam Jr. 91
    Amos, 79, 80, 82, 87
    Amos, Sr., 97
    Andrew, 2, 4, 8, 9, 10, 13, 14, 16,
        25, 27, 30, 32, 34, 36, 37, 39,
        40, 41, 43, 44, 48, 49, 52, 53,
        59, 63, 69, 76
    Andrew, Junr., 59, 69, 76
    Benjamin, 69, 79
    Caleb, 79, 82, 97, 99
    Christian, 76
    Elinor, 79, 82, 87
    Henry (Hanary), 5, 9, 11, 14, 16, 17,
        22, 24, 25, 27, 30, 32, 34, 36,
        39, 40, 41, 44, 48, 50, 59, 63,
        69, 70, 73, 76, 87, 92
    James, 89, 92, 96
    James, Jr., 97
    James, Sr., 97
    Jesse, 97
    Jobe, 18, 24, 48, 49, 59, 69, 79
    John, 6, 16, 25, 32, 34, 39, 40, 44,
        48, 49, 60, 64, 70, 76, 77, 79,
        82, 95, 97
    John, Sr., 97
    Joshua, 82
    Josiah, 99
    Luci, 80, 82
    Luke, 6, 15, 32, 34, 39, 43, 44, 45,
        48, 49, 53, 59, 63, 69
    Marmeduke, 2, 5, 8, 9, 11, 12, 13,
        27, 30, 34, 36, 37, 43, 57, 60,
        63, 64, 67, 74, 76
    Mermeduk, Jur., 38, 39, 42, 45, 53
    Marmeduke, Ser., 26, 32, 39, 40,
        41, 44, 48, 49
    Mathew, 80, 97
    Mathias, 82, 87, 92
    Moses, 62, 71
    Peter, 63
    Richard, 1, 4, 8, 10, 11, 13, 16, 26,
        28, 30, 33, 34, 36, 38, 39, 41,
        44, 49, 50, 54, 64, 75, 80, 82,
        87, 89, 91, 92, 97
    Richd., Jr., 54
    Sampson, 76, 79, 80, 82, 89, 90,
        91, 96
    Sampson, Jr., 96
    Samuel, 87, 97
    Samuel, Junr., 87, 92
    Samuel, Senr., 87, 92
    Sarah, 87
    Solomon, 77, 79, 92, 95, 96, 97
    Tart, 96
    Thoroughgood, 100
    Timothy, xvii, 57, 82, 87, 96
    William, 5, 15, 17, 26, 31, 37, 39,
        42, 44, 47, 48, 50, 73, 79, 80,
        82, 87, 89, 97, 100

Etheridge, Willis, 77, 79, 80, 82, 87, 92,
    97
    Willis, Junr., 26, 31, 87
    Willis, Senr., 87
Evans (Evens, Evins), Benjamin, 82, 87,
    89, 90, 96
    Catrine, 4
    Catarn 15
    Ezekiel, 90
    Henry 79, 82, 89, 90, 91
    Isaac, 87, 89, 90
    John, 2, 4, 8, 10, 13, 14, 16, 26, 27,
        33, 38, 41, 61
    Joseph, 79, 87, 89, 90, 96
    Rice, 79, 87, 91
    Robert, 99
    Sarah, 96
    Thomas, 1, 6, 7, 8, 9, 11, 13, 14,
        16, 23, 25, 26, 33, 35, 37, 42,
        62, 87, 89, 90, 91
Eyellet, David, 99
Everton, John, 96
    Thomas, 87, 99
Ewen, Robert, 84
Eyland, Richard, 28, 53
Fanshaw (Ffanshaw, Fancher, Fansha,
    Fansher, Fansow), Henry, 48, 49,
        53, 61, 70
    Isaiah, 43
    John, 9, 24, 26, 30, 33, 34, 39, 40,
        45, 48, 49, 53, 61, 64
    Moses, 77, 80, 82, 87, 92, 95, 97
    Richard, 33, 34, 39, 40, 45, 48, 49,
        61, 64, 70, 75, 77, 80, 82, 87,
        92, 95
    Thomas, 5, 7, 11, 13, 15, 26, 39,
        45, 48, 49, 61, 64, 70, 87
    Thomas, Jur., 9, 26, 30, 33, 34, 39,
        40, 45
    Thomas, Ser., 9, 26, 30, 33, 34, 40,
        42
Farrow (Faro, Farow), Chrostopher, 100
    Francis, 2, 4, 15, 16, 17, 26, 27, 33,
        35, 37, 39, 41, 42, 49, 52, 97
    Hezekiah, 80, 82, 84, 87, 92, 97
    Isaac, 84, 87, 92, 93, 97
    Jacob, xvi, 77, 80, 82, 83, 84, 86,
        87, 92
    Capt. Jacob, 84
    Jacob, Jr., 84, 87, 97, 100
    Jacob, Sr., 97
    John, 84
    Thomas, 97
    Vinah, 97
Fenton, Caleb, 60, 62, 93
    Isham, 93
    John, 37, 39, 40, 43, 44, 50, 57, 71
    Jno., Jur., 87
    Jno., Ser., 67, 71
    Richard, 67, 77, 80, 82, 87, 93
    Sarah, 97
    Thomas, 79, 82, 93
    Tho., Ser., 68
Ferebee, (Ferabee, Ferby, Ferreby,
    Furby), James, 97
    Jane, 87
    John, 76, 80, 82, 87, 92
    Joseph, 80, 82, 87, 92

Ferebee, Peter, 79, 97
    Sarah, 97
    Thomas, 79
    William, 77, 80, 82, 87, 92, 97
Ferrill, Richd, 4
Ffairecloth, [Torn], 32
Firrell, Wm., 77
Fisher, Adam, 82, 87, 91
    George, 97
    John, 79, 97
Fitz Jarret, William, 92
Fitzgarell, William, 87
Fletcher, Margaret, 97
    Robert, 80, 82, 87, 92, 95, 97
Flora (Florah, Florey, Flower, Flurrey),
    John, 48, 51, 59, 69, 73, 99
    Lazarus, 80, 82, 87, 92, 95
    Lucy, 97
    Thomas, 97
    Willam, 97
Focker, Wm., xvii
Forober, Matheyas, 43
Foster, Jeremiah, 97
Foulker, John, 86
Fowler, Mathins, 39, 45
Fremon, Zekiah, 77
Frost, Wm., 7
Fulcar, John, 87
Fulford, Josiah, 99
Fuller, Wm., 1
Fushore, John, 19
Galf, Edwd., 1
Gallap, [Tom]he, 31
Gallop, Jonah, 99
Gamewell, George, 84
Garnige, Fran, 57
Gammet, John, 97
Garnwell, James, xvii, 97
    John, 84, 99
    William, 100
Gard, Robt., 1
Garden, Peter, 97
Gardner, Adam, 95
Garrett (Garett, Garott, Garrot), Freeman
    92
    James, xvii, 80, 82, 84, 87, 92
    John, 82, 87, 92, 95
    Joseph, 92
Garrot, Truman, 87
Gaskins, Elinor, 80
    Levea, 82
    Leven, 97, 93
Geite, Hanary, 14
Gennet, Jabesh, 84
Gervis, Foster, 1
Gervis, Samuel, 91
    see Jarvis
Gespar, Richard, 1
Gespeno, Hen., 62
Getree, Daniel, 75
Gibbens, Joshua, 97
    Stephen, 82, 87, 89, 90, 91, 97
Gibbin, William, 91
Gibbs (Gibs), Henry, 4, 6, 10, 11, 15, 16,
    26, 27, 34, 35, 37, 39, 41, 42,
    49, 52, 75, 77
    Willm., 51, 54, 61, 62, 70
Gibson (Gipson), David, 97

106

Hutsun, Widdo, 7
Huttson, John, 17
Indian - D___, 63
    Davy, 58
    Lewis, 56, 62, 67
    Sue, 56
Insel, Anthony, 84
Island, Elizabeth, 80, 82, 88
    Richard, 42
Ives, 61
    [Torn], 73
    Abigail, 97
    John, 2, 8, 10, 11, 12, 13, 15, 25,
        26, 28, 33, 35, 37, 38, 40, 41,
        44, 49, 51, 52, 56, 62, 74, 84
    John, Jur., 30
    John, Ser., 26, 30
    Timothey, 4, 39, 45, 54, 62, 70, 76,
        77, 80, 82, 87, 88, 91, 97
    Timothey, Jur., 37, 42, 51, 56, 87,
        89, 90, 91
    Timothey, Ser., 37, 41, 42, 49, 51,
        60
    William, 39, 41, 45, 59, 63, 69, 80,
        87, 93
Jack, 1
Jackson, Tho., xii
Jacobs, Isack, 5, 7
Jacocks, Jonathon, 5
Jains, Thos., 1
James, Thomas, 32, 39, 42, 45, 48, 50,
    57
Jamison, George, 97
Jarrard, James, 97
Jarvis, Foster, 2, 4, 6, 7, 8, 10, 11, 12,
    13, 14, 15, 26, 28, 30, 33, 35,
    37, 38, 40, 41, 44, 50, 53, 58,
    62, 66, 74, 75, 76, 97
    Foster, Jur., 39, 43, 45
    Francis, 2, 5, 7, 8, 9, 11, 14, 15, 16,
        26, 28, 30, 33, 34, 36, 39, 40,
        42, 45, 48, 49, 61, 64
    Henry, 77
    James, 97
    John, 97
    Jonathan, 38, 76, 80, 82, 87, 88, 89,
        90, 91, 93
    Jonathan, Jr., 82
    Malichia, 100
    Martin, 80, 82, 83, 93
    Mary, 80
    Maximillian, 97
    Richd., 77
    Samuel, xvii, 76, 77, 80, 82, 83, 86,
        87, 89, 90, 91, 93, 97
    Solomon, 77, 80, 82, 92, 95, 97
    Thomas, xvii, 1, 41, 38, 40, 44, 51,
        56, 62, 67, 75, 89, 90, 97
    Wido, 70
    William, 80, 82, 83, 87, 93
Jeans, Thomas, 100
Jelfe, Edward, 1, 4
Jenes, Corn., 62
Jenkins, Chapan, 95
    Elisha, 97
    James, 80, 82, 88, 92
    Lewis, 77
Jennet, Easter, 97

Jennet, Jabez, 80, 82, 93, 100
    Jessie, 100
    Job, 100
    Joseph, 97
Jepson, Henry, 91
    John, 91
    Robert, 91
Jeshna, Malatto, 88
Jesper, Dorcas, 97
Joh_____, James, 79
Johnson, John Hiphaven 88
    Morris, 39, 45
    Richd., 4, 5, 13, 70
    Thomas, 1, 2, 5, 6, 7, 8, 14, 15, 26
    Wm., 2, 4, 6, 8, 15, 26, 37, 45
Joice, Edward, 93
Jon[Torn], Richard, 6
Jones [Torn] 32
    [Torn]gh 31
    Cornelas, 5, 71, 75, 77
    David, 14, 15, 49, 52, 75, 77, 99
    David, Jur., 4, 10, 16, 26, 31, 33,
        35, 39, 43, 47
    David, Ser., 4, 10, 11, 14, 16, 26,
        28, 31, 33, 35, 37, 39, 43, 47
    Davis, 67
    Edward, xii, 2, 5, 9, 10, 12, 13, 16,
        25, 26, 31
    Elizabeth, xvii, 80, 82, 87
    Evan, 77, 80, 82, 83, 87, 93
    Evan, Jr., 97
    Evan, Sr., 97
    Fra, 5
    George, 80, 82, 84, 88
    Henry, 38, 39, 44
    Isaac, 1, 4, 8, 9, 11, 13, 16, 26, 28,
        30, 33, 34, 36, 38, 40, 44
    James, 2, 5, 9, 10, 12, 13, 16
    John, 1, 4, 5, 12, 13, 24, 32, 37, 44,
        49, 50, 62, 66, 82, 87, 93, 100
    John, Jur., 4, 8, 10, 11, 20, 26, 28,
        30, 34, 38, 42
    John, Ser., 1, 8, 9, 11, 13, 16, 26,
        28, 30, 33, 35, 38, 43
    Jos., xvii
    Loyd, 82, 87
    Patrick, 77
    Randal, 80, 82, 83, 87, 93, 100
    Randal, Sr., 97
    Richard, 4, 11, 15, 36, 43, 77, 80,
        82, 87
    Robert, 1
    Samuell, xii, 2, 4, 8, 9, 10, 14, 16,
        26, 28, 30, 33, 34, 36, 39, 42,
        48, 49, 60, 64, 66, 79, 80, 82,
        87, 92
    Samll., Jr., 60, 64, 66
    Sarah, 97
    Sevel, 80, 82, 87
    Taylor, xvii, 93
    Thomas, 38, 41, 44, 49, 52, 60, 64,
        97
    William, 97
    Yoansis, 14
    Zadock, 97
Jons, David, 6, 7
    Edward, 6
    Hugh, 5

Jons, Jams, 6
    John, 6, 7
    Sam, 7
Jonson, Henry, 1
    John, 7
    Jonathon, 84
    Richd., 73
    Samuell, 40
    Thomas, 13
    Willm, 13, 54
Jonston, [Torn], 61
    James, 52
    Moris, 33, 34, 40, 48, 52
    Richard, 10, 11, 16, 26, 27, 33, 35,
        37, 43, 47
    Thomas, 10, 16, 26, 27, 30, 33, 35,
        48, 49
    William, 10, 16, 3133, 35, 39, 43,
        45
Jooler, [Torn], 32
Justice, James, 84
Justine, Isaac, 84
Kallehan, Patrick, 33, 35, 43, 47, 49
Kalse, [Torn], 32
Keath, James, 4, 15
Keaton, Hillary, 88
Kegley, John, 84
Keito, Wm., 61, 70
Kelly, 84
    James, 92
    John, 80, 82, 84, 88
Kemp, [Tom], 32
    Job, 81, 88
Kenndy, Abraham, 90
Kight, Amos, 92
Kilgoar, James, 88
Killam, Theophilus, 97
Killey, Nicholis, 95
King, Thomas, 97
Kinnian, John, 97
Kinnion, Daniel, 97
Kinsey, Henry, 80, 82, 93
Kirke, John, 33, 35, 37, 43
Kitching, Robert, 1
Kite, Amos, 88
    Chas., 59, 63
    John, 8
Kitt, Charles, 23, 25
    John, 9, 16, 25, 31, 33, 35
Knight, Elisha, 97
Lagit, John, 5, 7, 13
    see Legett
Lain, Joseph, 93
Laley, Henry, 10, 25, 32
Lamb, Gideon, xvii
    Tho., xii
Land, Richard, 97
Lankford, J. R., Jr., xvii
Lanly, Hanary, 7
Lawly, Henry, 15, 17, 30, 34, 39, 42, 45,
    47, 48, 52, 59
Leach, Jacob, 4
Leachfield, Edward, 80, 87
Leary, William, 38, 40, 41, 44, 49, 51
    Thos., 74
Ledah, Edward, 100
Ledget, Jno:, 2
Lee, Asa, 95

Lee, Asahel, 97
   Daniel, 77, 80, 82, 92, 95, 97
   Elias, 95
   Horatio, 95, 97
   Jean, 97
   John, 95, 100
   Josiah, 79, 97
   Linton, 95, 97
   Malachi, 79
   Nathan, 95, 97
   Samuel, 76, 77, 79, 82, 87, 92, 95
   Thomas, 95, 97
   William, 77, 79, 80, 82, 87, 92, 97
   William, Sr., 97
Legett (Legatt, Legat, Legit, Ledget, Liggett), Abner, 80, 82, 87, 92
   Absalom, 77, 80, 82, 87
   David, 12, 26, 27, 28, 33, 35, 36, 38, 41, 42, 48, 51, 57, 63, 67, 75, 76, 77, 80, 82
   John, 5, 8, 9, 11, 16, 26, 28, 30, 33, 35, 37, 39, 41, 42, 43, 48, 51, 53, 57, 63, 67, 75
   Thomas 33, 35, 77
Leichfield, Edward, 82
   Peter, 89, 90
Lemmond (Lemmons), Arthur, 88, 93, 99
   Caleb 93
   Henry, 99
Lerry, Tho., 56, 64
   William, 1, 4, 8, 9, 11, 12, 26, 28, 30, 33, 34, 36, 56
Lewin (Lewing), John, 1
   Joseph, 38, 44, 76, 80, 82, 88
Lewis (Lewist), John, 2, 4, 14, 15, 16, 17, 26, 28, 31, 33, 37, 39, 43, 47
   Joseph, 54
   Thomas, 38, 42, 44, 47
Lindsay (Lindsey, Linsey, Linsay, Linsy), _____, 8, 89
   Alexander, 97
   Ann, 80, 82
   Benjamin, 80, 82, 87, 89, 90, 91, 97
   Daniell, 1, 2, 4, 10, 12, 13, 14, 16, 26, 28, 31, 33, 35, 37, 39, 40, 42, 45, 51, 54, 82, 87, 90
   David, xvii, 4, 14, 15, 91, 100
   John, 87, 89, 90, 91, 97
   Joseph, 87, 80, 89, 90, 91
   Thomas, 97
Linn, Jo White, Mrs., xviii
Linqua, Charles, 25, 30, 33
Linton (Lenton), 82
   [Torn]n Senr 31
   Catron, 87
   John, 32, 35, 41, 75, 77
   Lemuel, 87, 95, 97
   Moses, 9, 11, 17, 26, 27, 30, 32, 34, 36, 39, 40, 41, 44, 48, 50, 59, 63, 69, 73, 75, 76, 77, 80, 82
   Richard, 26, 28, 31, 32, 34, 36, 39, 40, 41, 44, 48, 52, 71
   Saml., xvii
   William, 4, 15, 16, 17, 26, 31, 71, 75
   William Ser. 7, 28
Litchfield, Abraham, 97

Litchfield, Edward, 76, 91
   Edward, Junr., 91
   Jacob, 97
   Peter, 91, 97
Lonsdeall, Christopher, 8, 10, 16, 25, 30
Lorence, Mertensen, 38
Lorry, John, 63, 91
Love, Edward, 82, 91, 92
   John, 87, 91
   John, Junr., 89, 90
   Mary Willes, 47
   Ralph, 1, 4, 6, 8, 10, 11, 14, 15, 26, 28, 31, 33, 35, 36, 39, 41, 42, 45, 49, 52, 54, 61, 62, 70, 74
   Richard, 89
   Thomas, 80, 88, 89, 90
   William, 91
Low, Eman, 5
   John, 95
Lowd, Thomas, 1
Lowing, Ann, 24
Lowther, Thomas, 76, 77
Loyall, David, 45
   John, 45
Luffman, Daniel, 95, 97
   William, 2, 5, 8, 10, 12, 14, 15, 16, 22, 24, 25, 27, 30, 32, 36, 39, 40, 41, 44, 60, 63, 69, 75
   William, Jur., 2, 8, 33, 34, 39, 40, 44, 48, 49
   William, Ser., 7, 13, 34, 36, 48, 49
Luge Petter, 49
Luin, Joseph, 84
Lungren, Lawrence, 97
Lunn, Nicholas, 80, 84, 86, 91, 93, 97
Lurley, Thomas, 75
Lurry (Lurrey, Lurre), John, 82, 86, 88
   Mary, 97
   Orphans, 97
   Soloman 95
   Thomas, 62, 76
   William, 5, 7, 13, 16, 62, 77, 97
Lutts, Jacob, 80, 82
   Peter, 47, 52, 77, 89, 90
   William, 97
M_____, Alexdr., 45
   Ambros, 45
   Will, 45
Maccoy (Mackay, Makey), Alexr., 4, 33, 39, 40, 49, 51, 54
   Ambros, 4, 7, 8, 13, 15, 26, 39, 31, 33, 43, 47, 54
   Daniel, 11, 22, 27, 31, 36, 43, 53, 62, 71
   Elexsander, 15
   John, 97
   William, 39, 43, 47, 51, 54, 61, 77, 83, 86, 93
Macduel, Peter, 82
Mackay Daniell 27
Mackferson, Andrew, 27
   Daniell, 27
Macke, John, 93
Mackie, William, 80, 82, 88, 91
Mackuin [Torn]n 32
   John, 6
Macuing, John, 27, 39, 47
Madren, Ralph, xii

Magson, Sallay, 92
Mahorney, John, 97
Makefason, Andrew, 31, 71
   Ann, 62
   Daniel, 4, 14, 31, 71, 82
Makefurshon, John, 80, 82
Mallete, Lydia, 98
Man, James, 10, 15, 16, 39, 42, 47
   John, 10, 16, 26, 31, 33, 35, 39, 41, 45, 48, 51, 54, 70, 74, 75
   Wm., 82
Mandon, Epaphraditus, 98
Mank, John, 37, 82, 97
Mann, Edwd., 84, 86
   William, 80, 84, 86
Mannin, John, 4
Marchant, Caleb, 88
   Catherine, 98
   Christopher, Capt., xii
   Gideon, 88, 93
   John, 88
   Kedar, 88, 93, 100
   John, 100
   Malikia, 98
   Orphans, 98
   Willoughby, 14, 88, 98
Marsh, Jacob, 39, 40, 44
   Rd., 63
Marshall, Nicholas, 2, 8, 15, 26, 59, 63, 73, 76, 80, 82
   William, 80, 82, 88, 92
Martin, James, 2, 4, 6, 7, 8, 9, 13, 16
Martyn, Joseph, 84
Mas[Torn], Tho, 6
Mash, Jacob, 48, 59, 69, 73
   Ralph, 76
   Tho., 88
Mashew, George, 84
Mashie, John, 98
Mason, John, 1, 2, 4, 8, 10, 12, 13, 14, 16, 26, 28, 31, 33, 35, 37, 45, 99
   Josephus, 97
   Sally, 80, 82, 88
Matham (Mathon), Ralph, 4, 13, 14, 26, 31, 33, 35, 39, 40, 42, 51, 54, 75
Mathew, Joseph, 84
   Ralph, 62, 70
Matheyas, Towler, 37
Mathis, Tim, 5, 6, 15
Matthews, Timo, 4
Matthias, Matthew, 97
May, George, 98
   Joseph, 100
McCaney, Alexander, 90
McCastelton, Samuel, 88
McClure, Richard, 80
McCay, John, xvii
McClenahan, Walter, xii
McCoy, Daniell, 24
   Jno., 73
   William, 62, 80, 88, 89, 90
McCuen, Joseph, 84, 88, 92
McDaniel, Joshua, 97
McDowell, Peter, 88, 91
McFarson, John, 92

McFerson, Andrew, 11, 36, 40, 42, 43, 48, 51, 75, 92
    Daniell, 11, 36, 42, 53, 75, 92
McGee, John, 93
McGown, Andrew, 100
McPharson, Moses, 98
McPherson, Andrew, 88
    Daniel, 88, 98
    Daniel, Sr., 98
    John, 88
    William, 98
Mckay, Alixander, 35
    Ambros, 16, 17, 35
    Daniell, 17
Meckings, William, 80
Mecuing, Ann, 37, 43
    John, 28, 43, 47
Meekins (Mekins), Isaack, 93
    Jacob, 84, 93
    Roger, 98
    William, 82, 84, 88
Megg, John, 98
Melson, William, 97
Mercer, James, 80, 82, 88, 89, 90, 91
    James, Junr., 90
    Jeremiah, xvii, 80, 88, 92
    Jeremiah, Jr., 97
    Jeremiah, Sr., 97
    John, 76, 100
    Thomas, xvii, 80, 82, 88, 97, 100
Merchant, Cadar, 77, 80, 82
    Caleb, 77, 80, 82
    Christopher, xii
    Gideon, 80, 82
    John, 82
    Willobey, 4, 62, 77, 80, 82
    Witt, 71
Mereday, Thomas, 76
Mershal, Malachia, 62
    Nickcolas, 5, 9, 11, 16, 27, 30, 33, 34, 36, 39, 40, 41, 44, 48, 50, 89
Merten, James, 26, 28, 31, 33, 35, 37, 39, 43, 45, 47
    The Widow, 53
Mertint, Bowlen, 26
Meteer, James, 77
Michell, William, 88
Midget, Christopher, 98, 100
    Daniel, 98
    John, 98
    Joseph, 80, 82, 84, 86, 88, 98, 100
    Joseph, Junr., 88, 93
    Joseph, Senr., 88
    Matthew, 38, 43, 98
    Richard, 98
    Samuel, 84, 88, 93, 100
    Samuel, Jr., 97
    Samuel, Sr., 97
    Thomas, 80, 82, 84, 88, 93, 98
    William, 97
Miles, Moses, 99
Mill, Milborough, 97
Miller, Mr., 2
Miller, Caleb, 100
    Elizabeth, 88
    Even, 1, 4, 5, 6, 8, 10, 11, 12, 15, 26, 28, 31, 33, 34, 36, 38, 42,

Miller, Even, 43, 44, 45, 48, 50, 53, 57, 63, 67, 71, 75, 76, 77, 80, 82, 86, 91, 98, 99
    Evan, Junr., 91
    Isaac, 88
    James, 80, 82
    Johannah, 88
    John, 37, 42, 71
    Lidya, 33, 34
    Samuell, 6, 7, 17, 25, 27
    Soloman, 92
    Thomas, 2, 4, 5, 8, 9, 11, 12, 13, 14, 16, 23, 25, 26, 27, 30, 59, 77, 80, 82, 88, 91, 93, 98, 99
    Thomas, Jr., 82
    William, 98
    William, Senr., 88
    Willis, 77, 80, 98, 100
Millington, Jno., xii
Mills, John, 2, 4, 7, 8, 9, 13, 14, 15, 26, 31
    Thomas, 48, 52
Mitchel, William, 89
Mitchell, Ambrose, 97
Mixson, John, 5, 6
Mohun, James, 13
Moncreef, John, 82
    Thomas, 68, 75, 76, 77
    William, 30, 88, 88
Monke, John, 27, 63, 73
Moon, James, 6
Moore, [Torn], 32
    Abra., 1
Mor, Jonathan, 82
Morce, Benjamin, 99
Marmiduke, Elijah, 99
Moreral, Jeminah, 97
Morisset, Peter, 79, 88, 95
Morris, Fredarick, 7
    Hezekiah, 90
    John, 82, 93
    Margret, 4, 14
    Richardson 82
    Thomas, 80, 82, 88
    Willoughby, 97
Mors, Richard, 80
Morse, Caleb, 95
    Dickson, 95
    John, 80, 88
    Richardson, 77, 88
Morton, Richard, 4, 8, 10, 14, 17
Moscer Jer 77
Moseley, Conl Edward, xiii, 12, 13
Moue, Elizabeth, 98
    Francis, 97
    Malichia, 98
    Reuben, 98
    Richardson, 98
    Zachariah, 98
Mounk, 62
    Jno., 59
Mounticue, John, 99
Muldin, William, 98
Mulatto, James, 62
    Tom, 67
Mullen, Edward, 1
Muncke, John, 17, 75
Muncrief, Heziah, 98

Muncreef, John, 19, 24, 80, 92
    Thomas, 2, 4, 5, 6, 8, 10, 11, 13, 14, 16, 25, 27, 30, 33, 34, 36, 39, 40, 41, 43, 45, 53, 80, 63, 88
    William, 7, 10, 12, 15, 25, 28, 33, 34, 36, 39, 40, 41, 45, 48, 49, 60, 63, 79, 80, 82, 88, 89, 90, 91, 98
    Willoughby, 79
Munk, John, 39, 40, 41, 44, 48, 49, 69
Murphey, Joseph, xvii
Nal_____, Hen:, 63
Nash, John, 36
    Thomas, 42, 60, 63, 77
Navil, John, 14
Neal, John, 4, 77
    John G., Junr., 93
Neale, Luke, xii
Negro - Aron, 58
    Bada, 54, 62, 64
    Bess, 56, 58, 62, 63, 66, 68
    Betty, 54, 64
    Bridget, 88
    Cate, 66
    Cha, 70
    Criss, 58, 63, 68
    Cro 56
    Deb, 60, 64, 88
    Dick, 58, 63, 66
    Dina, 61
    Doll, 88
    Dynah, 64
    Eano, 67
    Elizabeth, 87
    Eron, 62
    Fillis, 54, 88
    Folls, 83
    Fran, 56, 60
    Frank, 62, 63, 64
    Grace, 60, 64
    Guy, 58, 63, 88
    Hannah, 56, 58, 62, 63, 66
    Henry, 88
    Hilly, 84
    Ishim, 57
    Ja, 60
    Jac, 56, 57, 58
    Jack, 56, 62, 63, 64, 66, 67, 88
    Jak, 83
    James, 64, 88
    Jase, 58
    Jeffrey, 63, 64, 68
    Jenny, 56, 58, 60, 62, 63, 64, 66, 68, 69, 79
    Jeremy, 68
    Jno., 58
    Juda, 58
    Judy, 63
    Kate, 58, 63
    Keah, 63
    Keto, 69
    Ketur, 60
    Kite, 70
    Lery, 58
    Maria, 62
    Marrose, 64
    Mingo, 64

Negro - Moll, 69, 88
Nan, 56, 62, 64, 68
Nanny, 62
Ned, 88
Oring, 60
Park, 60
Parker, 68
Pete, 57
Petter, 57, 62, 63
Phil, 58, 60
Philip, 63, 66
Philis, 64
Quash, 66, 88
Sam, 56, 60, 63, 69
Sampson, 60, 62, 64, 70
Sandfer, 62
Sarah, 54, 56, 60, 62, 63, 64, 66, 68, 69
Sciplo, 62
Sepeo 57
Sippias 67
Squash, 56, 62
Tom, 54, 56, 58, 60, 62, 63, 64, 66, 68
Tony, 54, 58, 63, 64, 66
Willee, 56, 62, 64
York 58
New England Company, 12, 28
Newby, Thomas, xvii
Newel, James, 99
Nicholas, Nichole, 98
Nichols, Jas., 57, 71, 77
Wm., 18
Nicholson, 88
Hannah, 82
Hunch 80
Josiah, 76, 77, 89, 90, 93
John, 91
Jonah, 98
Nicholas, 88
Wm., 5, 8, 58
Nickalls, Capt. William, 9, 11, 24, 28
Nickallson, William, 6, 7, 12, 14, 15, 26, 31, 33, 35, 37, 38, 42, 44, 45, 50, 63, 67
Wm., Jr., 63
Nickens, Ward, 95
Richard, 80, 82, 92
Nickolson, [Torn], 71
Nixson, John, 6
Noel, Christopher, 88
John, 88
Noesay, Jno., 75
Nolan, Jno:, 2
Northern, Benjamin, 88, 91
Northan, Elizabeth, 4, 13
Northen, John, 9, 10, 16, 18, 24, 26, 27, 30, 33, 34, 36, 37, 39, 40, 41, 43, 44, 48, 49, 52, 53, 60, 64, 70, 93, 95, 98
Orphans, 98
Philip, 76, 80, 82, 88, 92, 98
William, 95, 98
Norton, [Torn], 32
Asahel, 98
John, 35, 37, 39, 43, 45, 47, 49, 51, 54, 76, 98
Jonathan, 88, 89, 91

Norton, Orphans, 98
William, 91, 98
Nosay Jno 71
Noth[Torn], Widdo, 7
Nuby, Thomas, xvii
Nuton, 32
O Dowdy, Daiel, 77, 80, 82, 89, 90, 91
Daniel, Junr., 91
James, 82, 88, 89, 90
John, 88, 90
Joseph, 88, 89, 90, 91, 98
Richd., 77, 80
Thomas, 88, 89, 90
Wm., 77, 80, 91, 98
William, Junr., 90, 91
O Neal (Oneal), Charles, 66
Chrisr:, 80, 82, 83, 84, 92, 98, 99
John, 2, 4, 6, 8, 10, 11, 14, 15, 16, 26, 27, 33, 35, 37, 39, 43, 44, 47, 49, 52, 80, 83, 88, 92, 98
John, Jr., 82, 84
Michael, 5, 12, 14, 18, 24, 26, 28, 41, 58, 77, 80, 82, 88, 90, 91, 98
Michall, Jur., 15, 26, 30, 33, 34, 38, 40, 44, 50, 63, 66, 74
Michil, Senr., 7, 9, 11, 15, 30, 33, 34, 36, 38, 40, 50, 63, 66, 74
Richard, 89
Sarah, 98
Thomas, 84, 93, 98
William, 98
Oakley, Elizabeth, 98
Olds, Kedar, 98
Oright, Henry, 83
Osten, Cornealus, 81
Overington, Robert, 80
Overinton, Amos, 82
Overton, John, xvii
Robert, 77
Willis 98
P_____, Peter, 89
P__d_____, Wm J__, 62
Pa[Torn], Jams, 6
Paddrick, 84
Benjamin, 80, 83
Henry, 88, 98
John, 83, 88
Peter, 80, 83, 88, 98
Peter, Jr., xvii
Page, [Torn]hn, 31
Pane, Adam, 15
Pain (Paine), Samuel, 1, 4, 6, 7, 13, 14, 84, 88
Thomas, 80, 83, 84, 88, 96
Thomas, Sr., 98
Paint, Thomas, 93
Palin, Capt. John, 5
Palmer, John, 43, 52, 54, 61, 62, 70, 74, 84, 86, 93
Robert, 39, 41, 49, 52, 54, 61, 80, 88
Parker, _____, 62, 63, 79
Azaricam (Asaricum), 1, 4, 5, 7, 8, 9, 11, 12, 14, 15, 16, 19, 24, 26, 28, 30, 33, 34, 36, 38, 40, 41, 44, 48, 51, 56, 62, 66, 74, 76, 80, 82, 88, 90, 91, 98

Parker, Azariham, Jnr., 89, 90, 91
Azrikem, Senr., 89
Edw., 62
Gilbert, 77
Hilary, 89, 90
Isza, 75
James, 51, 58, 66, 74, 77, 80, 83, 88, 90, 91, 98
Jeminah, 98
John, 56, 62, 76
Peter, 1, 2, 4, 6, 7, 8, 10, 11, 13, 14, 15, 16, 26, 28, 30, 33, 34, 36, 38, 40, 41, 44, 48, 50, 57, 62, 67, 76, 77
Phebe, 98
Rebeckah, 88
Samuel, 75
Thomas, 38, 40, 44, 50, 56, 64, 66, 74, 75, 77, 80, 83, 88, 91, 95, 98
Wiker, 76
William, 1, 4, 6, 7, 8, 10, 11, 12, 14, 15, 16, 26, 28, 31, 33, 35, 37, 38, 40, 41, 42, 44, 48, 51, 57, 63, 71, 75, 76, 77, 88
William, Sr., 98
Parks, James, 49
Parkwood, Gilbert, 80
Parmac, Jam., 59
Parr, Daniel, 95, 98
Diniah, 98
Jesse, 98
Noah, 100
William, 76, 77, 80, 82, 88, 92
Parsoll, [Torn], 32
Patern, Robert, 75
Patesall, Jams, 8
Paton, Mr. Robert, 38
Patterson, William, 75, 88
Paul, George, 77
Robt., 77
Robt., Junr., 77
Pawlings, Wm., 77
Peacock, Andrew, 38, 40, 44
Pead, Timothy, 1
Peavey Payve, Peavy, Pave, Pavey),
Adam, 4, 7, 9, 13, 16, 17, 19, 24, 25, 30
Webly 33, 35, 39, 42, 44, 45, 48, 51, 57, 62, 66, 74
Peel, Francis, 83, 84, 88, 92
Pell, Etheridge John, 99
John, 1, 2, 4, 8, 9, 11, 12, 14, 15, 28, 33, 34, 36, 41, 44, 63, 66, 76, 77, 80, 83, 86, 88, 92
Stephen, 83
Penny, John, 26, 28, 31, 34, 36, 39, 41, 42, 48, 51, 54, 61, 62, 70, 74, 75
Perkins (Pirkens), Charles, xvii
Henry, 31, 80, 82, 88, 92, 95
Hanary, Junr., 7
Hanary Senr. 31
John, 7, 12, 14, 15, 19, 24, 26, 42, 45, 48, 50, 51, 57, 63, 67, 75, 76, 77, 82
John, Junr., 5, 8, 10, 28, 31, 33, 34, 36, 39, 42, 45, 80, 88, 92

Perkins, John, Senr., 6, 8, 9, 11, 18, 28, 31, 33, 35, 38, 39, 40, 44, 48, 82, 88
Joshua, 98
Mary, 88
Moses 80
Solo., 95
Thomas, 79, 92
William, xvii, 80, 82, 95, 98
Perry, John, 98
Thomas, 90, 91
Persons, Jos., 77
Petterson, Jacob, 1
Peugh, Stephen, 88
Pew, George, 88, 98
Peter, 90
Thomas, 88, 98
William, 98
Peyton, Mr. Robert, 39, 41, 42, 52, 61, 62, 70
Phillips, Ann, 98
Daniell, 39, 40, 42, 45, 48, 50, 60, 64, 71, 77, 80, 82, 95
David, 68
David, Jr., 68
James, 77, 80, 82, 83, 84, 86, 88, 91, 98
Jean, 98
Michell, 88
Orphans, 98
Samuel, xvii, 95
Wm., 59, 63, 81
Picketts, Jams., 83
Pieo, James, 84
Pierce, Peter, 91
Plummer, George, 98
John, 88
Moses, 100
Polk, John, 6
Pomar, John, 2
Popowell, William, 80, 83
Popplewell, George, 98
Popwith, William, 88
Portwood, Benjamin, 89, 90, 98
Gilbert, 58, 83, 88
Martin, 88, 91
Pos[Torn], Moses, 5
Powil, John, 6
Powell, William, 5, 8, 10, 15, 18, 25, 26, 31, 33, 38
Powers, Caleb, 92, 99
Caleb, Sr., 98
George, xvii, 63, 70, 75, 76, 77, 80, 82, 90, 92, 98
George, Jr., 98
Isabelah, 88
William, 80, 88, 92, 98
Poyner (Piner, Poiner, Poynar, Pyner),
Adam, 90, 98
Benjamin, 88, 89, 90, 91, 93
Edward, 2, 4, 7, 8, 9, 11, 12, 14, 15, 20, 24, 60, 69
Elizabeth, 15
Humphry, 80, 88, 91, 98
James, 2, 4, 5, 7, 8, 10, 14, 15, 20, 24, 28, 31, 33, 36, 39, 42, 44, 45, 48, 51, 57, 63, 67, 71, 75, 76, 77, 80, 83, 95

Poyner, Joel, 80, 83, 88, 89, 91, 98, 99
Joel, Jnr., 90
John, 83, 91
Jonathan, 80, 83, 88, 90, 91, 98
Joseph, 1, 4, 7, 8, 9, 11, 13, 15, 26, 28, 30, 33, 35, 36, 38, 40, 41, 48, 50, 57, 63, 79, 80, 82, 88, 92, 98
Joseph, Jr., 95
Joseph, Sr., 95
Nathan, xvii, 89, 90, 93, 98
Peter, 1, 5, 8, 9, 12, 13, 14, 15, 25, 26, 28, 30, 33, 34, 38, 42, 44, 45, 51, 58, 63, 66, 74, 75, 76, 77, 80, 83, 88, 91, 98
Peter, Jr., 4, 6
Peter, Senr., 4, 7, 13
Robert, xvii, 33, 34, 41, 42, 48, 50, 57, 67, 80, 83, 88, 90, 93, 98
Samuel, 2, 4, 5, 7, 8, 10, 12, 14, 15, 26, 27
Sarah, 80
Thomas, 1, 5, 7, 10, 14, 15, 19, 24, 26, 31, 33, 34, 36, 37, 38, 42, 44, 47, 75, 93, 100
Widow, 8, 9, 11, 26, 30
William, 2, 5, 6, 8, 9, 12, 13, 14, 15, 19, 24, 26, 28, 30, 39, 40, 41, 44, 48, 49, 60, 63, 69, 76, 83
William, Jur., 33, 35, 63
William, Ser., 33, 34, 36
Willis, 80, 83
Prescoat (Prescod, Prescot), Aron, 1, 4, 6, 8, 10, 11, 12, 14, 15, 17, 20, 24, 26, 28, 30, 33, 34, 36, 38, 40, 41, 44, 48, 50, 53, 67
Benjamin, 80, 83, 88, 89, 90, 91
Charles, 80, 91
Esb., 58
Jno., 63, 67
Moses, 15, 26, 53, 57, 63, 67
Pricket, Jno., 59
Prince, Joseph, 90
Privatt, Andrew, 77
Pursell, Edward, 88
Quidley, Thomas, 99
William, 98
R_____, Moses, 4
Radwell, Thomas, 84
Rale, Leah, 98
Ralf, Doo, 17
Ramsay, Moses, 12, 26, 27, 28, 33, 34, 36, 39, 41, 42, 45
Rebecka, 53
Randall, Giles, 37, 42, 75
Rannalls, John, 8
Raymond, [Torn], 32
Reading (Reeding), Lionel, 1, 4, 8, 9, 13, 14, 15, 16, 17, 23, 26, 31
Reed, William, 4, 8, 9, 11, 12, 14, 15, 16, 18, 24, 25, 26, 28, 30, 33, 34, 36, 38, 40, 41, 44, 52, 64, 98
Rees, Wm., 13
Regnaud, Benjamin, xii
Relf, Thos., xvii
Relph, John, 42
Renalls, John, 11, 16
Rencher (Renger), Samuel 25, 31, 32

Reynaud, Benjamin, xii
Mary, xii
Morgan, xii
Olimpa, xii
Rich, Obediah, 8, 10, 11, 18, 26, 27, 30
Richards, George, 1
John, 88, 90
Rickets, James, 33, 35, 59, 69
Rigby, Paul, 70
Riggs, James, 100
Right Henry   88
Rignnow, Moses, 54
Rigsby, James, 99
Rinor, Moses, 15
Riordan, Denis, 5, 31, 37, 39, 40, 42, 45, 48, 51, 57, 63, 67, 75
Robb (Rob), Thomas, 77, 80, 83, 88, 98
Thomas, Senr., 88
Robard, Tucker, 15
Roberson, John, 89
Roberts, John, 80, 84
William, 88
Wrencher, 99
Robertson, George, 99
John, 10, 16, 26, 27, 84, 88, 89
John, Jr., 90, 98
John, Sr., 98
Thomas, 99
Robinson, Francis, 92
John, 83, 91
[Tom]mas, 31
William, 80, 83, 88, 92
Robison, Ffra., xii
Roe, James, 2, 10, 18
Rogar, Cornelas, 6
Rogers, Samuel, 88
Spencer, 84, 86, 99
Roggers, Major, 98
Roirdors, Giles, 71
Rolin, Wm, 6
Roling, Robert, 80, 83
Rolland, Robert, 92
Rollenson, Frances, 84, 98
William, 6, 77, 83, 84, 98
William, Sr., 98
Rollins, Ezekial, 98
Rolls, Wm, 6
Ronnalls, John, 44
Roo, James, 14, 15
Rose (Roos, Ros), William, 6, 7, 11, 15, 17, 20, 24, 26, 27, 43
Ross, Wm., 2
Rothen, William, 88
Rowe, James, 4, 8
Rowland, George, 88, 92, 95, 98
Rowlin Robert   88
Royall, Cornelyus, 17
Timothey, 2, 7, 8, 10, 14, 18, 25, 27
Royonal, Mosis, 2
Russell, Thomas, 77, 83, 88, 89, 90, 91
Thomas, Jnr., 90
William, 1, 4, 5, 6, 8, 10, 12, 13, 16, 22, 26, 27, 33, 35, 66, 99
Willis, 89, 90
Ryan, James, 98
Rynard, Moses, 39, 40, 42, 45
Ryno, Moses, 28, 31, 33, 35, 37, 52
Salsbary, George, 2

111

CURRITUCK COUNTY TAX AND MILITIA RECORDS

Stafford, Edward, 2, 8, 9, 15, 16, 25, 27,
    William, xii, 2, 5, 7, 8, 9, 11, 13, 14,
       16, 17, 19, 24, 25, 27, 30, 33,
       34, 36, 39, 40, 41, 43, 44, 48,
       49, 59, 63, 69, 73, 76
Stanley, Even, xvii, 81, 83
    John, xvii, 98
    Richard, 80, 83, 88, 98
    Thomas, 98
Stearing, George, 39, 43, 47, 48, 52, 54,
    61, 70, 74
Stearns, Jeremiah, 92
Steel, William, 1, 7, 38
Stephens (Stevens), Diniah, 98
    Jeremiah, 77, 81, 83, 84, 89
    John, 76, 88, 89, 90
    William, 5, 28, 30, 33, 35
Stewart, John, 98
    Peter, 81, 83
Stickway, Cha:, 2
Still, Robert, 89
Stone, George, 93
Stonhouse, Thomas, 11, 28
Stow, Benjamin, 99
    Daniel, 99
    Jeremiah, 100
    Samuel, 89, 99
    Samuel, Junr., 84
    Samuel, Senr., 84
    Susanna, 99
    Thomas, 84
Stroud, John, xii
Stuart, John, xvii
    Robert, 42, 53, 71
Suel, Dan:, 2
Sumner, James, xvii
Supple, Anthony, 98
Swann, Thomas, 5, 7, 8, 10, 12, 13, 14,
    15, 16, 22, 24, 26, 33, 35, 36,
    37, 39, 41, 42, 45, 48, 50, 60,
    63, 69
    William, 1, 2, 4, 6, 8, 10, 12, 13, 14,
    15, 22, 23, 24, 25, 26, 28, 31,
    33, 35, 37, 38, 42, 44, 45, 48,
    51, 56, 62, 67, 71
Sweny (Swinny), Daniel, 88, 92
Swilndal, Baker, 81
    John, 1, 4, 6, 8, 10, 13, 14, 26, 30
    Parker, 76, 77, 83, 88, 92, 98
Tatum, John, 95, 99
    Thomas, 81, 83, 89
    William, 95, 99
Taylor (Tayler), Mr., 27
    [Torn], 63
    Benjamin, 81, 83, 89, 90, 91, 99
    Caleb, 100
    Ebenezer, 81, 83, 89, 90, 99
    Edward, 1, 50, 58, 66, 74, 75, 77,
       99
    John, 83, 89, 90, 91, 99
    Jonathan, 89, 99
    Joseph, 99
    Joshua, 79, 89, 91, 99
    Reuben, 89, 90, 99
    Thomas, xi, xii, 1, 5, 6, 8, 11, 12,
    14, 15, 17, 23, 27, 31, 34, 36,
    44, 58, 76, 81, 83, 89, 93, 99

Taylor, Thomas, Jur., 4, 9, 11, 15, 26, 28,
    30, 33, 34, 36, 38, 40, 41, 44,
    50, 63, 66, 75, 76
    Thomas, Ser., 5, 8, 9, 13, 14, 15,
    26, 28, 30, 33, 38, 40, 41, 43,
    50, 58, 63, 66, 74, 75, 99
    Thomason, 99
Taylor, William, 84, 89
Templeman, Richd., 98
Tharp, Richard, 6
Thethom, Thomas, 91
Thomas, free Negro, 89
Thomas, Charles, 47, 48, 54
    George, 68
    James, 99
    Jeremiah, 89, 92
    Peter, 90
    Robert, 99
    Susan, 63
    Susanna (Shusana), 38, 42, 44, 45,
       50, 68
    Sil, 58
    William, 99
Thompson (Thomson, Tomson), 37, 95
    Ann, 10
    Evan, 95, 99
    George, 2, 4, 5, 6, 8, 12, 14, 16, 25,
    30, 32, 34, 39, 42, 44, 47
    John, 81, 83, 89, 99
    Mary, 99
    Robert, 95
    Thomas, 91
    William, 81, 89, 91, 99
Thorogood, Jno., xii
Thorp, Richard, 17, 22, 25
Tiller, William, 47
Tillett (Tillit), Mr., 54
    Edward, 89
    Isaac, 84
    John, 77, 84, 89
    John, Snr., 81, 83
    Rw., 84
    Thomas, 84, 99
    William, 26, 27, 33, 35, 39, 43, 45,
       48
Tobe, John, 5
Toller, Caleb, 84
    James, 84, 99
    Mathw., 74
    Matthias, 84, 99
    Patk., 61
Tolley, Celly, 95
Tom_____, Jeremiah, 79
Towler, Daniel, 81
    James, 76, 81, 83, 89
    Matheyas, 1, 4, 13, 14, 45, 49, 51,
       54, 62, 70, 77
Townsend, Jacob, 95
    Job, 95
    John, 99
Tronbole, Aron, 63
    Jno., 63
Tucke, Will, 75
Tucker, Robert, 10, 12, 16, 22, 24, 26,
    28, 37, 57, 63
    Robert, Jur., 33, 35, 39, 42, 45, 47
    Robert, Ser., 31, 33, 35, 37, 39, 42,
       45

Tucker, William, 48, 52, 57, 63, 71
Tulle (Tull, Tully), Benjamin, xi, 4, 5, 7, 8,
    9, 11, 12, 13, 14, 16, 18, 24,
    28, 33, 35, 37, 38, 40, 41, 44,
    50, 59, 63, 68, 71
    Mark, 1
    Thomas, 1
    William, 76
Tulls, Thomas, xii
Tully, John, xii
Turner, George, 77
Turton, Abner, 99
    Thomas, 81, 83, 89
Twifford, Bartholomew, 90
Underwood, Thomas, 5, 31
Valentine, Henry, 81, 83, 89, 93
Vandermulen, Jane, xii
    Thomas, xii, 1, 4, 6, 7, 8, 10, 11,
    13, 14, 15, 25, 26, 28, 30, 33,
    34, 36, 38, 40, 41, 44, 48, 50
Varden, Brian, 83, 89, 92
    Silvester, 79, 83, 89, 92
Vince, Mr., 1
    Humphry, 1, 2, 4, 6, 8, 9, 11, 12,
    14, 15, 23, 25, 26, 28, 31, 33,
    35, 38, 40, 41, 44, 48, 50, 57,
    67, 71, 76
    Thomas, 1, 4, 7, 8, 9, 11, 12, 13,
    14, 15, 26, 28, 31, 33, 35, 38,
    40, 41, 44, 48, 50, 57, 62, 63,
    67, 71
W.[Torn], Corni., 7
W[Torn], Joseph, 7
Wabstar, John, 12, 14
Wade, John, 5
Wahab, James, 81, 83, 84, 89, 92, 99
    William, 99
Wakefeeld, Paul, 12
Walker, 89
    Caleb, 89, 90, 99
    John, 1, 4, 7, 28, 36, 38, 40, 41, 44,
    50, 58, 66, 74, 75, 76, 89, 91,
    100
    John, Junr., 81, 83, 89, 90, 91
    Neal, 91
    Oneel, 89, 90, 99
    Samuel, xvii
    Thomas, xvii, 99
    Willis, 90, 99
Wallis, 20, 24
    John, 5, 20
    Joshua, 100
    William, 5, 12, 20, 24
Walls, Joshua, 89
Walls, Joshua, 92
    Joshua, Junr., 92
    Thomas, 93
Walstar, Capt. John, 5
Walston, Jonathan, 99
Wamoth, Robt, 5
    Wm, 5
Waran, Tho:, 58
Ward, Jonathan, 95
    Joseph, 6
Wardin, William, 89
Warding (Warden), James, 27, 36, 42,
    53, 59, 70
Warill, John, 39

113

Waril, Thomas, 31
Waring (Warren), Edward, xii
    Eliz., xii
    John, 7, 9, 11, 17, 26, 27, 30, 32,
        34, 36, 42, 44, 47, 48, 52, 83
    Thomas, 25, 30, 32, 35, 43, 47, 52
Waterfield, Abraham, 99
    John, 99
    Michael, 81, 83, 89, 93, 100
Watkins, John, xvii
Waymouth, Wm., 44
Weaser, James, 89
Weasley, Jacob, 93
Webster, Capt John, 36
Wells, Joshua, 83
    William, 2, 4, 10, 11, 15, 16, 17, 24,
        26, 27, 33, 37, 38, 39, 43
Wenter, Michl., 1
Wentworth, Saml., & Co., 60
Weonses, The Widdow, 54
Wescoat, John, 86
Wescote, Stephen, 84
West, Absolem, 92
    Capt: Benjemen, 37
    Daniell, 11, 27, 36, 42, 48, 50, 59,
        63, 69, 73
    John, 77, 83
    Nathaniel, 93
    Nathaniel Spence, 89, 93
Weymouth, William, 38
Whaley, Jonathan, 84, 93
    Rachel, 89
Wheatley, John, 81, 83, 91, 95
    Robert, 99
    Thomas 95
Whed[bee], [Torn], 74
Whidbe (Whedbe, Whittbee, Whidbey),
    John, 4, 7, 8, 10, 12, 14, 16, 22, 24,
        26, 27, 33, 35, 37, 39, 43, 45,
        47, 52, 54, 61, 62, 70, 77, 81,
        83, 84, 89, 92, 99
    William, 99
White, [Torn]neser, 31
    [Torn]k, 71
    Easter, Widow, 89
    Henry, 38, 40, 41, 44, 50, 58, 63,
        66, 74, 81, 83, 84, 89
    Hillary, 81, 83, 86, 89, 92, 93
    James, xvii
    Jamima, 99
    Jos., 13
    Joshua, 77, 83, 86, 89, 91, 92, 93
    Josiah, 4, 8, 10, 16
    Lamuell, Junr., 95
    Luke, 4, 6, 8, 9, 11, 13, 14, 15, 16,
        24, 25, 26, 27, 28, 31, 33, 34,
        36, 38, 40, 41, 44, 48, 50, 58,
        63, 67, 75, 77, 81, 83, 89
    Margret, 89
    Orphans, 99
    Patrick, 81, 83
    Vinson, 89, 93
    William, 77, 81, 83, 89, 93
    Willoughby, 95, 99
Whitehall, Alexr. Legrand, 99
    Robert, 84, 86, 89, 91
    Thomas, 89
Whitehurst, Gideon, 77, 81, 83, 89

Whitehurst, John, 81, 83, 92
    Jonathan, 79
Wicker, Elizabeth, 89
    Jno:, 2, 6
    Joseph, 2, 5, 7, 9, 10, 12, 13, 14,
        15, 16, 25, 26, 28, 30, 33, 34,
        36, 38, 40, 44, 48, 50, 58, 63,
        68, 71
    Richard, 77, 89
Wilkins, William, 100
Will[torn], John, 60
Willey, 61
    Jno., 62, 70, 74
Williams, 84
    Charles, 81, 83, 89, 93
    Comfort, 99
    Elizabeth, 4, 12, 14, 37, 43
    Holloway, 93
    Jacob, 99
    James, xvii, 63, 83, 99
    John, 62, 77, 83, 84, 89, 93, 100
    Joseph, 81, 83, 89, 93, 100
    Lewis, xvii, 84, 90, 99
    Mathew, 91
    Nicholas, 89
    Phillip, 84, 89, 99
    Robert, 25, 27, 59
    Samuel, 76
    Stephen, 56, 62, 68, 76, 77, 81, 83,
        84, 86, 91
    Thomas, Jur., 45
    Thomas, 2, 5, 7, 8, 10, 11, 12, 13,
        14, 16, 27, 28, 30, 33, 34, 36,
        37, 38, 39, 41, 43, 44, 48, 49,
        50, 54, 61, 64, 68, 71, 76, 81,
        83, 84, 89, 93
    William, xii, 1, 5, 6, 8, 10, 12, 13,
        14, 15, 22, 25, 26, 27, 28, 30,
        31, 33, 34, 36, 38, 40, 41, 44,
        48, 50, 53, 56, 62, 68, 71, 83,
        86, 89, 90, 92
Williamson, Charles, 10, 16
    Mathew, 89, 90
    Richard, 52
    Stephen, 89
    Thomas, 2, 5, 7, 8, 10, 13, 15, 16,
        26, 33, 38, 44
    William, 77, 81, 89, 89, 90, 91, 99
Willm, [Torn], 32
Wills, Joshua, 84
Wilson, Caleb, 81, 83, 84
    Francis, 89
    James, 71
    Jno., 63
    Sarah, Widow, 89
    Soloman, 81, 83
    Tom, 56
    William, 1, 4, 7, 8, 9, 11, 12, 13, 16,
        17, 24, 26, 28, 30, 33, 34, 36,
        38, 40, 41, 44, 49, 51, 62, 64
Winter, Malecay (Mallykay, Mallica), 12,
        13, 14, 26, 30, 33, 34, 36, 38,
        40, 41, 44, 51, 74
    Mat, 64
    Mck., 56
    Michall, 4, 9, 15, 17, 23
Wipole, John, 84
Woll, Wm., 20

Wood, John, 84, 86, 92
Woodhouse, [Torn]nce, 38
    Azachia, 91
    Hadley, 99
    Henry, 1, 4, 5, 6, 8, 9, 13, 16, 26,
        28, 30, 33, 34, 36, 38, 40, 41,
        44, 49, 50, 54, 62, 64, 73, 77
    Hezekiah, 81, 83, 89, 90
    John, xvi, 1, 4, 5, 6, 8, 9, 11, 14, 15,
        16, 26, 28, 30, 33, 34, 36, 38,
        40, 41, 44, 49, 51, 56, 62, 66,
        74, 77, 81, 83, 84, 86, 89, 90,
        93
    William, 99
Woods, John, 81, 83, 89
Wooten, Wm., xvii
Wooton, William, xvii
Worden, Jams, 63, 73, 75
Worrill, John, 5
Wrensher, Samuell, 35
Wright, 84
Write, Luke, 76
Wroten, William, 99
Wuntworth, Saml, 4
Wyatt, John, 95
Young, Thomas, 1
Younghusband, Thomas, 99
[Smeared]man 61
[Torn], Andrew, 8
[Torn], Backlon 32
[Torn], Hanary, 6, 7
[Torn], Henry, 79
[Torn], J_____ , 79
[Torn], Jams. 62, 63
[Torn], James 44
[Torn], John, 7, 38, 79
[Torn], Marma[Torn], 6
[Torn], Moses, 79
[Torn], R 62
[Torn], Ralph 45
[Torn], Richard 93
[Torn], Richardson 93
[Torn], Samuel, Sr., 79
[Torn], Tho., 7, 67
[Torn], Thos:, Junr. 71
[Torn], W_____ , 79
[Torn], William 89
[Torn], William, Jr., 79
[Torn]athern B___ 81
[Torn]awkins 32
[Torn]berry Geo. 63
[Torn]ghan 32
[Torn]ight 32
[Torn]illor 32
[Torn]oges 84
[Torn]rharey 32
[Torn]son 63
[Torn]rbush 32
[Torn]regin 32
[Torn]riffin 32
[Torn]ton Jno. Jur. 63
[Torn]un, Richard, 7

www.ingramcontent.com/pod-product-compliance
Lightning Source LLC
Chambersburg PA
CBHW080242270326
41926CB00020B/4344